W9-BDE-669

Reclaiming the Wesleyan Tradition:

JOHN WESLEY'S SERMONS FOR TODAY

Douglas M. Strong

Sarah Babylon Dorrance

Robert P. McDonald-Walker

Ingrid Y. Wang

Kevin M. Watson

DISCIPLESHIP RESOURCES

PO BOX 340003 • NASHVILLE, TN 37203-0003
www.discipleshipresources.org

Cover design by Shawn Lancaster.

ISBN 13: 978-0-8177-519-8

Library of Congress Cataloging-in-Publication Data

Reclaiming the Wesleyan tradition : John Wesley's sermons for today /
Douglas M. Strong ... [et al.].
    p. cm.
 Includes bibliographical references and index.
 ISBN 978-0-88177-519-8 (alk. paper)
 1. Wesley, John, 1703-1791. 2. Wesley, John, 1703-1791--Sermons. I.
Strong, Douglas M., 1956-
  BX8495.W5R43 2007
  252'.07--dc22
                   2007027550

RECLAIMING THE WESLEYAN TRADITION: John Wesley's Sermons for Today. Copyright © 2007 Discipleship Resources. All rights reserved. No part of this book may be reproduced in any form whatsoever, print or electronic, without written permission. For information regarding rights and permissions, contact Discipleship Resources, PO Box 340003, Nashville TN 37203-0003; fax 615-340-1789.

Discipleship Resources® and design logos are trademarks owned by GBOD®, Nashville, Tennessee. All rights reserved.

Acknowledgements and Permissions

Sermons of John and Charles Wesley. These documents were adapted from the Christian Classics Ethereal Library server. These versions had been designed for the Wesley homepages on the General Board of Global Ministries, The United Methodist Church Web Server at http://gbgm-umc.org. Last modified by the GBGM on October 24, 2000. Modified by the authors.

- *Awake, Thou That Sleepest*: Edited anonymously at the Memorial University of Newfoundland with corrections by George Lyons for the Wesley Center for Applied Theology, Northwest Nazarene University at Nampa, Idaho.
- *Catholic Spirit*: Edited anonymously at the Memorial University of Newfoundland with corrections by George Lyons for the Wesley Center for Applied Theology.
- *Justification By Faith*: Edited anonymously at the Memorial University of Newfoundland with corrections by George Lyons for the Wesley Center for Applied Theology.
- *Original Sin*: Edited by George Lyons at Northwest Nazarene, for the Wesley Center for Applied Theology.
- *The Almost Christian*: Edited anonymously at the Memorial University of Newfoundland with corrections by George Lyons of Northwest Nazarene University for the Wesley Center for Applied Theology.
- *The Circumcision of the Heart*: Originally edited by Dave Giles (student at Northwest Nazarene University) with corrections by George Lyons of Northwest Nazarene University for the Wesley Center for Applied Theology.
- *The Danger of Riches*: Edited by Ralph E. Neil, Chair of the Division of Philosophy and Religion at Northwest Nazarene University, with corrections by George Lyons for the Wesley Center for Applied Theology.
- *The General Spread of the Gospel*: Edited by Syl Hunt IV, student at Northwest Nazarene University, with corrections by George Lyons for the Wesley Center for Applied Theology.
- *The Means of Grace*: Edited by Darin Million, student at Northwest Nazarene University, with corrections by George Lyons for the Wesley Center for Applied Theology.
- *The New Birth*: Edited by Michael Anderson, student at Northwest Nazarene University, with corrections by George Lyons for the Wesley Center for Applied Theology.
- *The New Creation*: Edited by Jennette Descalzo, student at Northwest Nazarene University, with corrections by George Lyons for the Wesley Center for Applied Theology.
- *The Scripture Way of Salvation*: Edited by Anne-Elizabeth Powell, Librarian at Point Loma Nazarene University, with corrections by George Lyons for the Wesley Center for Applied Theology.

Other sermons of John Wesley:

- *The One Thing Needful*: Retyped from Albert C. Outler and Richard P. Heitzenrater, Editors, *John Wesley's Sermons: An Anthology*. Nashville: Abingdon Press, 1991, pp. 34-38. Modified by the authors.

The Hymns of Charles Wesley:

- *Collection of Hymns for the Use of the People Called Methodists*, edited by the Rev. John Wesley, 1889 (public domain through the General Board of Global Ministries: http://gbgm-umc.org/umhistory/wesley/hymns/#hymns).
- *Cyber Hymnal*: http://www.cyberhymnal.org/bio/w/e/s/wesley_c.htm.
- *Hymns of Faith and Life*: Free Methodist Church and The Wesleyan Church, Winona Lake, Indiana: Light and Life Press, 1976.
- *Sing To The Lord*, Church of Nazarene Hymnal, Kansas City: Lillenas Publishing Company, 1993.

- *The African Methodist Episcopal Church Bicentennial Hymnal*, The African Methodist Episcopal Church. Nashville: 1984.
- *The United Methodist Hymnal*, Nashville: The United Methodist Publishing House, 1989.

Permissions:

- Unless otherwise indicated, all Scripture quotations are from the King James Version of the Holy Bible or are the personal translations by John Wesley.
- NIV: Scripture quotations marked NIV are taken from the Holy Bible, New International Version TM. NIV®. Copyright © 1973, 1978, 1984 by International Bible Society. Used by permission of Zondervan. All rights reserved.
- NKJV: Scripture quotations marked NKJV are taken from the New King James Version®. Copyright © 1982 by Thomas Nelson, Inc. Used by permission. All rights reserved.
- NRSV: Scripture quotations marked NRSV are from the New Revised Standard Version Bible, copyright © 1989, Division of Christian Education of the National Council of the Churches of Christ in the United States of America. Used by permission. All rights reserved.
- TNIV: Scripture quotations marked TNIV are taken from the Holy Bible, Today's New International Version TM. TNIV®. Copyright © 2001, 2005 by International Bible Society®. Used by permission of Zondervan. All rights reserved worldwide.

Other Acknowledgements:

- Meaning of Terms Used by John and Charles Wesley in Modern English" (Appendix C) originated from a list compiled by Dr. Howard A. Snyder of Asbury Theological Seminary for The Wesley Center for Applied Theology, Northwest Nazarene University (http://wesley.nnu.edu/john_wesley/wesley-vocabulary.htm).
- Teachers and students from the following churches provided comments that were incorporated into the text: Bethany United Methodist Church, Ellicott City, Maryland (two classes); Calvary United Methodist Church, Mount Airy, Maryland (two classes); Lamont United Methodist Church, Lamont, Oklahoma; and Oakdale Emory United Methodist Church, Olney, Maryland.
- The authors would like to acknowledge the extensive assistance provided by Howertine Farrell Duncan, Head of Public Services and (formerly) Reference/Serials Librarian, Wesley Theological Seminary. Technical assistance was also provided by Sara Sheppard, Course of Study Registrar.

PREFACE

John Wesley's teachings demonstrate his fervent desire for people to become committed disciples of Jesus Christ. His sermons, in particular, have relevance for those who desire to live faithfully in today's culture. However, it is evident that, within our churches generally, there is a lack of understanding about Wesleyan theology. Even people from the Methodist tradition are largely uninformed about Wesley's "Way of Salvation." As students, former students, and faculty of Wesley Theological Seminary—all of whom are working in congregational settings—we share a common passion for communicating the theological understanding of John Wesley.

Consequently, we have drawn together an easy-to-understand study of the central themes of Wesley's theology of salvation by using his sermons and related Scripture. This series of lessons is a tool that will enable people in small-group settings to return to their roots by studying Christian doctrine on topics such as salvation, sin, grace, justification, sanctification, ethical living, and the work of Jesus Christ. *Reclaiming the Wesleyan Tradition* is a resource for the members of local churches to acquire a better comprehension of Wesley's theology in lay terms.

Our aim is to help people understand and apply Wesley's teachings to their lives, especially his Way of Salvation. The Way of Salvation is a spiritual road map of the journey of humanity toward God—a pathway of grace—in which we respond to God with increasing self-awareness of our separation from God (and other people), and our consequent need to come back home to God. This spiritual foundation in Wesleyan theology is needed in order for congregations to be motivated once again by the early Methodist mission to "spread scriptural holiness over the land." It is also needed so that congregants will be empowered to pursue Wesley's biblically grounded goal of being renewed in God's image. Through this study, we pray that individuals and entire churches will be energized by the Holy Spirit to be transformed from being "almost Christians" to being "altogether Christians."

As a thirteen-week study, *Reclaiming the Wesleyan Tradition* works effectively as a series for a small study group, adult Sunday school class, home fellowship group, campus ministry group, Emmaus community, women's or men's fellowship, or new membership class. It also serves as an excellent follow-up for a group that has worked with *Disciple Bible Study, Jesus in the Gospels,* or *Christian Believer* (all available from Abingdon Press), and would then like to learn more about their particular theological heritage.

From the outset, this study may look difficult. Do not let it intimidate you. We encourage you not to give up quickly. Studying Wesley's sermons—even though the eighteenth century wording can sometimes be challenging to decipher—has transformed our lives, and we are convinced that it can reshape your spiritual life as well. There may be times when you become frustrated with the older English usage. For example, as a product of eighteenth century British culture, Wesley used the word *man* when he was referencing all of humanity, as did all writers of his era. If, however, you allow yourself to read past his use of sometimes archaic terms, you will find that there will be many times when you will be inspired, rejuvenated, spiritually awakened, and brought into a deeper communion with God.

Take the time to ponder the questions found on the last page of each lesson. Reflect upon them, meditate on them, and ask them of your friends, family, and small-group members.

In the words of John Wesley, "The best of all is, God is with us!"

CONTENTS

HOW TO USE THIS STUDY

This study series is designed to help people understand John Wesley's Way of Salvation, thereby generating theological dialogue within local congregations and inspiring individuals who are searching for spiritual growth. The weaving of Scripture, hymns, and theological insights contained in Wesley's sermons will make an impact on participants so that their own study of Scripture will become more meaningful and their desire to grow in Christ-likeness will increase. The result, we trust, will be nothing less than the stirring up of a spiritual revival in the Wesleyan tradition.

This study series has several components. Lesson One presents a short biographical description of John Wesley's life, allowing study participants to examine key elements in Wesley's ministry and helping them to understand how his theology developed over his lifetime. Each of the remaining twelve lessons is based on a theme that corresponds to one of Wesley's sermons. The text of the sermon to be studied for the week follows each of the lessons.

Class members will read the sermon text during the week. While reading and preparing, participants are encouraged to pray that the Holy Spirit would show them how Wesley's teaching from the sermon applies to their own spiritual life, their church life, and the life of their community. The suggested weekly reading and study time outside of class is one to two hours. Parts of the sermon that do not directly pertain to the lesson are indented in order to indicate they are optional for a first reading.

Prior to each sermon is a lesson of about six pages. Class members will prepare notes and answers to questions that are asked at the end of the lesson. The first page identifies "Our Starting Point," the assignment of readings from the sermon, a reflection statement, and a prayer. The second page provides a place for the class members to write their notes or to pose questions from the readings. Since Wesley's sermons were written in eighteenth century English, it is expected that participants may have questions of clarification; such questions should be written down on the second page of the lesson and brought to the class session.

The third, fourth, and fifth pages of each lesson discuss the topic in more depth. Additional material that expands on this discussion is presented in the right-hand columns of these pages, with more space provided for student notes. For example, relevant Scripture passages are quoted, and citations from other authors are used to inspire an interest within the student to read relevant supplementary works on Wesley's theology. Selected verses from one or more hymns by Charles Wesley are given in each lesson to emphasize the theme of the week. The last page of the lesson is a page of application. This is where participants apply the concepts of the lesson to their own lives and to the life of the church and community.

Appendix A provides extra information for facilitating class discussions, and Appendix B has a list of resources. The glossary of theological terms (Appendix C) also includes a list (Section C.3) that defines several out-of-date terms found in the sermons; these are marked with an asterisk (*) on first use.

Lesson 1–Introducing the Wesleys

This one thing I do: forgetting what lies behind and straining forward to what lies ahead,
I press on toward the goal for the prize of the heavenly call of God in Christ Jesus.

Philippians 3: 13-14, NRSV

I soon found what spirit he [Mr. Spangenberg] was of; and asked his advice with regard
to my own conduct. He said, "My brother, I must first ask you one or two questions. Have you the
witness within yourself? Does the Spirit of God bear witness with your spirit, that you are a child of
God? I was surprised, and knew not what to answer. He observed it, and asked, "Do you know
Jesus Christ? I paused, and said, "I know he is the Savior of the world." True," replied he; "but do
you know he has saved you? I answered, "I hope he has died to save me." He only added,
"Do you know yourself? I said, "I do." But I fear they were vain words.

John Wesley, Journal; February 7, 1736

My gracious Master and my God, assist me to proclaim,
to spread through all the earth abroad the honors of thy name.

Charles Wesley, "O For a Thousand Tongues to Sing" (1739)

OUR STARTING POINT

Concrete events make a deep impact on our lives. The family that we are raised in and major milestones in our lives—these leave lasting marks. God has been at work since the beginning of creation, reaching out to God's people through the experiences of their lives in order to make divine grace, mercy, and love known to all.

As we begin our study of the Wesleyan "Way of Salvation," it is important to have a basic understanding of the person who first articulated this "way," based on his understanding of Scripture. John Wesley is commonly regarded as the founder of the Methodist movement and of the theology that bears his name. One of the most compelling aspects of the narrative of John Wesley is to see how God was at work throughout each part of his life.

In this introductory chapter, we will take a brief look at the major stages in Wesley's journey of faith. Understanding Wesley's background will demonstrate his importance for the Methodist revival and his continuing importance for those who seek to recover a Wesleyan heritage.

REFLECTION

You have searched me, Lord,
    and you know me.
  For you created my inmost being;
    You knit me together in my mother's womb.
I praise you because I am fearfully and wonderfully made;
    your works are wonderful,
    I know that full well.

Ps. 139:1, 13-14; TNIV

PRAYER

Lord God, Creator of the Heavens and the Earth,

It amazes me that you have been reaching out to me, seeking to show me your love and grace, even before I was born. And you continue to work in my life through all that happens in it.

Thank you for allowing us to see you at work not just in our own lives, but also in the lives of others. As we begin our study of Reclaiming the Wesleyan Tradition, *enable us to see you at work in the lives of John and Charles Wesley and help us to come to understand you more fully through reading and studying the words of their sermons and hymns.*

In all that we do, it is our desire to see your face and come to know and love you and your Son, Jesus Christ, more deeply. Amen.

Prayer concerns for this week:

Note: Terms found in the sermon texts marked with an asterisk (*) have changed meanings since their use by the Wesleys in the 18th Century; these are listed with modern English equivalents in the Glossary, Appendix C, Part C.3. Footnotes are explained at the end of each lesson.

John Wesley: Man on a Mission

John Wesley started a revival in England that not only spread throughout Britain but also caught on in the British colonies in America, soon to become the United States. Wesley and his followers were often called "Methodists," because they were methodical in their daily practice of reading Scripture and prayer and they were incredibly disciplined in ordering their lives together in faith. The Methodist movement grew and thrived under John Wesley's direction and piercing gaze.

In this study, we will seek to recover a sense of the Wesleyan heritage through reading sermons and hymns written by John and Charles Wesley. This gives us the benefit of learning about Wesleyan theology from its founders. Clearly, John Wesley is a crucial figure in the Christian tradition. But who was he? Why is he so important?

A Brand Plucked from the Burning

John Wesley was born on June 17, 1703, in Epworth, England. His father, Samuel, was an Anglican pastor; and his mother, Susanna—an amazing, self-educated woman—was kept busy raising and teaching their many children. Wesley was the fifteenth of nineteen children, nine of whom died as infants. Susanna Wesley played a very important role in her children's lives. Her discipline and focus were especially instilled in her son John, as would be evident later in his life in his habit of rising early every morning and his determination to avoid wasting time.

One of the most important events of Wesley's childhood occurred on February 9, 1709. On this night, the house that the Wesleys lived in caught fire. Samuel and Susanna thought everyone had escaped safely from the house, but when John stood up on a chest to be seen from his second-story window, his father panicked. A few neighbors saw John; one climbed onto the back of another, and they pulled him out of the window just before the roof of the burning house collapsed.

Wesley's parents were understandably affected by his dramatic rescue. Susanna especially felt that God's hand was upon her son's life and that it was her responsibility to raise him as God intended. Perhaps more importantly, John Wesley powerfully

NOTES, REFLECTIONS, AND QUESTIONS

The Methodist Mission

John Wesley believed that the mission of the people called Methodists was "to reform the nation; particularly the church, and to spread Scriptural holiness over the land."[1]

Revival and Renewal of the Anglican Church

John and Charles Wesley talked about reforming the church because they were priests in the Church of England (Anglicans), and they saw the Methodist movement as a renewal movement within the Anglican Church.

Journal of John Wesley

One of the reasons it is so easy to see the major stages in John Wesley's life is due to his practice of journaling. It is in Wesley's journals that we find some of the most vivid descriptions of his faith journey on the Way of Salvation.

I do intend to be more particularly careful of the soul of this child, that thou hast so mercifully provided for, than ever I have been, that I may do my endeavor to instill into his mind the principles of thy true religion and virtue.[2]
Susanna Wesley, *Journal Notebook*, 1711

experienced God's providence and came to feel that the Lord had a special plan for his life that would not be thwarted.

It is tempting to gloss over Wesley's spiritual journey by portraying him as simply getting up after being rescued from the fire, brushing the ashes off of his face, and immediately beginning a revival of English Christianity. However, Wesley's journey from being a "brand plucked from the burning" to a zealous and effective servant of the Lord included several dramatic shifts.

Oxford Methodists

The first major step came when the Wesley brothers went to Oxford University. During the time John was at Oxford, he read two books that had a lasting influence on him: Jeremy Taylor's *Holy Living* and Thomas à Kempis's *Imitation of Christ*. In 1725, as a result of reading these books, John Wesley became convinced that he must give every part of his life to God. With astonishing dedication and perseverance, he sought to live this out. A few years later, Charles Wesley, John's younger brother, invited John to join a small group of young men who began meeting together in order to encourage each other to do God's work. Other Oxford students soon mockingly labeled this group "The Holy Club." The name "Methodist" was not initially a compliment or a self-given name, but another name given to the group by those who ridiculed them. It was during this time that the seeds of accountability and a method for living out the Christian life were first planted and took root.

Voyage to the Americas

Yet, there was still much that God needed to do before Wesley would be responsible for anything that could be called a "Revival." The next stage of the journey for Wesley entailed a trip to America. In 1735, he set sail for the British colony of Georgia. This trip bore no fruit for John Wesley's attempts to spread the gospel. In fact, the most important result of this trip was that Wesley realized that something was wrong with his experience of God and his approach to Christianity.

During a turbulent storm on his way to Georgia, when Wesley feared for his life, he noticed a group of German Christians. These Moravians possessed a spirit of calm throughout the voyage, even in the face of death. When confronted with a group of Christians who had such peace during a life-threatening experience, Wesley realized that his faith was lacking. While he believed that Jesus was the savior of the world, he did not know Jesus to be his personal savior. He did not **know** that Christ died for **him**. He lacked what others would call "assurance" (see Lesson 7).

Wesley's time in Georgia was nowhere near the success he had hoped it would be. The low point came when Wesley, after jealously refusing to serve communion to a recently married woman with whom he earlier had a romantic interest, was brought up on charges before a grand jury in Savannah. After posting bail, Wesley fled the colony before the case could come to trial. Although his ministry in Georgia was a failure, he made progress in his journey of Christian discipleship by first taking a few steps backward.

Is not this a brand plucked out of the burning?
Zech. 3:2; *KJV*

Teach me to do your will, for you are my God.
Ps. 143:10; *NRSV*

In the midst of the psalm wherewith their service began, the sea broke over, split the main-sail in pieces, covered the ship, and poured in between the decks, as if the great deep had already swallowed us up. A terrible screaming began among the English. The Germans calmly sung on. I asked one of them afterwards, "Was you not afraid? He answered, "I thank God, no." I asked, "But were your women and children afraid? He replied mildly, "No; our women and children are not afraid to die."
John Wesley, *Journal*, January 25, 1736

I went to America, to convert the Indians; but O! who shall convert me? Who, what is he that will deliver me from this evil heart of unbelief? I have a fair summer religion. I can talk well; nay, and believe myself, while no danger is near: But let death look me in the face, and my spirit is troubled. Nor can I say, "To die is gain!"
John Wesley, *Journal*; January 24, 1738

Although he never returned to America, he indirectly had a major impact there; indeed, the revival that began in England eventually overflowed into what became the United States.

Aldersgate Experience

When Wesley returned to England, he pursued the assurance of salvation that he witnessed in the Moravians. In particular, Wesley began meeting with a Moravian minister named Peter Böhler. Wesley had many conversations with Böhler and others about salvation by faith. The personal faith that others were emphasizing Wesley found confirmed in Scripture. Ultimately, Wesley experienced a spiritual crisis when he came to believe that one could be forgiven solely through faith by God's grace. There was nothing that anyone could do in order to merit God's forgiveness.

After Wesley wrestled with this for some weeks, on May 24, 1738, he had an experience at a small-group meeting on Aldersgate Street, London, that confirmed in his heart what he had come to be convinced of intellectually. As Wesley heard someone reading from the preface to Martin Luther's commentary on the Epistle to the Romans, he received the assurance that he had been searching for—that his sins were forgiven because of his faith in Jesus Christ. This experience gave Wesley a renewed zeal for doing God's work, and he found, by God's grace, that his ministry began to bear fruit.

Submitting To Be More Vile: Field Preaching

A crucial change became visible in Wesley's approach to ministry after his experience of assurance. Before Aldersgate, Wesley was very concerned with order and ceremony, sometimes to a fault. Afterwards, he increasingly became open to the ways that God seemed to be working. If the Holy Spirit was doing something in his midst, Wesley wanted to cooperate with it rather than be an obstacle to it. This was most clearly seen in Wesley's decision to embrace outdoor preaching, known as "field preaching." Initially, it was difficult for Wesley to see preaching outside of a church as anything other than "vile."

However, he ultimately "submitted to be more vile" because he realized that God was at work. Although field preaching would never become second nature for Wesley, it did become one of the major ways that many people heard and responded to the Methodist message.

Charles Wesley, Fellow Pilgrim

Charles Wesley does not often receive the attention he deserves in discussions of the rise of Methodism. Charles was a part of the first group of Oxford Methodists, before John joined the group. Charles also experienced a similar assurance of the forgiveness of his sins, which occurred three days before John's. While John was the organizational leader and the voice of the movement, Charles was in some sense the heart and soul behind the movement. While the distinctions between them should not

For by grace you have been saved through faith, and this is not your own doing; it is the gift of God—not the result of works, so that no one may boast.

Eph. 2:8-9; *NRSV*

*In the evening I went very unwillingly to a society [small group] in Aldersgate-Street, where one was reading Luther's preface to the Epistle to the Romans. About a quarter before nine, while he was describing the change which God works in the heart through faith in Christ, I felt my heart strangely warmed. I felt I did trust in Christ, Christ alone for salvation: And an assurance was given me, that he had taken away **my** sins, even **mine,** and saved **me** from the law of sin and death.*

John Wesley, *Journal,* May 24, 1738 (§14)

At four in the afternoon, I submitted to be more vile, and proclaimed in the highways the glad tidings of salvation, speaking from a little eminence in a ground adjoining to the city, to about three thousand people.

John Wesley, *Journal,* April 2, 1739

be overstated, if John were the intellectual force of Methodism, writing sermons and publishing responses to attacks on Methodist doctrine, Charles was the one who helped the "head knowledge" become "heart knowledge." Charles Wesley was a prolific poet and hymn writer, having penned over 5,500 hymns![3] He made major contributions to the Christian faith with cherished hymns such as "Hark! The Herald Angels Sing," "Love Divine, All Loves Excelling" and "Christ the Lord Is Risen Today." Although the two brothers did not always agree, they complemented each other's strengths beautifully.

The Importance of Wesley's Sermons

Although the brothers continued to work together throughout much of their ministry, John Wesley was the indisputable leader of the Methodist movement. It was his voice more than any other that articulated the theology behind the revival. Of the sermons we will read as a part of this study, twelve were written by John Wesley and one by Charles Wesley.[4] They were written by the Wesleys as a guide to the preachers and teachers in the Methodist movement. These sermons were sometimes used by other preachers as sermons themselves, but more often they were used as a guide and illustration of what Methodists believe and why.

Wesley's sermons continue to guide, direct, and challenge those who hear and read them. Wesley's sermons continue to have the weight of authority; indeed, Wesley's sermons are part of the doctrinal standards of all Methodist and Wesleyan denominations today. It is no accident that Methodist beliefs are outlined in sermons, because these comprised the primary medium that Wesley used to teach what it meant to be a faithful Christian. Today, there is still no better place to look to discover what it means to be Wesleyan than in John Wesley's sermons!

NOTES, REFLECTIONS, AND QUESTIONS

Hail the heaven-born Prince of Peace!
Hail the Sun of Righteousness!
Light and life to all he brings,
risen with healing in his wings.

Mild he lays his glory by,
born that we no more may die,
Born to raise us from the earth,
born to give us second birth.

Hark! the herald angels sing,
"Glory to the new-born King!"

Charles Wesley, "Hark, the Herald Angels Sing" (1739)—UM Hymnal #240; AME Hymnal #115; CME Hymnal #58; Afr. Amer. Heritage Hymnal #214, 217; Free Methodist Ch. & The Wesleyan Ch. Hymnal #117; Ch. of Nazarene Hymnal #191

RESPONDING FAITHFULLY

What did you know about John and Charles Wesley before you began this lesson?

Were any of these ideas challenged or changed?

How do you relate to Wesley's experience at Aldersgate Street?

_____

_____

_____

_____

_____

Peter Böhler mentored John Wesley spiritually. Can you think of people in your own life who have encouraged you to grow in your faith? How did they do so?

_____

_____

_____

_____

_____

Field preaching was a scandalous way of sharing Christ in Wesley's day. Can you think of something comparable to field preaching where your church could more effectively reach those who have not heard the gospel?

_____

_____

_____

_____

_____

LEARNING MORE

More on Wesley's writing[5]:
- John Wesley's *Journal* (especially up to May 24, 1738).

Other Resources:
- Charles Yrigoyen, Jr., *John Wesley: Holiness of Heart and Life*.
- Kenneth J. Collins, *A Real Christian*.
- Richard P. Heitzenrater, *Wesley and the People Called Methodists*.
- Henry D. Rack, *Reasonable Enthusiast: John Wesley and the Rise of Methodism*.

LOOKING AHEAD

Next Lesson. Created in the Image of God—the necessity of being restored to a right relationship with God.

Teacher Helps provides follow-up questions that may be useful in class discussions.

END NOTES

[1] See, for example, John Wesley, *The General Spread of the Gospel*, §§13-14; and *On God's Vineyard*, §II.8.

[2] Susanna Wesley, *Journal Notebook (1709-1718)*, May 17, 1711, Headingley Manuscript A, Wesley College, Bristol, England. See Charles Wallace, Jr., Editor, *Susanna Wesley: The Complete Writings*, New York: Oxford University Press, 1997 [Entry 47], p. 235.

[3] According to John R. Tyson, "Recent research suggests that he [Charles] wrote over 9,000 hymns and sacred poems, though fewer than half that number were published in his lifetime." Tyson, John R. *Charles Wesley on Sanctification: A Biographical and Theological Study.* Grand Rapids, Michigan, Asbury Press, 1986, p. 47.

[4] One complete sermon is provided for each of Lessons 2 to 12. Lesson 13 has parts of two sermons of John Wesley as assigned reading.

[5] Full bibliographic references for suggested resources are provided in Appendix B.

Lesson 2—Created in the Image of God

One thing is needful.

Luke 10:42; NRSV

Now, that the recovery of the image of God, of this glorious liberty, of this perfect soundness, is the one thing needful upon earth, appears first from hence, that the enjoyment of them was the one end of our creation. For to this end was man created, to love God; and this end alone, even to love the Lord his God with all his heart, and soul, and mind, and strength. But love is the very image of God: it is the brightness of his glory.

John Wesley, The One Thing Needful, §II.2

OUR STARTING POINT

God created humanity "good" and in God's own image. For Wesley, that image has been destroyed as a result of the creature's disobedience in the Fall. Moreover, there is one thing needful for restoring the relationship of the human creature to God.

READING

Read daily the reflection and prayer (below) about God's good creation. Wesley wrote *The One Thing Needful* in 1734, prior to his Aldersgate experience. This sermon is foundational in Wesley's understanding of Christian salvation: that salvation comes in the restoration of humans to the image of God.

- Day 1   Scan the entire sermon *The One Thing Needful.* Scan Lesson 2.
- Day 2   Carefully read the four-part introduction to this sermon.
- Day 3   Read Part I (§§I.1-5). What is the one thing needful?
- Day 4   Read Part II (§§II.1-5). Proving the one thing needful.
- Day 5   Read Part III (§§III.1-3). Exhortation.
- Day 6   Read the creation narrative in Gen. 1:1-2:3. Reread the lesson and answer the questions at the end.
- Day 7   Rest.

REFLECTION

So God created humankind in his image, in the image of God he created them; male and female he created them. God blessed them . . . . God saw everything that he had made, and indeed, it was very good.

Gen. 1:27-28, 31; NRSV

PRAYER

Pray daily before study:

O Great Creator and Healer of my soul,

When I meditate upon all of your good creation, including humankind, and then think about the way things have become, it makes my soul cry out in despair. How can there be so much brokenness and evil in the good world that you created?

Then I think about how you created each of us in your good and perfect image. We have fallen far away from that image. I pray for your mercy and grace so that your perfect image can be restored in my soul. Help me use your means of grace and place my trust in Christ's work for me on the cross so that I may be restored back to you. Amen.

Prayer concerns for this week:

Daily Reflections

Day 1   Scan the entire sermon *The One Thing Needful*. Scan Lesson 2.

Meaning for me:

Day 2   Carefully read the four-part introduction to this sermon.

Meaning for me:

Day 3   Read Part I (§§I.1-5). What is the one thing needful?

Meaning for me:

Day 4   Read Part II (§§II.1-5). Proving the one thing needful.

Meaning for me:

Day 5   Read Part III (§§III.1-3). Exhortation.

Meaning for me:

Day 6   Read the creation narrative in Gen. 1:1-2:3.
Reread the lesson and answer the questions at the end.

Meaning for me:

The Doctrine of Salvation

Salvation. How are we saved? What *is* salvation? Salvation is reconciliation with God. For John Wesley, the way to reconciliation both in the present and in the future is restoring the image of God (*imago Dei*). Humanity's need for restoration to the image of God was a consistent theme throughout Wesley's ministry.

For Wesley, we must "exchange the image of Satan for the image of God" [*The One Thing Needful*, §I.5 (Section I.5)]. *We* are responsible for our sins, not the good God who created us in the divine image. Humanity is now in a state of sinfulness and corruption. Humanity needs healing. Jesus is the one who gives us power over sin. We need to recover the image that was lost. The one thing needful is to be restored to the perfect image of God. The Way of Salvation is the journey toward that restoration.

This sermon points us toward our entire life's goal as a Christian believer. We should not be discouraged if our journey so far has only taken us a few small steps. The main thing is that we have begun to move forward.

In *The One Thing Needful*, Wesley used the powerful imagery of healing, in which sin is an infirmity of human nature (e.g., "loathsome sores" and a "fatal leprosy") and the human soul is diseased. Humanity's original situation was that humans were created "good" by God, but then humanity fell. Now we are born evil and must seek a sense of renewal. Humanity must be restored again and healed of its disease.

How the Image of God Is Restored. Wesley's theological goal for humanity (the renewal of the image of God) remained the same over the course of his lifetime. However, his understanding of the method by which humans are restored to the image of God changed. His own experience of the new birth and receiving forgiveness of sin led him to a more complete understanding of the role that *grace* plays (see Lesson 4) in the restoration of the image of God in humanity.

Works Versus Faith. Early in his career, Wesley tried everything in his power to be accepted by God. He met regularly with a small group of fellow Christians, who joined together in doing good works in acts of charity [works of love]. He was trying to understand how faith fit in with good works.

Wesley's early understanding of the restoration of humanity to the image of God (as expressed in this sermon) was by acting in charity (works of love), righteousness, and humility; and in recognizing our sinful state. Change would occur in our humility; humility was worked out in charity; and charity affected our actions in the way we live.[1] Note that phrases in the sermon, such as the following, seem to point to our "works" assisting us in achieving saving faith: "The one work we have to do" (§I.5); "one thing we have to do"(§III.1); "Let us then labor" (§III.3); and "to attain" (§III.3).

Later in his ministry, Wesley viewed the idea of "doing" and "laboring" in order to please God as "works righteousness"—which he rejected since our works are not sufficient for

NOTES, REFLECTIONS, AND QUESTIONS

[God] has given us his very great and precious promises, so that through them you may participate in the divine nature and escape the corruption in the world caused by evil desires.

2 Peter 1:4; *NIV*

When he [humanity] lost his innocence [due to sin], he lost his happiness.

John Wesley, *The Fall of Man*, §I.2

I wait my vigour to renew,
Thine image to retrieve,
The veil of outward things pass through,
And gasp in thee to live.

I work, and own the labor vain,
And thus from works I cease;
I strive, and see my fruitless pain,
Till God create my peace.

Charles Wesley, "Still, for Thy Loving Kindness"—*AME Hymnal* #289

To recover our first estate, from which we are thus fallen, is the one thing now needful—to re-exchange the image of Satan for the image of God, bondage for freedom, sickness for health. Our one great business is to raze out of our souls the likeness of our destroyer . . . to be formed anew after the likeness of our creator.

John Wesley, *The One Thing Needful*, §I.5

our salvation—and thereafter he strongly emphasized reliance on God's grace for faith. After his Aldersgate experience, he understood that humanity is restored to God's image not by good works, but only by God's mercy. He then exhorted his listeners and readers to use all the means of grace given by God (see Lesson 8), in order to allow for the restoration of the image of God in humanity.

In his mature theology, Wesley came to a more grace-filled understanding of how to be renewed in the image of our creator. This emphasis on grace became the basis for his entire message of salvation.

What Is the Image of God?

In part, Wesley understood the original, ideal human condition to be a mirror reflecting the image of God. According to theologian Theodore Runyon, Wesley's understanding of the image of God can be described as a "vocation or calling to which human beings are called, the fulfillment of which constitutes their true destiny…. It resides in the way the creature lives out his or her life in relation to the Creator, using whatever gifts and capacities have been received to be in communion with their source and to reflect that source in the world."[2] This image of God can also be described as the relationship in which the creature receives blessings from God, and in turn transmits that which is received to the rest of creation. "'God is love.' Accordingly, man at his creation was full of love; which was the sole principle of all his tempers, thoughts, words, and actions. God is full of justice, mercy, and truth; so was man as he came from the hands of his Creator."[3]

Will and Freedom

For Wesley, the human native state is freedom. Creaturely freedom was designed for positive, intimate relationship with the Creator,[4] but it had the potential to be abused. "Human beings misused this freedom. They have revolted against their Creator, distorting the relationship for which they were created."[5]

Nature of Evil. Evil, for Wesley, was the result of our misuse of human freedom to "construct a self-sufficient world."[6] Wesley believed that the material world was part of God's good creation. When the human spirit, which was also originally created as "good," rebelled against this good creation, the result was evil. At the moment of human disobedience:

A whole army of evils, totally new, totally unknown till then, broke in upon rebel man, and all other creatures, and overspread the face of the earth.[7]

Wesley's Perspective on the Christian Life

John Wesley had a perspective of what the Christian life was all about. While it was not unlike the perspectives of many other Christian theologians, Wesley had an especially compelling way of portraying Christian discipleship.

Freedom for Humanity Is Part of the Salvation Plan

He [God] made man in his own image, a spirit endued with understanding and liberty. Man abusing that liberty produced evil, [and] brought sin and pain into the world. This God permitted in order to [receive] a fuller manifestation of his wisdom, justice, and mercy, by bestowing on all who would receive it an infinitely greater happiness than they could possibly have attained. . . . [So once again,] If Adam had not fallen, then Christ would not have died.

John Wesley, *God's Love to Fallen Man*, §§II.15 & I.1

Man found out to himself many inventions of happiness independent of God, [then man] threw not only himself but the whole creation, which was intimately connected with him, into disorder, misery, and death.

John Wesley, *God's Approbation of His Works*, §II.3

So God created man in his own image: in the image of God created he him!' . . . God did not make him mere matter, a piece of senseless, unintelligent clay, but a spirit like himself . . . As such he was endued with understanding, with a will, including various affections, and with liberty, a power of using them in a right or wrong manner, of choosing good or evil. Otherwise neither his understanding nor his will would have been to any purpose; for he must have been as incapable of virtue or holiness as the stock of a tree. Adam, in whom all mankind were then contained, freely preferred evil to good. He chose to do his own will rather than the will of his Creator. He 'was not deceived', but knowingly and deliberately rebelled against his Father and his King. In that moment he lost the moral image of God, and, in part, the natural. He commenced unholy, foolish, and unhappy. And 'in Adam all died.' He entitled all his posterity to error, guilt, sorrow, fear; pain, diseases, and death.

John Wesley, *On The Fall of Man*, §II.6

For Wesley, something is broken and needs to be fixed. That brokenness is our human nature. God is about the task of fixing the brokenness. God's whole reason for being incarnated in this world was to repair and heal this brokenness through Christ's life, death, and resurrection.

We are to envision ourselves as part of this process. We are to be participants in God's own work of renewing creation. We can be full participants with God through Christ in the work that God has for us.

That work is to renew the whole of creation to what God intended it to be. It begins with us. Then it moves out to our communities and to the world. Wesley's understanding of the Gospel message can be summarized as this: humanity has sinned, the world is a fallen place, but God's desire, God's full intent is to bring the whole world, as well as us, back to restoration and reconciliation. As this salvation occurs, humans begin to experience the restored image of God for themselves.

NOTES, REFLECTIONS, AND QUESTIONS

[You] have clothed yourself with the new self, which is being renewed in knowledge according to the image of its creator.

Col. 3:10; *NRSV*

RESPONDING FAITHFULLY

What is the "one thing needful" (that is, the one essential priority) in your life?

Do you think people are basically "good"?

How do you account for people who are "good" yet do not seem to be Christian?

What is the image of God? How can you become restored in the image of God?

_____

_____

_____

_____

_____

_____

_____

How can we as a community of faith become participants in God's own work of renewing all of creation?

_____

_____

_____

_____

_____

_____

_____

LEARNING MORE

The following sermons by Wesley will also speak of the fall of humanity and the need for a restored image of God (web sites are noted in Appendix B):

- *God's Approbation of His Works*
- *The Fall of Man*
- *The Great Privilege of Those Born of God.*

The following books outline Wesley's full theology:

- Randy L. Maddox, *Responsible Grace: John Wesley's Practical Theology*
- Theodore Runyon, *The New Creation: John Wesley's Theology Today.*

LOOKING AHEAD

Next Lesson. Original Sin—more on our natural human condition.

Teacher Helps provides follow-up questions that may be useful in class discussions.

ENDNOTES

[1] John Wesley, *The Image of God*, §III.1-2.
[2] John Wesley, *The New Birth*, §I.1.
[3] Theodore Runyon, *The New Creation: John Wesley's Theology Today.* Nashville: Abingdon Press, 1998, p. 13-14.
[4] Runyon, *op.cit.*, p. 11.
[5] *Ibid.*, p. 10 .
[6] *Ibid*, p. 11.
[7] John Wesley, *God's Approbation of His Works*, §II.1.

Reading for Lesson 2: The One Thing Needful (1734)

One thing is needful (Luke 10:42).

Introduction

1. Could we suppose an intelligent being, entirely a stranger to the state of this world and its inhabitants, to take a view of their various enterprises and employments, and thence conjecture the end* of their existence, he would surely conclude that these creatures were designed to be busied about many things. While he observed not only the infinite difference of the ends which different men were pursuing, but how vast a multitude of objects were successively pursued by almost every different person, he might fairly infer that for all these things were the sons of men placed upon the earth, even to gratify their several* desires with sensual pleasure, or riches, or honor, or power.

2. How surprised then would he be to hear their Creator declare to all, without distinction, "One thing is needful! But how much more when he knew that this one thing needful for men, their one business, the one end of their existence, was none of all those things which men were troubled about, none of all those ends they were pursuing, none of all those businesses wherein they were so deeply engaged, which filled their hearts and employed their hands. Nay, that it was an end not only distinct from but contrary to them all—as contrary as light and darkness, heaven and hell, the kingdom of God and that of Satan!

3. The only thought he could form in their favor must be that they had a surplus of time at their command; that they therefore trifled a few hours, because they were assured of thousands of years wherein to work. But how beyond measure would he be amazed when he heard further that these were creatures of a day; that as they yesterday arose out of the dust, so tomorrow they were to sink into it again; that the time they had for their great work was but a span long, a moment; and that they had no manner of assurance of not being snatched away in the midst of this moment, or indeed at the very beginning of it! When he saw that all men were placed on a narrow, weak, tottering bridge, whereof either end was swallowed up in eternity; that the waves and storms which went over it were continually bearing away one after another, in an hour when they looked not for it; and that they who yet stood, knew not but they should plunge into the great gulf the very next instant, but well knew that if they fell before they had finished their work they were lost, destroyed, undone—for ever: how would all utterance, nay, all thought, be lost! How would he express, how would he conceive the senselessness, the madness, of those creatures who, being in such a situation, could think of anything else, could talk of anything else, could do anything besides, could find time for any other design, or care, but that of ensuring the one thing needful!

4. It cannot, therefore, be an improper employment for us, first, to observe what this one thing needful is; and, secondly, to consider a few of the numberless reasons that prove* this to be the one thing needful.

I.

1. We may observe what this one thing is, in which, 'tis true, many things are comprised—as are all the works of our callings, all that properly belong to our several stations in the world, insomuch that whoever neglects any of these so far neglects the one thing needful. And this indeed can no otherwise be pursued than by performing all the works of our calling, but performing them in such a manner as in and by everyone to advance our great work.

2. Now this great work, this one thing needful, is the renewal of our fallen nature. In the image of God was man made, but a little lower than the angels. His nature was perfect, angelical, divine. He was an incorruptible picture of the God of glory. He bore his stamp on every part of his soul; the brightness of his Creator shone mightily upon him. But sin has now effaced the image of God. He is no longer nearly allied to angels. He is sunk lower than the very beasts of the field. His soul is not only earthly and sensual but devilish. Thus is the mighty fallen! The glory is departed from him! His brightness is swallowed up in utter darkness!

3. From the glorious liberty wherein he was made, he is fallen into the basest bondage. The devil, whose slave he now is, to work his will, hath him so fast in prison that he cannot get forth. He hath bound him with

---

* Words and phrases marked with an asterisk (*) have an unusual meaning and are further explained in the Glossary. (See Appendix C, Section C.3.)

a thousand chains, the heavy chains of his own vile affections. For every inordinate appetite, every unholy passion, as it is the express image of the god of this world, so it is the most galling yoke, the most grievous chain, that can bind a free-born spirit. And with these is every child of Adam, everyone that is born into this world, so loaded that he cannot lift up an eye, a thought to heaven, that his whole soul cleaves unto the dust!

4. But these chains of darkness under which we groan do not only hold us in on every side, but they are within us, too; they enter into our soul; they pierce through its inmost substance. Vile affections are not only so many chains, but likewise so many diseases. Our nature is distempered, as well as enslaved; the whole head is faint, and the whole heart sick. Our body, soul, and spirit are infected, overspread, consumed, with the most fatal leprosy. We are all over, within and without, in the eye of God, full of diseases, and wounds, and putrefying sores. Every one of our brutal passions and diabolical tempers*, every kind of sensuality, pride, selfishness, is one of those deadly wounds, of those loathsome sores, full of corruption, and of all uncleanness.

5. To recover our first estate, from which we are thus fallen, is the one thing now needful—to re-exchange the image of Satan for the image of God, bondage for freedom, sickness for health. Our one great business is to raze out of our souls the likeness of our destroyer, and to be born again, to be formed anew after the likeness of our Creator. It is our one concern to shake off this servile yoke and to regain our native freedom; to throw off every chain, every passion and desire that does not suit an angelical nature. The one work we have to do is to return from the gates of death to perfect soundness; to have our diseases cured, our wounds healed, and our uncleanness done away.

II.

1. Let us in the second place consider a few of the numberless reasons which prove that this is the one thing needful; so needful that this alone is to be had in view, and pursued at all times and in all places; not indeed by neglecting our temporal affairs, but by making them all minister unto it; by so conducting them all, that every step therein may be a step to this higher end.

2. Now, that the recovery of the image of God, of this glorious liberty, of this perfect soundness, is the one thing needful upon earth, appears first from hence, that the enjoyment of them was the one end of our creation. For to this end was man created, to love God; and to this end alone, even to love the Lord his God with all his heart, and soul, and mind, and strength. But love is the very image of God: it is the brightness of his glory. By love man is not only made like God, but in some sense one with him. "If any man love God, God loveth him, and cometh to him, and maketh his abode with him." He "dwelleth in God, and God in him"; and "he that is thus joined to the Lord is one spirit."[1] Love is perfect freedom. As there is no fear, or pain, so there is no constraint in love. Whoever acts from this principle alone, he doth whatsoever he will. All his thoughts move freely; they follow the bent of his own mind, they run after the beloved object. All his words flow easy and unconstrained; for it is the abundance of the heart that dictates. All his actions are the result of pure choice: the thing he would, that he does, and that only. Love is the health of the soul, the full exertion of all its powers, the perfection of all its faculties. Therefore, since the enjoyment of these was the one end of our creation, the recovering of them is the one thing now needful.

3. May not the same truth appear, secondly, from hence, that this was the one end of our redemption; of all our blessed Lord did and suffered for us; of his incarnation, his life, his death? All these miracles of love were wrought with no other view than to restore us to health and freedom. Thus [he] himself testifies of the end of his coming into the world: "The Spirit of the Lord is upon me; he hath sent me to heal the brokenhearted, to preach deliverance to the captives"[2]; or, as the prophet expresses it, "to preach good tidings to the meek, to bind up the broken-hearted, to proclaim liberty to the captives, and the opening of the prison to them that are bound."[3] For this only he lived, that he might heal every disease, every spiritual sickness of our nature. For this only he died, that he might deliver those who were all their lifetime subject to bondage. And it was in pursuance of the very same design that he gave us his merciful law. The end of his commandment, too, was only our health, liberty, perfection, or, to say all in one word, charity*. All the parts of it center in this one point, our renewal in the love of God; either enjoining what is necessary for our recovery thereof, or forbidding what is obstructive of it. Therefore this, being the one end of our redemption as well as our creation, is the one thing needful for us upon earth.

[1] Ed: John 14:23; 1 Jn. 4:12; and 1 Cor. 6:17.
[2] Ed: Luke 4:18.
[3] Ed: Isa. 61:1.

4. This is the one thing needful, thirdly, because it is the one end of all God's providential dispensations. Pleasure and pain, health and sickness, riches and poverty, honor and dishonor, friends and enemies, are all bestowed by his unerring wisdom and goodness with a view to this one thing. The will of God, in allotting us our several portions of all these, is solely our sanctification; our recovery from that vile bondage, the love of his creatures, to the free love of our Creator. All his providences, be they mild or severe, point at no other end than this. They are all designed either to wean us from what is not, or to unite us to what is worthy our affection. Are they pleasing? Then they are designed to lift up our hearts to the Parent of all good. Are they painful? Then they are means of rooting out those passions that forcibly withhold us from him. So that all lead that same way, either directly or indirectly, either by gratitude or mortification. For to those that have ears to hear, every loss, especially of what was nearest and dearest to them, speaks as clearly as if it were an articulate voice from heaven, "Little children, keep yourselves from idols."[4] Every pain cries aloud, "Love not the world, neither the things of the world."[5] And every pleasure says, with a still small voice, "Thou shalt love the Lord thy God with all thy heart."[6]

5. To the same end are all the internal dispensations of God, all the influences of his Holy Spirit. Whether he gives us joy or sorrow of heart, whether he inspires us with vigor and cheerfulness, or permits us to sink into numbness of soul, into dryness of heaviness, 'tis all with the same view, viz., to restore us to health, to liberty, to holiness. These are all designed to heal those inbred diseases of our nature, self-love, and the love of the world. They are all given together with the daily bread of his external dispensations, to enable us to turn that into proper nourishment, and so recover his love, the health of our souls. Therefore the renewal of our nature in this love being not only the one end of our creation and our redemption, but likewise of all the providences of God over us, and all the operations of his Spirit in us, must be, as the eternal wisdom of God hath declared, the one thing needful.

III. Exhortation

1. How great reason is there, then, even in the Christian world, to resume the Apostle's exhortation, "Awake thou that sleepest, and arise from the dead!"[7] Hath not Christ given thee light? Why then sittest thou still in the shadow of death? What slumber is this which hangs on thy temples? Knowest thou not that only one thing is needful?

What then are all these? Why hath any but that the least place in thy thoughts, the least share in thy affections? Is the entertainment of the senses the one thing needful? Or the gratifying [of] the imagination with uncommon, or great, or beautiful objects? Our Lord saith not so. Saith he then that the one thing is to acquire a fortune, or to increase that thou hast already? I tell you, nay: these may be the thoughts of those that dream, but they cannot [be those] of waking men. Is it to obtain honor, power, reputation, or (as the phrase is) to get preferment? Is the one thing to gain a large share in that fairest of the fruits of earth, learning? No.

Though any of these may sometimes be conducive to, none of them is, the one thing needful. That is simply to escape out of the snare of the devil, to regain an angelic nature; to recover the image wherein we were formed; to be like the Most High. This, this alone, is the one end of our abode here; for this alone are we placed on the earth; for this alone did the Son of God pour out his blood; for this alone doth his Holy Spirit watch over us. One thing we have to do, to press towards this mark of the prize of our high calling; to emerge out of chains, diseases, death, into liberty, health, and life immortal!

2. Let us well observe, that our Lord doth not call this our main concern, our great business, the chief thing needful, but the *one* thing—all others being either parts of this or quite foreign to the end of life. On this then let us fix our single view, our pure unmixed intention; regarding nothing at all, small or great, but as it stands referred to this. We must use many means; but let us ever remember we have but one end. For as while our eye is single, our whole body will be full of light, so, should it ever cease to be single, in that moment our whole body would be full of darkness.

---

[4] Ed: 1 Jn. 5:21.
[5] Ed: 1 Jn. 2:15.
[6] Ed: Deut. 6:5; 30:6; Matt. 22:37; Mark 12:30; and Luke 10:27.
[7] Ed: Eph. 4:14.

3. Be we then continually jealous over our souls, that there be no mixture in our intention. Be it our one view in all our thoughts, and words, and works, to be partakers of the divine nature, to regain the highest measure we can of that faith which works by love, and makes us become one spirit with God. I say, the highest measure we can; for who will plead for any abatement of health, liberty, life, and glory? Let us then labor to be made perfectly whole, to burst every bond asunder; to attain the fullest conquest over this body of death, the most entire renovation of our nature; knowing this, that when the Son of man shall send forth his angels to cast the double-minded into outer darkness, then shall the single of heart receive the one thing they sought, and shine forth as the sun in the kingdom of their Father!

Now to God the Father, God the Son, and God the Holy Ghost,
be ascribed all honor and glory, adoration and worship, both now and for ever. Amen.

Lesson 3—The Effects of Sin

The LORD saw that the wickedness of humankind was great in the earth,
and that every inclination of the thoughts of their hearts was only evil continually.

Gen. 6:5; NRSV

Ye know that the great end of religion is, to renew our hearts in the image of God,
to repair that total loss of righteousness and true holiness which we sustained by the sin
of our first parent. Ye know that all religion which does not answer this end, all that stops short of this,
the renewal of our soul in the image of God, after the likeness of him that created it,
is no other than a poor farce, and a mere mockery of God, to the destruction of our own soul.

John Wesley, Original Sin, §III.2

OUR STARTING POINT

We have noted that God created humanity "good" and in the image of God, but the creature's disobedience in the Fall has defaced that image. We now consider the effects of such disobedience, often called "original sin."

Wesley taught that our present human condition is one of sin, since "corruption pervades every human faculty and power," leaving us unable to save ourselves in restoring the image of God intended for each of us. We realize that the general human problem has become *my* problem, that human sin is *my* sin. We wonder if there is any hope for reconciliation with God—any hope for salvation.

READING

Read daily the reflection and prayer, and use the following readings in your daily study of *Original Sin* (1759), found at the end of this lesson:

Day 1   Read through the entire sermon, treating as optional those sections that are indented with a smaller font. Scan Lesson 3.

Day 2   Reread the four-part Introduction. True human nature.

Day 3   Read Genesis 4-6 and Part I (§§I.1-5) of the sermon. The nature of sin.

Day 4   Read Part II (§§II.1-11). The present corrupt human condition.

Day 5   Read Part III (§§III.1-5). Implications for Christians today.

Day 6   Reread *Original Sin* and make notes of what you think must occur to overcome our loss of the image of God. Reread the lesson and answer the questions at the end.

Day 7   Rest.

REFLECTION

Have mercy on me, O God, according to your steadfast love; according to your abundant mercy blot out my transgressions. Wash me thoroughly from my iniquity, and cleanse me from my sin. For I know my transgressions, and my sin is ever before me. Against you, you alone, have I sinned, and done what is evil in your sight, so that you are justified in your sentence and blameless when you pass judgment. Indeed, I was born guilty, a sinner when my mother conceived me. You desire truth in the inward being; therefore teach me wisdom in my secret heart. Purge me with hyssop, and I shall be clean; wash me, and I shall be whiter than snow.

Ps. 51:1-7; NRSV

PRAYER

Merciful God and Healer of my soul, how could it be that we have become so separated from you that we no longer have you as a constant source of life? Have we really lost the image of your divine self that is given to each of us?

Teach me how to seek you. Show me how to love you. Do not judge me as I am, but rather have mercy on me. Take away my guilt and shame. Cleanse me from my sin. I long for your wisdom to enter my inward being. I am lost without your steadfast love. Accept me as I am and then transform me as you wish. Amen.

Prayer concerns for this week:

Daily Reflections

Day 1   Read through the entire sermon, treating as optional those sections that are indented with a smaller font. Read Lesson 3.

Meaning for me:

Day 2   Reread the four-part Introduction. True human nature.

Meaning for me:

Day 3   Genesis 4-6 and Part I (§§I.1-5) of the sermon. The nature of sin.

Meaning for me:

Day 4   Read Part II (§§II.1-11). The present human condition.

Meaning for me:

Day 5   Read Part III (§§III.1-5). Implications for Christians today.

Meaning for me:

Day 6   Reread *Original Sin* and make notes of what you think must occur to overcome our loss of the image of God. Reread the lesson and answer the questions at the end.

Meaning for me:

The Way of Salvation

Human Condition. For John Wesley, the Way of Salvation is restoring the image of God. He eventually came to see that there is nothing we can do on our own to recover what has been lost. Before we can know the powerful and transforming nature of God's grace, we need to consider carefully the current human condition, including our own complicity in it.

At one time, humans reflected the image of God in all their thoughts and actions. In this state, people knew and loved God, and their behavior reflected that knowledge and love. Yet God granted people freedom of thought and action. God chose not to impose the divine self; rather, God sought a relationship with human beings in which people *choose* harmony with God and with all creation.

The Fall. The biblical story affirms that people from their earliest beginnings have used their freedom to turn away from God and pursue human-defined goals and objects. The Fall from God involved not simply disobedience, but also separation from God (and God's creation). Men and women focus on their own happiness and universally experience false pride, anxiety, and irresponsibility.[1] Human actions are often directed to futile, even perverse, ends. Relationships are dominated by fear and not love. People abandon God's call for stewardship of creation and substitute its exploitation.

Implications of the Fall. Human sin is the result of unbelief and separation from God. People left in this condition can progressively move farther and farther away from God until they have stifled any hope of being renewed in the image of God. Unbelief and separation from God leads to further evils such as pride and self-will. Sadly, people in such a condition have lost the ability to do anything to cooperate with God's will; they are unable—even in their best moments—to convey to others God's blessing and love. People who are completely separated from God's loving presence find "the life of God was extinguished in [their] soul. [They] lost the whole moral image of God, righteousness and true holiness. [They were] unholy; . . . unhappy; . . . full of sin, full of guilt and tormenting fears."[2]

All creation groans to God under the exploitation and cruelty of humankind [Rom. 8:19-22]. As creation's caretakers, we have rebelled against our Creator God and abandoned the direction God intended for us. All creation suffers from human sin. People no longer seek God night and day, no longer continually call on God's name, and no longer sing God's praises with joyful thanksgiving for life. God searches and we are not found. God speaks and we do not answer. The conduit of God's blessing of life and fullness of life lies dormant. God bears the pain of creation and especially of human sin.[4]

Salvation. Salvation—reconciliation with God—comes by faith, which itself is a gift of God. This salvation is available here and now: God saving each of us from sin, original and actual, past and present; and saving each of us from sin's guilt and the power

The disposition of sin is not immorality and wrong-doing, but the disposition of self-realization—I am my own god . . . it has . . . one basis, my claim to my right to myself.[3]
Oswald Chambers, *My Utmost for His Highest*

Upright, both in heart and will,
We by our God were made;
But we turn'd from good to ill,
And o'er the creatures stray'd;
Multiplied our wandering thought,
Which first was fix'd on God alone;
In ten thousand objects sought
The bliss we lost in one.

Charles Wesley, "Upright, Both in Heart and Will"—*Methodist 1889 Hymnal*, #98

Long my imprisoned spirit lay,
fast bound in sin and nature's night . . .

Charles Wesley, "And Can It Be that I Should Gain" (1739)—*UM Hymnal* #363; *AME Hymnal* #459; *Free Methodist Ch. & The Wesleyan Ch. Hymnal* #273; *Ch. of Nazarene Hymnal* #225

What is more natural to us than to seek happiness in the creature, instead of the Creator?—to seek that satisfaction in the works of his hands, which can be found in God only? What more natural than "the desire of the flesh? That is, of the pleasure of sense in every kind?"
John Wesley, *Original Sin*, §II.9

of that sin. We are also saved from fear: fear of torment, of punishment, and of the wrath of God. We are treated as adopted children by an indulgent and merciful Father.

In salvation, we have peace, hope, and love of God in our hearts. By faith, we are enabled to avoid habitual sin, willful sin, sinful desire—sin in act, word, or thought. This is a high standard! We are able to be saved from sin and the consequences of sin by the atonement of Christ actually applied to the soul. This is expressed by the concept of "justification." Those saved by faith are born again.[5] (See Lesson 6 on Justification and Lesson 7 on New Birth.)

Notes for Understanding the Sermon, *Original Sin*

In Part I, Wesley considers the biblical human condition. He observes that human hearts are evil, rejecting humanity's own moral goodness, the nature of God, the divine will, and the image of God. The Scripture for this sermon (Gen. 6:5) asserts that "every inclination of the thoughts of their hearts was only evil continually." The evil state of humankind begins with a turning away from God that leads to the human choice of separation from God. Some implications of this evil state are human mortality; suffering; and broken relationships with God, with each other, and with the rest of creation.

In Part II, Wesley considers the human condition in the present day. Wesley uses the term "natural state" to characterize the human condition outside of and unassisted by God's initiative of grace and the gift of love. "In this state, humanity is blind to the things of God and is not sensible of its spiritual needs."[6] There is no love of God and no fear of God. In this state, "all people are rank idolaters" [§II.7], filled with "pride, self-will, and love of the world" [§III.1].

In Part III, Wesley draws some implications from his understanding of the human condition without the effects of God's grace." [Other religions] knew not that all men were empty of all good, and filled with all manner of evil. They were wholly ignorant of the entire depravation of the whole human nature, of every man born into the world, in every faculty of his soul, not so much by those particular vices which reign in particular persons, as by the general flood of atheism and idolatry, of pride, self-will, and love of the world." Moreover, "the great end of [true] religion is, to renew our hearts in the image of God, to repair that total loss of righteousness and true holiness which we sustained by the sin of our first parent" (§III.5).

Theology of the Sermon, *Original Sin*

Wesley understood the "ideal state of humanity [as] created in God's Image and living in God's Likeness."[7] The Fall is a "result of the human preference to compete with God as God's equal, rather than accepting our need for participating in the Divine gifts."[8]

Original sin is understood by some biblical interpreters as guilt inherited from human posterity. Other interpreters suggest that the guilt becomes ours when we imitate the sin of our

NOTES, REFLECTIONS, AND QUESTIONS

Do Not Be Discouraged

Despite Wesley's realistic assessment of human nature, sin is not the dominant note of his theology. The triumph of God's grace is never obscured by human sinfulness.

[Our own sins], considered with regard to ourselves, are chains of iron and fetters of brass. They are wounds wherewith the world, the flesh, and the devil, have gashed and mangled us all over. They are diseases that drink up our blood and spirits, that bring us down to the chambers of the grave. But considered . . . with regard to God, they are debts, immense and numberless.

John Wesley, *Upon Our Lord's Sermon on the Mount:* Discourse Six, §III.13 (commentary on the Lord's Prayer)

ancestors. Yet even after the Fall, men and women retained the ability to cooperate with divine grace and are thus accountable for responding to that grace.[9]

Three forms of original sin that mirror satanic evil are atheism (unbelief), pride, and self will. A fourth form is love of the world and its components (actual sins; see 1 Jn. 2:16): desire of the flesh, desire of the eye, and pride of life.

In our posture before God, we stand guilty and in need of forgiveness. In characterizing the state of the sinner, Wesley often used therapeutic (medical) language, in which sin is described as an infirmity of human nature (e.g., a "loathsome leprosy") and the human soul as diseased. After Wesley wrote this sermon, in the latter years of his ministry, Wesley tended to use the term "inbeing sin" instead of "original sin" to express his conviction that "the issue of guilt [is located in] our own sins rather than the sin of our ancestors."[10] People are universally sinful, but the guilt for their sin is not inherited. "No one is damned for Adam's sin alone."[11]

Inbeing sin is seen as the "present infection of our nature." Inbeing sin is a result of our own separation from God, and it is the source of actual sins. Spiritual corruption of inbeing sin takes such forms as (1) our will being "seized by wrong tempers," (2) our liberty being lost, and (3) our conscience being "left without a standard."[12]

Yet, as we will see, our gracious God has provided the opportunity and power to overcome our sin.

Ah whither should I go,
Burdened, and sick, and faint?

To whom should I my troubles show,
And pour out my complaint?

My Savior bids me come,
Ah! why do I delay?

He calls the weary sinner home,
And yet from him I stay!

What is it keeps me back,
From which I cannot part,

Which will not let my Savior take,
Possession of my heart?

Some cursed thing unknown
Must surely lurk within,

Some idol, which I will not own,
Some secret bosom-sin.

Charles Wesley, "Ah Whither Should I Go"—
AME Hymnal #368

. . . there is in the heart of every child of man, an inexhaustible fund of ungodliness and unrighteousness, so deeply and strongly rooted in the soul, that nothing less than almighty grace can cure it.
John Wesley, *The Deceitfulness of the Human Heart*, §II.4

RESPONDING FAITHFULLY

Would you agree that human sinfulness is universal?

How do you react to the description of our sinful nature as a "disease of the soul"?

Wesley says, "Know your disease, know your cure" (§III.5). What is the cure to sin?

In §II.7, Wesley says that we have set up idols in our hearts and we worship them. What are your idols?

LEARNING MORE

The following sermons by Wesley also speak of the fall of humanity and the need for a restored image of God:
- *On the Deceitfulness of the Human Heart*
- *The New Birth*
- *On Working Out Our Own Salvation.*

Read and reflect on Rom. 5:12-21 and Ps. 51.
Consult the following books on Wesley's theology:
- Kenneth J. Collins, *The Scripture Way of Salvation* (especially Ch. 1)
- Randy L. Maddox, *Responsible Grace: John Wesley's Practical Theology*
- Theodore Runyon, *The New Creation: John Wesley's Theology Today.*

LOOKING AHEAD

Next Lesson. Prevenient Grace—God takes the initiative to overcome our universal sinful condition.

Teacher Helps provides follow-up questions that may be useful in class discussions.

END NOTES

[1] Theodore Runyon, *The New Creation: John Wesley's Theology Today.* Nashville. Abingdon Press, 1998, p. 20.
[2] Kenneth J. Collins, *The Scripture Way of Salvation: The Heart of John Wesley's Theology.* Nashville: Abingdon Press, 1997, pp. 27, 30, 35-36.
[3] Oswald Chambers, *My Utmost for His Highest.* New York: Dodd, Mead and Company, 1935, p. 279.
[4] Paraphrased from John Wesley, *The Doctrine of Original Sin*, III.2 (a treatise: *Works*, IX, 318-319).
[5] John Wesley, *Salvation By Faith*, Part II, 1738 (preached just eighteen days after his Aldersgate experience!).
[6] Kenneth J. Collins, *Wesley on Salvation: A Study in the Standard Sermons.* Grand Rapids. Francis Asbury Press, 1989, p. 21.
[7] Randy L. Maddox, *Responsible Grace: John Wesley's Practical Theology.* Nashville: Kingswood Books, Abingdon Press, 1994, p. 73.
[8] *Ibid.*, p. 66.
[9] *Ibid.*
[10] *Ibid.*, pp. 74-76.
[11] C. H. Spurgeon, Sermon 140, *A Simple Sermon for Seeking Souls*, July 12, 1857, §3. " . . . no man was ever yet damned for Adam's sin alone."
[12] Maddox, op. cit., pp. 81-82.

Reading for Lesson 3: Original Sin (1759)[1]

And God saw that the wickedness of man was great in the earth,
and that every imagination of the thoughts of his heart was only evil continually (Gen. 6:5).

Introduction

1. How widely different is this [Gen. 6:5] from the fair pictures of human nature which men have drawn in all ages! The writings of many of the ancients abound with gay* descriptions of the dignity of man; whom some of them paint as having all virtue and happiness in his composition, or, at least, entirely in his power, without being beholden to any other being; yea, as self-sufficient, able to live on his own stock, and little inferior to God himself.

2. Nor have heathens alone, men who were guided in their researches by little more than the dim light of reason, but many likewise of them that bear the name of Christ, and to whom are entrusted the oracles of God, spoken as magnificently concerning the nature of man as if it were all innocence and perfection. Accounts of this kind have particularly abounded in the present [18th] century; and perhaps in no part of the world more than in our own country [England]. Here not a few persons of strong understanding, as well as extensive learning, have employed their utmost abilities to show what they termed, "the fair side of human nature." And it must be acknowledged that, if their accounts of him be just, man is still but "a little lower than the angels"[1]; or, as the words may be more literally rendered, "a little less than God."

3. Is it any wonder that these accounts are very readily received by the generality of men? For who is not easily persuaded to think favorably of himself? Accordingly, writers of this kind are almost universally read, admired, applauded. And innumerable are the converts they have made, not only in the gay [sophisticated], but the learned world. So that it is now quite unfashionable to talk otherwise, to say anything to the disparagement of human nature; which is generally allowed, notwithstanding a few infirmities, to be very innocent, and wise, and virtuous!

4. But, in the meantime, what must we do with our Bibles?—for they will never agree with this. These accounts, however pleasing to flesh and blood, are utterly irreconcilable with the scriptural. The Scripture avers that "by one man's disobedience all men were constituted sinners"; that "in Adam all died," spiritually died, lost the life and the image of God; that fallen, sinful Adam then "begat a son in his own likeness"—nor was it possible he should beget him in any other; for "who can bring a clean thing out of an unclean?"—that consequently we, as well as other men, were by nature "dead in trespasses and sins," "without hope, without God in the world," and therefore "children of wrath"; that every man may say, "I was shaped in wickedness, and in sin did my mother conceive me"; that "there is no difference," in that "all have sinned and come short of the glory of God," of that glorious image of God wherein man was originally created.[2] And hence, when "the Lord looked down from heaven upon the children of men, he saw they were all gone out of the way; they were altogether become abominable, there was none righteous, no, not one," none that truly "sought after God." Just agreeable [is] this, to what is declared by the Holy Ghost in the words above recited, "God saw," when he looked down from heaven before, "that the wickedness of man was great in the earth"; so great that "every imagination of the thoughts of his heart was only evil continually."

This is God's account of man, from which I shall take occasion,
I. First, to show what men were before the flood;
II. Secondly, to inquire, whether they are not the same now; and,
III. Thirdly, to add some inferences.

I.

1. I am, first, by opening* the words of the text, to show what men were before the flood. And we may fully depend on the account here given. For God saw it, and he cannot be deceived. He "saw that the wickedness of man was great"—not of this or that man; not of a few men only; not barely of the greater part, but of man in general; of men universally. The word includes the whole human race, every partaker of human nature.

---

[1] Ed: Some text in many of the sermons has been indented and presented with smaller font; such sections may be skipped when the sermon is scanned initially. The indentation is not in the original.
[2] Ps. 8:5; Heb. 2:7,9 (footnotes with citations are not in the original).

And it is not easy for us to compute their numbers, to tell how many thousands and millions they were. The earth then retained much of its primeval beauty and original fruitfulness. The face of the globe was not rent and torn as it is now; and spring and summer went hand in hand. 'Tis therefore probable [that] it afforded sustenance for far more inhabitants than it is now capable of sustaining; and these must be immensely multiplied, while men begat sons and daughters for seven or eight hundred years together. Yet, among all this inconceivable number, *only* "Noah found favor with God." He alone (perhaps including part of his household) was an exception from the universal wickedness, which, by the just judgment of God, in a short time after brought on universal destruction. All the rest were partakers in the same guilt, as they were in the same punishment.

2. "God saw all the imaginations of the thoughts of his heart"—of his soul, his inward man, the spirit within him, the principle of all his inward and outward motions. He "saw all the imaginations." It is not possible to find a word of a more extensive signification. It includes whatever is formed, made, fabricated within; all that is or passes in the soul; every inclination, affection, passion, appetite; every temper, design, thought. It must of consequence include every word and action, as naturally flowing from these fountains, and being either good or evil according to the fountain from which they severally flow.

3. Now God saw that all this, the whole thereof, was evil—contrary to moral rectitude; contrary to the nature of God, which necessarily includes all good; contrary to the divine will, the eternal standard of good and evil; contrary to the pure, holy image of God, wherein man was originally created, and wherein he stood when God, surveying the works of his hands, saw them all to be "very good"; contrary to justice, mercy, and truth, and to the essential relations which each man bore to his Creator and his fellow-creatures.

4. But was there not good mingled with the evil? Was there not light intermixed with the darkness? No; none at all: "God saw that the whole imagination of the heart of man was only evil." It cannot indeed be denied but many of them, perhaps all, had good motions put into their hearts; for the Spirit of God did then also "strive with man," if haply he might repent, more especially during that gracious reprieve, the hundred and twenty years, while the ark was preparing. But still "in his flesh dwelt no good thing"; all his nature was purely evil. It was wholly consistent with itself, and unmixed with anything of any opposite nature.[3]

5. However, it may still be [a] matter of inquiry, "Was there no intermission of this evil? Were there no lucid intervals, wherein something good might be found in the heart of man? We are not here to consider what the grace of God might occasionally work in his soul; and, abstracting from this, we have no reason to believe there was any intermission of that evil. For God, who "saw the whole imagination of the thoughts of his heart to be only evil," saw likewise that it was always the same, that it "was only evil continually"—every year, every day, every hour, every moment. He never deviated into good.

II.

Such is the authentic account of the whole race of mankind which he who knoweth what is in man, who searcheth the heart and trieth the reins, hath left upon record for our instruction. Such were all men before God brought the flood upon the earth. We are, secondly, to inquire, whether they are the same now.

1. And this is certain, the Scripture gives us no reason to think any otherwise of them. On the contrary, all the above-cited passages of Scripture refer to those who lived after the flood. It was above a thousand years after that God declared by David concerning the children of men, "They are all gone out of the way" of truth and holiness; "there is none righteous, no, not one." And to this bear all the prophets witness, in their several generations. So Isaiah, concerning God's peculiar* people (and certainly the heathens were in *no better* condition), "The whole head is sick, and the whole heart faint. From the sole of the foot even unto the head there is no soundness; but wounds, and bruises, and putrefying sores." The same account is given by all the apostles, yea, by the whole tenor of the oracles of God. From all these we learn, concerning man in his natural state, unassisted by the grace of God, that "all the imaginations of the thoughts of his heart are" still "evil, only evil," and that "continually."

2. And this account of the present state of man is confirmed by daily experience. It is true, the natural man discerns it not. And this is not to be wondered at. So long as a man born blind continues so, he is scarce sensible of his want*. Much less, could we suppose a place where all were born without sight, would they be

---

[3] Rom. 5:19; 1 Cor. 15:22; Gen. 5:3; Rom. 3:23.

sensible of the want of it. In like manner, so long as men remain in their natural blindness of understanding, they are not sensible of their spiritual wants, and of this in particular. But as soon as God opens the eyes of their understanding, they see the state they were in before; they are then deeply convinced that "every man living," themselves especially, are, by nature, "altogether vanity"; that is, folly and ignorance, sin and wickedness.

3. We see, when God opens our eyes, that we were before *atheoi en toi kosmoi*—without God, or, rather, atheists, in the world. We had, by nature, no knowledge of God, no acquaintance with him. It is true, as soon as we came to the use of reason, we learned "the invisible things of God, even his eternal power and Godhead, from the things that are made." From the things that are seen we inferred the existence of an eternal, powerful being that is not seen. But still, although we acknowledged his being we had no acquaintance with him. As we know there is an emperor of China, whom yet we do not know; so we knew there was a King of all the earth, yet we knew him not. Indeed we could not by any of our natural faculties. By none of these could we attain the knowledge of God. We could no more perceive him by our natural understanding, than we could see him with our eyes. For "no one knoweth the Father but the Son, and he to whom the Son willeth to reveal him. And no one knoweth the Son but the Father, and he to whom the Father revealeth him."

4. We read of an ancient king, who, being desirous to know what was the natural language of men, in order to bring the matter to a certain issue, made the following experiment: he ordered two infants, as soon as they were born, to be conveyed to a place prepared for them, where they were brought up without any instruction at all, and without ever hearing a human voice. And what was the event*? Why that, when they were at length brought out of their confinement, they spoke no language at all; they uttered only inarticulate sounds, like those of other animals. Were two infants in like manner to be brought up from the womb without being instructed in any religion, there is little room to doubt but (unless the grace of God interposed) the event would be just the same. They would have no religion at all. They would have no more knowledge of God than the beasts of the field, than the wild ass's colt. Such is natural religion, abstracted from traditional, and from the influences of God's Spirit!

5. And having no knowledge, we can have no love of God: We cannot love him we know not. Most men *talk* indeed of loving God, and perhaps imagine that they do. At least, few will acknowledge they do not love him. But the fact is too plain to be denied. No man loves God by nature, no more than he does a stone, or the earth he treads upon. What we love we delight in: but no man has naturally any delight in God. In our natural state we cannot conceive how anyone should delight in him. We take no pleasure in him at all; he is utterly tasteless to us. To love God! It is far above, out of our sight. We cannot, naturally, attain unto it.

6. We have by nature, not only no love, but no fear of God. It is allowed, indeed, that most men have, sooner or later, a kind of senseless, irrational fear, properly called "superstition"; though the blundering Epicureans gave it the name of religion. Yet even this is not natural, but acquired; chiefly by conversation* or from example. By nature "God is not in all our thoughts." We leave him to manage his own affairs, to sit quietly, as we imagine, in heaven, and leave us on earth to manage ours. So that we have no more of the fear of God before our eyes, than of the love of God in our hearts.

7. Thus are all men "atheists in the world." But atheism itself does not screen us from *idolatry*. In his natural state, every man born into the world is a rank idolater. Perhaps, indeed, we may not be such in the vulgar* sense of the word. We do not, like the idolatrous heathens, worship molten or graven images. We do not bow down to the stock of a tree, to the work of our own hands. We do not pray to the angels or saints in heaven, any more than to the saints that are upon the earth. But what then? We have "set up our idols in our heart"; and to these we bow down and worship them. We worship ourselves, when we pay that honor to ourselves which is due to God only. Therefore all pride is idolatry; it is ascribing to ourselves what is due to God alone. And although pride was not made for man, yet where is the man that is born without it? But thereby we rob God of his unalienable right, and idolatrously usurp his glory.

8. But pride is not the only sort of idolatry which we are all by nature guilty of. Satan has stamped his own image on our heart in self-will also. "I will," said he, before he was cast out of heaven, "I will sit upon the sides of the north"; I will do my own will and pleasure, independently of that of my Creator. The same does every man born into the world say, and that in a thousand instances; nay, and avow it too, without ever blushing upon the account, without either fear or shame. Ask the man, "Why did you do this? He answers, "Because I had a mind to it." What is this but, "Because it was my will"; that is, in effect, because the devil and I are agreed; because Satan and I govern our actions by one and the same principle. The will of God, meantime, is not in his thoughts, is not considered in the least degree; although it be the supreme rule of every intelligent creature, whether in heaven or earth, resulting from the essential, unalterable relation which all creatures bear to their Creator.

9. So far we bear the image of the devil, and tread in his steps. But at the next step we leave Satan behind; we run into an idolatry whereof he is not guilty: I mean *love of the world*; which is now as natural to every man as to love his own will. What is more natural to us than to seek happiness in the creature instead of the Creator?—to seek that satisfaction in the works of his hands, which can be found in God only? What more natural than "the desire of the flesh?"—that is, of the pleasure of sense in every kind? Men indeed talk magnificently of despising these low pleasures, particularly men of learning and education. They affect to sit loose to the gratification of those appetites wherein they stand, on a level with the beasts that perish. But it is mere affectation; for every man is conscious to himself that in this respect he is, by nature, a very beast. Sensual appetites, even those of the lowest kind, have, more or less, the dominion over him. They lead him captive; they drag him to and fro, in spite of his boasted reason. The man, with all his good breeding, and other accomplishments, has no pre-eminence over the goat. Nay, it is much to be doubted whether the beast has not the pre-eminence over him! Certainly he has, if we may hearken to one of their modern oracles, who very decently tells us,

Once in a season beasts too taste of love;
Only the beast of reason is its slave,
And in that folly drudges all the year.

A considerable difference indeed, it must be allowed, there is between man and man, arising (beside that wrought by preventing grace) from difference of constitution and of education. But, notwithstanding this, who that is not utterly ignorant of himself, can here cast the first stone at another? Who can abide the test of our blessed Lord's comment on the Seventh Commandment: "He that looketh upon a woman to lust after her hath committed adultery with her already in his heart?" So that one knows not which to wonder at most, the ignorance or the insolence of those men who speak with such disdain of them that are overcome by desires which every man has felt in his own breast! The desire of every pleasure of sense, innocent or not, being natural to every child of man.

10. And so is "the desire of the eye"; the desire of the pleasures of the imagination. These arise either from great, or beautiful, or uncommon objects—if the two former do not coincide with the latter; for perhaps it would appear, upon a diligent inquiry, that neither grand nor beautiful objects please any longer than they are new; that when the novelty of them is over, the greatest part, at least, of the pleasure they give is over; and in the same proportion as they become familiar, they become flat and insipid. But let us experience this ever so often, the same desire will remain still. The inbred thirst continues fixed in the soul; nay, the more it is indulged, the more it increases, and incites us to follow after another, and yet another object; although we leave everyone with an abortive hope, and a deluded expectation. Yea,

The hoary fool, who many days
 Has struggled with continued sorrow,
Renews his hope, and fondly lays
 The desperate bet upon tomorrow!

Tomorrow comes! 'Tis noon! 'Tis night!
 This day, like all the former, flies:
Yet on he goes, to seek delight
 Tomorrow, till tonight he dies!

11. A third symptom of this fatal disease, the love of the world, which is so deeply rooted in our nature, is "the pride of life"; the desire of praise, of the honor that cometh of men. This the greatest admirers of human nature allow to be strictly natural—as natural as the sight, or hearing, or any other of the external senses. And are they ashamed of it, even men of letters, men of refined and improved understanding? So far from it that they glory therein! They applaud themselves for their love of applause! Yea, eminent Christians, so called, make no difficulty of adopting the saying of the old, vain heathen, *Animi dissoluti est et nequam negligere quid de se homines sentiant*: "Not to regard what men think of us is the mark of a wicked and abandoned mind." So that to go calm and unmoved through "honor and dishonor, through evil report and good report," is with them a sign of one that is, indeed, "not fit to live; away with such a fellow from the earth." But would one imagine that these men had ever heard of Jesus Christ or his apostles; or that they knew who it was that said, "How can ye believe who receive honor one of another, and seek not the honor which cometh of God only? But if this be really so, if it be impossible to believe, and consequently to please God, so long as we "receive (or seek) honor one of another, and seek not the honor which cometh of God only"—then in what a condition are all mankind! The Christians as well as the heathens! Since they all "seek honor one of another"! Since it is as natural for them so to do, themselves being the judges, as it is to see the light which strikes upon their eye, or to hear the sound which enters their ear; yea, since they account it the sign of a virtuous mind to seek the praise of men, and of a vicious one to be content with the honor which cometh of God only!

III.

1. I proceed to draw a few inferences from what has been said. And, first, from hence we may learn one grand, fundamental difference between Christianity, considered as a system of doctrines, and the most refined heathenism. Many of the ancient heathens have largely described the vices of particular men. They have spoken much against their covetousness or cruelty, their luxury or prodigality. Some have dared to say that "no man is born without vices of one kind or another." But still, as none of them were apprized of the fall of man, so none of them knew [of] his total corruption. They knew not that all men were empty of all good, and filled with all manner of evil. They were wholly ignorant of the entire depravation of the whole human nature, of every man born into the world, in every faculty of his soul, not so much by those particular vices which reign in particular persons, as by the general flood of atheism and idolatry, of pride, self-will, and love of the world. This, therefore, is the first, grand, distinguishing point between heathenism and Christianity. The one acknowledges that many men are infected with many vices, and even born with a proneness to them; but supposes withal that in some the natural good much over-balances the evil. The other declares that "all men are conceived in sin," and "shaped in wickedness"—that hence there is in every man a "carnal mind, which is enmity against God, which is not, cannot be, subject to his *law*; and which so infects the whole soul that "there dwelleth in" him, "in his flesh," in his natural state, "no good thing"; but "all the imagination of the thoughts of his heart is evil," "only evil, and that "continually."

2. Hence we may, secondly, learn that all who deny this—call it "original sin" or by any other title—are but heathens still, in the fundamental point which differentiates heathenism from Christianity. They may, indeed, allow that men have many vices; that some are born with us; and that, consequently, we are not born altogether so wise or so virtuous as we should be; there being few that will roundly affirm, "We are born with as much propensity to good as to evil, and that every man is, by nature, as virtuous and wise as Adam was at his creation." But here is the *shibboleth:* Is man by nature filled with all manner of evil? Is he void of all good? Is he wholly fallen? Is his soul totally corrupted? Or, to come back to the text, is "every imagination of the thoughts of his heart only evil continually"? Allow this, and you are so far a Christian. Deny it, and you are but a heathen still.

3. We may learn from hence, in the third place, what is the proper nature of religion, of the religion of Jesus Christ. It is *therapeia psyches*, God's method of healing a soul which is thus diseased. Hereby the great Physician of souls applies medicine to heal this sickness, to restore human nature, totally corrupted in all its faculties. God heals all our atheism by the knowledge of himself, and of Jesus Christ whom he hath sent; by giving us faith, a divine evidence and conviction of God, and of the things of God—in particular, of this important truth, "Christ loved me"—and gave himself for *me*. By repentance and lowliness of heart, the deadly disease of pride is healed; that of self-will by resignation, a meek and thankful submission to the will of God; and for the love of the world in all its branches, the love of God is the sovereign remedy. Now this is properly religion, "faith" thus "working by love"; working the genuine, meek humility, entire deadness to the world, with a loving, thankful acquiescence in, and conformity to, the whole will and Word of God.

4. Indeed, if man were not thus fallen, there would be no need of all this. There would be no occasion for this work in the heart, this renewal in the spirit of our mind. The superfluity of godliness would then be a more proper expression than the "superfluity of naughtiness." For an outside religion, without any godliness at all, would suffice to all rational intents and purposes. It does, accordingly, suffice, in the judgment of those who deny this corruption of our nature. They make very little more of religion than the famous Mr. Hobbes did of reason. According to him, reason is only "a well-ordered train of words": according to them, religion is only a well-ordered train of words and actions. And they speak consistently with themselves; for if the inside be not full of wickedness, if this be clean already, what remains, but to "cleanse the outside of the cup?" Outward reformation, if their supposition be just, is indeed the one thing needful.

5. But ye have not so learned the oracles of God. Ye know that he who seeth what is in man gives a far different account both of nature and grace, of our fall and our recovery. Ye know that the great end of religion is to renew our hearts in the image of God, to repair that total loss of righteousness and true holiness which we sustained by the sin of our first parent. Ye know that all religion which does not answer this end, all that stops short of this, the renewal of our soul in the image of God, after the likeness of him that created it, is no other than a poor farce, and a mere mockery of God, to the destruction of our own soul. O beware of all those teachers of lies who would palm this upon you for Christianity! Regard them not, although they should come unto you with all the deceivableness of unrighteousness; with all smoothness of language, all decency, yea, beauty and elegance of expression, all professions of earnest goodwill to you, and reverence for the Holy Scriptures. Keep to the plain, old faith, "once delivered to the saints," and delivered by the Spirit of God to your hearts. Know your disease! Know your cure! Ye were born in sin; therefore, "ye must be born again," born of God. By nature ye are wholly corrupted. By grace ye shall be wholly renewed. In Adam ye all died: In the second Adam, "in Christ, ye all are made alive." You "that were dead in sins hath he quickened." He hath already given you a principle of life, even faith in him who loved *you* and gave himself for *you*! Now, "go on from faith to faith," until your whole sickness be healed; and all that "mind be in you which was also in Christ Jesus"!

Lesson 4–Prevenient Grace:
God's Loving Initiative

Sleeper, awake! Rise from the dead, and Christ will shine on you.

Eph. 5:14; *NRSV*

How encouraging a consideration is this, that whosoever thou art who obeyest his call,
thou canst not seek his face in vain. If thou even now 'awakest and arisest from the dead,' he hath
bound himself to 'give thee light.' 'The Lord shall give thee grace and glory'; the light of his grace....
God is light, and will give himself to every awakened sinner that waiteth for him.

Charles Wesley, *Awake, Thou That Sleepest*, §§III.1,2

OUR STARTING POINT

We were created to be in close fellowship with God, but our self-centered will has created a situation in which we are far away from God. Only by God's grace through the work of Jesus Christ can we be awakened to our sinful condition and be given the opportunity to turn back to God.

READING

Read daily the reflection and prayer about God's grace, which has been given because God "offers salvation to all people," in order that we may live holy lives now, and claim the promise of eternal life.

This sermon was preached at Oxford University in 1742 by Charles Wesley, John Wesley's younger brother. Charles's theology was nearly identical to that of John's, and John included this sermon in his collection of "standard" sermons. This sermon describes our need to be made aware of our sinfulness, so that we can turn away from our sins and turn towards salvation through Jesus Christ.

Day 1   Scan *Awake, Thou That Sleepest* and read §§I.1-3 of Part I. People are unawakened sinners in their natural state. Scan Lesson 4.
Day 2   Read §§I.4-12. Describing those who are "sleepers."
Day 3   Read §§II.1-13. A summons for sinners to awaken from their sleep.
Day 4   Read §§III.1-5. Christ gives grace to all.
Day 5   Read §§III.6-15. Now is the time to wake up.
Day 6   Reread the lesson and answer the questions at the end.
Day 7   Rest.

REFLECTION

For the grace of God has appeared that offers salvation to all people. It teaches us to say "No" to ungodliness and worldly passions, and to live self-controlled, upright, and godly lives in this present age, while we wait for the blessed hope—the appearing of the glory of our great God and Savior, Jesus Christ, who gave himself for us to redeem us from all wickedness and to purify for himself a people that are his very own, eager to do what is good.

Titus 2:11-14; *TNIV*

PRAYER

Gracious and loving God,

Though I was made in your image, my sin has distanced me from you and from my neighbors. I have been ignorant of many of the ways that you have been there for me all along. But now I ask that you would wake me up to the reality of my situation before you. Help me to be aware of my true condition and my need for your continual grace. Convince me of my sin and give me the grace to turn around so that I can truly trust you and make a commitment to your way for my life. Amen.

Prayer concerns for this week:

Daily Reflections

Day 1   Scan *Awake, Thou That Sleepest* and read §§I.1-3 of Part I. People are unawakened sinners in their natural state. Scan Lesson 4.

Meaning for me:

Day 2   Read §§I.4-12. Describing those who are "sleepers."

Meaning for me:

Day 3   Read §§II.1-13. A summons for sinners to awaken from their sleep.

Meaning for me:

Day 4   Read §§III.1-5. Christ gives grace to all.

Meaning for me:

Day 5   Read §§III.6-15. Now is the time to wake up.

Meaning for me:

Day 6   Read this lesson and answer the questions at the end.

Meaning for me:

Free Grace

When we recognize the reality of original sin and the enormity of our own willful participation in sinful behavior, we can become overwhelmed. Thankfully, God has acted in Jesus Christ to do something about our diseased wills. Through the redemption offered to us by Jesus' death on the cross, God has provided us with a way to be restored to God's image: grace. Grace is God's unmerited love, given to us in spite of our sin. Because of our great need, God has lavished us with great love. The Wesley brothers (John and Charles) taught a lot about the spiritual power of the grace of God. Their deep pessimism regarding human nature was offset by their bold optimism regarding the immense potential for human fulfillment due to divine mercy. God has given us a universal remedy (grace) for a universal evil (sin).

In the sermon *Free Grace*, John Wesley wrote that "the grace or love of God…is free *in* all, and free *for* all." It is free *in* all because "it does not in any wise depend on the good works or righteousness of the receiver; not on anything [the person] has done, or anything [the person] is."[1] We don't have to depend on our being good enough to please God!

This grace is also free *for* all because (in contrast to the Calvinist view of predestination) the Wesleys read in the Bible that God "so loved the [entire] world, that he gave his only begotten son, that *whosoever* believeth on him should not perish but have eternal life" (John 3:16, *KJV*). "The gracious words which came out of [Jesus'] mouth," John Wesley wrote, "are full of invitations to *all* sinners,"[2] not just to some. Jesus "really is the Savior of the world" (John 4:42; *TNIV*). This divine grace is bestowed universally and experienced personally.

Universal Grace

God loves us extravagantly and indiscriminately. Grace is provided for all people, not only a few. No one is excluded from the offer of salvation, though we may resist God's initiative. "The God of love is willing to save all the souls that he has made . . . . But he will not force them to accept of it."[3] God desires that we choose to follow as disciples of Jesus Christ, and to accept the acceptance that God has already offered to us.

The life of grace is an upward call to be made more and more like Christ, in the image of God (see Phil. 3:13-14), which the Wesleys called the "Way of Salvation." Since people are at different places in this process of the restoration of the image of God, God's grace may be thought of as having different purposes at different times in a person's life. God's grace can be seen, for example, as <u>prevenient</u> (the grace that prepares us to respond to God by faith), <u>justifying</u> (the grace that forgives us our sins through faith in Christ), and <u>sanctifying</u> (the grace that empowers us to become increasingly like Christ in holiness). These are not three graces, but one grace that meets us at our particular points of need. Grace is always singular, because grace is personified in the life and work of Jesus Christ. Christ is the source and

NOTES, REFLECTIONS,
AND QUESTIONS

He is the atoning sacrifice for our sins, and not for ours only but also for the sins of the whole world.

1 Jn. 2:2; *NRSV*

He who did not withhold his own Son, but gave him up **for all of us**—will he not with him also give us everything else?

Rom. 8:32; *NRSV*

I abhor the doctrine of predestination.
John Wesley, *Free Grace*, §VII.4

Pure, Universal Love thou art. **To me, to all**, thy mercies move, thy nature and thy name is Love.
Charles Wesley, "Come, O Thou Traveler Unknown" (1742)—*UM Hymnal* #386-387; *Free Methodist Ch. & The Wesleyan Ch. Hymnal* #317

The Lord . . . is patient with you, not wanting anyone to perish, but everyone to come to repentance.

2 Peter 3:9; *TNIV*

Come, sinners, to the gospel feast;
let every soul be Jesus' guest.
Ye need not one be left behind,
for God hath bid all humankind.
Sent by my Lord, on you I call;
the invitation is to all.
Come, all the world! Come, sinner, thou!
All things in Christ are ready now.
This is the time, no more delay!
This is the Lord's accepted day.
Come thou, this moment, at his call,
and live for him who died for all.

Charles Wesley, "Come, Sinners, to the Gospel Feast" (1747)—*UM Hymnal* #339; *AME Hymnal* #234

foundation of salvation, and from him alone comes the grace that we experience personally.

Prevenient Grace

Prevenient grace is a term used to describe the grace that comes before we recognize that God is working in our lives. (The word "prevenient" literally means to "come before.") It refers to God's activity prior to when we turn to God, including our "conscience"—our sense of right and wrong. As with all grace, prevenient grace works totally apart from human activity. Therefore, even the first step in the Way of Salvation is God's. Only by divine favor are we able to respond to God. Sometimes, the Wesleys called this "preventing" grace, since God's mercy has frequently prevented us from falling further into sin or trouble than we would have, if left to our own devices.

Faith in Christ is possible only due to grace. "For by grace you have been saved through faith, and this [faith] is not of your own doing; it is the gift of God" (Eph. 2:8-9; *NRSV*). Prevenient grace gives us the power to decide for God. Our trust and acceptance of God (faith) is grace-empowered. But the Wesleys did not emphasize prevenient grace as much as justifying and sanctifying grace (which will be discussed in later lessons). The Wesleys didn't want us to stay in a state of prevenient grace; they wanted us to push onward and upward toward forgiveness and holiness.

It is commonly said that "God accepts us just the way we are"—a popular expression that refers to God's free grace. It is true that God loves us unconditionally, but God doesn't want to *leave* us the way we are! God wants us to change and become more and more like Christ, through the power of the Holy Spirit.

Awakening

Due to God's prevenient grace, God is active in our lives without our knowledge of it. This "preventing" grace is *constantly* at work in our lives. God finds us; we do not find God. In the words of Charles Wesley, "'Tis mercy all, immense and free, for O my God, it found out me."[4] It is through prevenient grace that our hardened souls are awakened due to the hearing of a sermon, a life circumstance, or perhaps a conversation with a friend. Our hardened hearts melt, and we see the way that God has been active in our lives.

In a similar way, the first step of our conscious awareness is described in the sermon, *Awake, Thou That Sleepest*, when Charles Wesley describes the "deep sleep of the soul" that is our typical human condition until "the voice of God awakes" us (*Awake, Thou That Sleepest*, §I.1). The spiritually asleep individual "has no knowledge of himself" (§I.2). He or she does not know that the one thing needful "in the present world is to recover from his fall, to regain that image of God wherein he was created" (§I.2). Spiritual restoration will come about only through an "inward universal change"—the new birth, "which is the beginning of that total renovation" (§I.2).

[Salvation includes] all that is wrought in the soul by what is frequently termed 'natural conscience,' but more properly 'preventing grace'; all the 'drawings' of 'the Father', the desires after God, which, if we yield to them, increase more and more; all that 'light' wherewith the Son of God 'enlighteneth everyone that cometh into the world', showing every man 'to do justly, to love mercy, and to walk humbly with his God'; all the convictions which his Spirit from time to time works in every child of man.

John Wesley, *The Scripture Way of Salvation*, §I.2

There is no man, unless he has quenched the Spirit, that is wholly void of the grace of God . . . Everyone has some measure of that light, some faint glimmering ray, which sooner or later, more or less, enlightens every man that cometh into the world. And everyone . . . feels more or less uneasy when he acts contrary to the light of his own conscience. So that no man sins because he has not grace, but because he does not use the grace which he hath.

John Wesley, *On Working Out Our Own Salvation*, §III.4

By some awful providence [bad personal circumstances], or by his Word applied with the demonstration of his Spirit, God touches the heart of him that lay asleep in darkness and in the shadow of death. He is terribly shaken out of his sleep, and awakes into a consciousness of his danger. Perhaps in a moment, perhaps by degrees, the eyes of his understanding are opened, and now . . . discern[s] the real state he is in.

John Wesley, *The Spirit of Bondage and Adoption*, §II.1

Like waking up from the longest dream—How real it seemed, until Your love broke through. I was lost in a fantasy that blinded me, until Your love broke through.[5]

Keith Green, "Your Love Broke Through" (1972)

Sadly, many people are in a kind of dream (actually, a kind of nightmare) in which they imagine themselves to be "in perfect health"—"a sinner satisfied in his sins, contented to remain in his fallen state, to live and die without the image of God; one who is ignorant both of his disease and of the only remedy for it" (§I.4).

Charles Wesley exhorts his readers: "Awake, thou everlasting spirit, out of thy dream of worldly happiness. Did not God create thee for himself? Then thou canst not rest till thou resteth in him" (§II.5).

Wesley declared that if anyone would obey God's call, then that one "canst not seek his face in vain. . . . The Lord shall give thee grace and glory" (§III.1). The great promise is that "God is light, and will give himself to every awakened sinner that waiteth for him" (§III.2).

God's light, through Jesus Christ, makes people aware of their true condition before God and "convicts" or "convinces" them of their sin—a kind of godly despair—which leads them to repentance. This "convicting" or "convincing grace" is another stage on our Way of Salvation. God is working to turn us around and bring us to a point of decision for Christ. After being awakened to our need and convinced of our sin, then our response to God's gracious offer of salvation should be evident: "Choose life" (Deut. 30:19; NRSV).

What difference would it make if people truly experienced God's grace as free *in* all and free *for* all? (See page 40.)

RESPONDING FAITHFULLY

Share an example of when God's grace was working in your life, before you were even aware of it.

_____

_____

_____

What is the role of prevenient grace in our lives?

_____

_____

_____

How does the concept of prevenient grace differ from the commonly held belief that God "accepts us just as we are"—as if God were indifferent about our sin?

_____

_____

_____

_____

NOTES, REFLECTIONS, AND QUESTIONS

. . . you have made us for yourself, and our heart is restless until it comes to rest in you.[6]
Augustine of Hippo, *Confessions*, fourth century

The true light, which enlightens everyone, was coming into the world.
John 1:9; *NRSV*

While God has overlooked the times of human ignorance, now he commands all people everywhere to repent.
Acts 17:30; *NRSV*

Upon your present choice depends your eternal lot. Choose Christ and his ways, and you are blessed forever; refuse, and you are undone forever.
John Wesley "Directions for Renewing Our Covenant With God" (1780)[7]

Come home, come home; you who are weary, come home; earnestly, tenderly, Jesus is calling, calling, O sinner, come home!

Will L. Thompson, "Softly and Tenderly, Jesus Is Calling" (1880); *UM Hymnal* #348; *AME Church Hymnal* #261

Medical Image for Spiritual Awakening

A cancer survivor once remarked that the Wesleys' understanding of spiritual awakening is like a CT scan that alerts us to the malignancy in our souls and sends us scurrying to the Physician who can heal us.

How can we help awaken someone who does not know Jesus to recognize God's prevenient grace at work in their lives?

_____

_____

_____

LEARNING MORE

The following sermons by John Wesley have sections that deal with prevenient grace:

- *The Spirit of Bondage and Adoption*, §II.1
- *The Scripture Way of Salvation*, §I.2
- *On Working Out Our Own Salvation*, §III.4.

The following books describe the theology of Charles Wesley:

- Charles Yrigoyen, *Praising the Grace of God: The Theology of Charles Wesley's Hymns*
- John R. Tyson, Editor, *Charles Wesley: A Reader*.

The following book has a theological description of prevenient grace:

- Randy L. Maddox, *Responsible Grace*.

LOOKING AHEAD

Next Lesson. Becoming a Real Christian.

Teacher Helps provides follow-up questions that may be useful in class discussions.

END NOTES

[1] John Wesley, *Free Grace* (1739), Part 1 (first paragraph).
[2] John Wesley, *Free Grace*, §VII.1.
[3] John Wesley, *On the Wedding Garment* (1790), §19.
[4] Charles Wesley, "And Can it Be that I Should Gain" (1739).
[5] Keith Green, *Your Love Broke Through: The Worship Songs of Keith Green*, Volume 1 (The Ministry Years 1977-1979), Recording, Sparrow Records, February 1, 2002 (cd006521).
[6] Henry Chadwick (translator), Saint Augustine of Hippo, *Confessions*. Oxford: Oxford University Press, 1991, Book I, p. 3.
[7] §I, p. 3 [Whaling 1981, p. 134].

Depth of mercy! Can there be mercy still reserved for me? Can my God his wrath forbear, me, the chief of sinners, spare?

I have long withstood his grace, long provoked him to his face, would not hearken to his calls, grieved him by a thousand falls.

Charles Wesley, "Depth of Mercy" (1740)—*UM Hymnal* #355; *AME Hymnal* #262; *CME Hymnal* #240; *Free Methodist Ch. & The Wesleyan Ch.* Hymnal #249

Reading for Lesson 4. Awake, Thou That Sleepest
(Charles Wesley, 1742)

Preached on Sunday April 4, 1742, before the University of Oxford,
by the Rev. Charles Wesley, M.A. student of Christ-Church

Awake, thou that sleepest, and arise from the dead, and Christ shall give thee light (Eph. 5:14).

Introduction

In discoursing on these words, I shall, with the help of God,
First, describe the sleepers, to whom they are spoken;
Secondly, enforce the exhortation, "Awake, thou that sleepest, and arise from the dead"; and,
Thirdly, explain the promise made to such as do awake and arise: "Christ shall give thee light."

I.

1. And first, as to the sleepers here spoken to. By sleep is signified the natural state of man; that deep sleep of the soul, into which the sin of Adam hath cast all who spring from his loins—that supineness, indolence, and stupidity, that insensibility of his real condition, wherein every man comes into the world, and continues till the voice of God awakes him.

2. Now, "they that sleep, sleep in the night." The state of nature is a state of utter darkness; a state wherein "darkness covers the earth, and gross darkness the people." The poor unawakened sinner, how much knowledge soever he may have as to other things, has no knowledge of himself: in this respect "he knoweth nothing yet as he ought to know." He knows not that he is a fallen spirit, whose only business in the present world is to recover from his fall, to regain that image of God wherein he was created. He sees *no necessity* for the *one thing needful*, even that inward universal change, that "birth from above," figured out by baptism, which is the beginning of that total renovation—that sanctification of spirit, soul, and body, "without which no man shall see the Lord."

3. Full of all diseases as he is, he fancies himself in perfect health. Fast bound in misery and iron, he dreams that he is happy and at liberty. He says, "Peace! Peace!" while the devil, as "a strong, man armed," is in full possession of his soul. He sleeps on still and takes his rest, though hell is moved from beneath to meet him; though the pit from whence there is no return hath opened its mouth to swallow him up. A fire is kindled around him, yet he knoweth it not; yea, it burns him, yet he lays it not to heart.

4. By one who sleeps we are, therefore, to understand (and would to God we might all understand it!) a sinner satisfied in his sins, contented to remain in his fallen state, to live and die without the image of God; one who is ignorant both of his disease and of the only remedy for it; one who never was warned, or never regarded the warning voice of God, "to flee from the wrath to come"; one that never yet saw he was in danger of hell-fire, or cried out in the earnestness of his soul, "What must I do to be saved?"

5. If this sleeper be not outwardly vicious, his sleep is usually the deepest of all: whether he be of the Laodicean spirit, "neither cold nor hot," but a quiet, rational, inoffensive, good-natured professor of the religion of his fathers; or whether he be zealous and orthodox, and, "after the most straitest sect of our religion," lives "a Pharisee"; that is, according to the scriptural account, one that justifies himself; one that labors to establish his own righteousness, as the ground of his acceptance with God.

6. This is he who, "having a form of godliness, denies the power thereof"; yea, and probably reviles it, wheresoever it is found, as mere extravagance and delusion. Meanwhile, the wretched self-deceiver thanks God that he is "not as other men are; adulterers, unjust, extortioners." No, he doeth no wrong to any man. He "fasts twice in a week," uses all the means of grace, is constant at church and sacrament, yea, and "gives tithes of all that he has"; does all the good that he can. "Touching the righteousness of the law," he is "blameless"—he wants nothing of godliness but the power; nothing of religion but the spirit; nothing of Christianity but the truth and the life.

7. But know ye not that, however highly esteemed among men such a Christian as this may be, he is an abomination in the sight of God, and an heir of every woe which the Son of God, yesterday, today, and for ever, denounces against "scribes and Pharisees, hypocrites"? He hath "made clean the outside of the cup and the platter," but within is full of all filthiness. "An evil disease cleaveth still unto him, so that his inward parts

are very wickedness." Our Lord fitly compares him to a "painted sepulcher," which "appears beautiful without"; but nevertheless is "full of dead men's bones, and of all uncleanness." The bones indeed are no longer dry; the sinews and flesh are come up upon them, and the skin covers them above: but there is no breath in them, no Spirit of the living God. And, "if any man have not the Spirit of Christ, he is none of his." "Ye are Christ's, if so be that the Spirit of God dwell in you"; but, if not, God knoweth that ye abide in death, even until now.

8. This is another character of the sleeper here spoken to. He abides in death, though he knows it not. He is dead unto God, "dead in trespasses and sins." For "to be carnally minded is death." Even as it is written, "By one man sin entered into the world, and death by sin; and so death passed upon all men"—not only temporal death, but likewise spiritual and eternal. "In the day that thou eatest," said God to Adam, "thou shalt surely die"; not bodily (unless as he then became mortal), but spiritually: thou shalt lose the life of thy soul; thou shalt die to God: shalt be separated from him, thy essential life and happiness.

9. Thus first was dissolved the vital union of our soul with God; insomuch that "in the midst of" natural "life, we are" now in spiritual "death." And herein we remain till the Second Adam becomes a quickening Spirit to us; till he raises the dead, the dead in sin, in pleasure, riches, or honors. But, before any dead soul can live, he "hears" (hearkens to) "the voice of the Son of God": he is made sensible of his lost estate, and receives the sentence of death in himself. He knows himself to be "dead while he liveth"; dead to God, and all the things of God; having no more power to perform the actions of a living Christian than a dead body to perform the functions of a living man.

10. And most certain it is that one dead in sin has not "senses exercised to discern spiritual good and evil." "Having eyes, he sees not; he hath ears, and hears not." He doth not "taste and see that the Lord is gracious." He "hath not seen God at any time," nor "heard his voice," nor "handled the Word of life." In vain is the name of Jesus "like ointment poured forth, and all his garments smell of myrrh, aloes, and cassia." The soul that sleepeth in death hath no perception of any objects of this kind. His heart is "past feeling," and understandeth none of these things.

11. And hence, having no spiritual senses, no inlets of spiritual knowledge, the natural man receiveth not the things of the Spirit of God; nay, he is so far from receiving them that whatsoever is spiritually discerned is mere foolishness unto him. He is not content with being utterly ignorant of spiritual things, but he denies the very existence of them. And spiritual sensation itself is to him the foolishness of folly. "How," saith he, "can these things be? How can any man *know* that he is alive to God? Even as you know that your body is now alive. Faith is the life of the soul; and, if ye have this life abiding in you, ye want no marks to evidence it *to yourself*, but *elegchos pneumatos*, that divine consciousness, that *witness* of God, which is more and greater than ten thousand human witnesses.

12. If he doth not now bear witness with thy spirit that thou art a child of God, O that he might convince thee, thou poor unawakened sinner, by his demonstration and power, that thou art a child of the devil! O that, as I prophesy, there might now be "a noise and a shaking"; and may "the bones come together, bone to his bone!" Then "come from the four winds, O Breath! and breathe on these slain, that they may live!" And do not ye harden your hearts, and resist the Holy Ghost, who even now is come to convince you of sin, "because you believe not on the name of the only-begotten Son of God."

II.

1. Wherefore, "Awake, thou that sleepest, and arise from the dead"? God calleth thee now by my mouth; and bids thee know thyself, thou fallen spirit, thy true state and only concern below. "What meanest thou, O sleeper? Arise! Call upon thy God, if so be thy God will think upon thee, that thou perish not." A mighty tempest is stirred up round about thee, and thou art sinking into the depths of perdition, the gulf of God's judgments. If thou wouldst escape them, cast thyself into them. "Judge thyself, and thou shalt not be judged of the Lord."

2. Awake, awake! Stand up this moment, lest thou "drink at the Lord's hand the cup of his fury." Stir up thyself to lay hold on the Lord, the Lord thy Righteousness, mighty to save!" "Shake thyself from the dust." At least, let the earthquake of God's threatenings shake thee. Awake, and cry out with the trembling [jailer], "What must I do to be saved?" And never rest till thou believest on the Lord Jesus, with a faith which is his gift, by the operation of his Spirit.

3. If I speak to any one of you, more than to another, it is to thee who thinkest thyself unconcerned in this exhortation. "I have a message from God unto thee." In his name, I warn thee "to flee from the wrath to come." Thou unholy soul, see thy picture in condemned Peter, lying in the dark dungeon, between the soldiers, bound with two chains, the keepers before the door keeping the prison. The night is far spent, the morning is at hand,

when thou art to be brought forth to execution. And in these dreadful circumstances, thou art fast asleep; thou art fast asleep in the devil's arms, on the brink of the pit, in the jaws of everlasting destruction!

4. O may the angel of the Lord come upon thee, and the light shine into thy prison! And mayest thou feel the stroke of an almighty hand, raising thee, with, "Arise up quickly, gird thyself, and bind on thy sandals, cast thy garment about thee, and follow me."

5. Awake, thou everlasting spirit, out of thy dream of worldly happiness! Did not God create thee for himself? Then thou canst not rest till thou resteth in him. Return, thou wanderer! Fly back to thy ark. "This is not thy home." Think not of building tabernacles here. Thou art but a stranger, a sojourner upon earth; a creature of a day, but just launching out into an unchangeable state. Make haste; eternity is at hand. Eternity depends on this moment: an eternity of happiness, or an eternity of misery!

6. In what state is thy soul? Was God, while I am yet speaking, to require it of thee, art thou ready to meet death and judgment? Canst thou stand in his sight, who is of "purer eyes than to behold iniquity"? Art thou "meet* to be partaker of the inheritance of the saints in light"? Hast thou "fought a good fight, and kept the faith"? Hast thou secured the one thing needful? Hast thou recovered the image of God, even righteousness and true holiness? Hast thou put off the old man, and put on the new? Art thou "clothed upon with Christ"?

7. Hast thou oil in thy lamp? Grace in thy heart? Dost thou "love the Lord thy God with all thy heart, and with all thy mind, and with all thy soul, and with all thy strength"? Is that "mind in thee, which was also in Christ Jesus"? Art thou a Christian indeed, that is, a new creature? Are "old things passed away, and all things become new"?

8. Art thou a "partaker of the divine nature"? Knowest thou not, that "Christ is in thee, except thou be reprobate"? Knowest thou that God "dwelleth in thee, and thou in God, by his Spirit, which he hath given thee"? Knowest thou not that "thy body is a temple of the Holy Ghost, which thou hast of God"? Hast thou the "witness in thyself"? the "earnest of thine inheritance"? Art thou sealed by that Spirit of promise unto the day of redemption? Hast thou "received the Holy Ghost"? Or dost thou start at the question, not knowing "whether there be any Holy Ghost"?

9. If it offends thee, be thou assured that thou neither art a Christian nor desires to be one. Nay, thy "very prayer is turned into sin"; and thou hast solemnly mocked God this very day, by praying for the "inspiration of his Holy Spirit" when thou didst not believe there was any such thing to be received.

10. Yet, on the authority of God's Word, and our own Church, I must repeat the question, "Hast thou received the Holy Ghost?" If thou hast not, thou art not yet a Christian. For a Christian is a man that is "anointed with the Holy Ghost and with power." Thou art not yet made a partaker of pure religion and undefiled. Dost thou know what religion is?—that it is a participation of the divine nature; the life of God in the soul of man: "Christ formed in the heart"; "Christ in thee, the hope of glory"; happiness and holiness; heaven begun upon earth; "a kingdom of God within thee"; "not meat and drink," no outward thing, "but righteousness, and peace, and joy in the Holy Ghost"; an everlasting kingdom brought into thy soul; a "peace of God that passeth all understanding"; a "joy unspeakable and full of glory"?

11. Knowest thou that "in Jesus Christ, neither circumcision availeth anything, nor uncircumcision; but faith that worketh by love"; but a new creation? Seest thou the necessity of that inward change, that spiritual birth, that life from the dead, that holiness? And art thou thoroughly convinced that "without it no man shall see the Lord"? Art thou laboring after it?—"giving all diligence to make thy calling and election sure," "working out thy salvation with fear and trembling," "agonizing to enter in at the strait gate"? Art thou in *earnest* about thy soul? And canst thou tell the Searcher of hearts, "Thou, O God, art the thing that I long for! Lord, thou knowest all things; thou knowest that I *would* love thee!"

12. Thou hopest to be saved; but what reason hast thou to give of the hope that is in thee? Is it because thou hast done no harm? Or because thou hast done much good? Or because thou art not like other men, but wise, or learned, or honest, and morally good; esteemed of men, and of a fair reputation? Alas! all this will never bring thee to God. It is in his account lighter than vanity. Dost thou know "Jesus Christ, whom he hath sent"? Hath he taught thee that "by grace we are saved through faith, and that not of ourselves—it is the gift of God: not of works, lest any man should boast"? Hast thou received the faithful saying as the whole foundation of thy hope, "that Jesus Christ came into the world to save sinners"? Hast thou learned what that meaneth, "I came not to call the righteous, but sinners to repentance? I am not sent, but unto the lost sheep"? Art thou (he that heareth, let him understand!) lost, dead, *damned already*? Dost thou know thy deserts? Dost thou feel thy wants? Art thou "poor in spirit"? Mourning for God, and refusing to be comforted? Is the prodigal "come to himself," and well content to be therefore thought "beside himself" by those who are still feeding upon the

husks which he hath left? Art thou willing to "live godly in Christ Jesus"? And dost thou therefore suffer persecution? Do "men say all manner of evil against thee falsely, for the Son of Man's sake"?

13. O that in all these questions ye may hear the voice that wakes the dead, and feel that hammer of the Word which "breaketh the rock in pieces"! "If ye will hear his voice today, while it is called today, harden not your hearts." Now, "awake, thou that sleepest" in spiritual death, that thou sleep not in death eternal! Feel thy lost estate, and "arise from the dead." Leave thine old companions in sin and death. Follow thou Jesus, and let the dead bury their dead. "Save thyself from this untoward generation." "Come out from among them, and be thou separate, and touch not the unclean thing, and the Lord shall receive thee." "Christ shall give thee light."

III.

1. This promise, I come, lastly, to explain. And how encouraging a consideration is this, that whosoever thou art who obeyest his call, thou canst not seek his face in vain! If thou even now "awakest and arisest from the dead," he hath bound himself to "give thee light." "The Lord shall give thee grace and glory"; the light of his grace here, and the light of his glory when thou receivest "the crown that fadeth not away." "Thy light shall break forth as the morning, and thy darkness be as the noonday." "God, who commanded the light to shine out of darkness, shall shine in thy heart; to give the knowledge of the glory of God in the face of Jesus Christ." On them that fear the Lord shall "the Sun of Righteousness arise with healing in his wings." And in that day it shall be said unto thee, "Arise, shine; for thy light is come, and the glory of the Lord is risen upon thee." For Christ shall reveal himself in thee, and he is the true Light.

2. God is light, and will give himself to every awakened sinner that waiteth for him; and thou shalt then be a temple of the living God, and Christ shall "dwell in thy heart by faith"; and, "being rooted and grounded in love, thou shalt be able to comprehend with all saints, what is the breadth, and length, and depth, and height of that love of Christ which passeth knowledge, that thou mayest be filled with all the fullness of God."

3. Ye see your calling, brethren. We are called to be "an habitation of God through his Spirit"; and, through his Spirit dwelling in us, "to be saints here," and "partakers of the inheritance of the saints in light." So "exceeding great are the promises which are given unto us," actually given unto us who believe. For by faith "we receive, not the spirit of the world, but the Spirit which is of God"—the sum of all the promises—"that we may know the things that are freely given to us of God."

4. The Spirit of Christ is that great gift of God, which at sundry times, and in divers* manners, he hath promised to man, and hath fully bestowed since the time that Christ was glorified. Those promises, before made to the fathers, he hath thus fulfilled: "I will put my Spirit within you, and cause you to walk in my statutes" (Ezek. 36:27). "I will pour water upon him that is thirsty, and floods upon the dry ground; I will pour my Spirit upon thy seed, and my blessing upon thine offspring" (Isa. 44:3).

5. Ye may all be living witnesses of these things; of remission of sins, and the gift of the Holy Ghost. "If thou canst believe, all things are possible to him that believeth." "Who among you is there that feareth the Lord," and yet walketh on in "darkness, and hath no light? I ask thee, in the name of Jesus, believest thou that "his arm is not shortened at all"? That he is still "mighty to save"? That he is "the same yesterday, today, and for ever"? That "he hath now power on earth to forgive sins"? "Son, be of good cheer; thy sins are forgiven." God, for Christ's sake, hath forgiven thee. Receive this, "not as the word of man; but as it is, indeed, the Word of God"; and thou art "justified freely through faith." Thou shalt be sanctified also through faith which is in Jesus, and shalt set to thy seal, even thine, that "God hath given unto us eternal life, and this life is in his Son."

6. Men and brethren, let me freely speak unto you, and suffer ye the word of exhortation, even from one the least esteemed in the church. Your conscience beareth you witness in the Holy Ghost that these things are so, "if so be ye have tasted that the Lord is gracious." "This is eternal life, to know the only true God, and Jesus Christ, whom he hath sent." This experimental* knowledge, and this alone, is true Christianity. He is a Christian who hath received the Spirit of Christ. He is not a Christian who hath not received him. Neither is it possible to have received him and not know it. For, "at that day" (when he cometh, saith the Lord), "ye shall know that I am in my Father, and you in me, and I in you" (John 14:20). This is that "Spirit of Truth, whom the world cannot receive, because it seeth him not, neither knoweth him—but ye know him; for he dwelleth with you, and shall be in you."

7. The world cannot receive him, but utterly rejecteth the promise of the Father, contradicting and blaspheming. But every spirit which confesseth not this is not of God. Yea, "this is that spirit of antichrist, whereof ye have heard that it should come into the world; and even now it is in the world." He is antichrist whosoever denies the inspiration of the Holy Ghost, or that the indwelling Spirit of God is the common privilege of all believers, the blessing of the gospel, the unspeakable gift, the universal promise, the criterion of a real Christian.

8. It nothing helps them to say, "We do not deny the *assistance* of God's Spirit; but only this *inspiration*, this *receiving the Holy Ghost* and being *sensible* of it. It is only this *feeling* of the Spirit, this being *moved* by the Spirit, or *filled* with it, which we deny to have any place in sound religion." But in *only* denying this, you deny the whole Scriptures; the whole truth, and promise, and testimony of God.

9. Our own excellent Church knows nothing of this devilish distinction; but speaks plainly of "feeling the Spirit of Christ" [Article 17]; of being "moved by the Holy Ghost" [Office of Consecrating Priests (i.e., Deacons)] and knowing and "feeling there is no other name than that of Jesus," [Visitation of the Sick] whereby we can receive any salvation." She teaches us also to pray for the "inspiration of the Holy Spirit" [Collect before Holy Communion]; yea, that we may be "filled with the Holy Ghost" [Order of Confirmation]. Nay, and every presbyter of hers professes to "receive the Holy Ghost by the imposition of hands." Therefore, to deny any of these is, in effect, to renounce the Church of England, as well as the whole Christian revelation.

10. But "the wisdom of God" was always "foolishness with men." No marvel, then, that the great mystery of the gospel should be now also "hid from the wise and prudent," as well as in the days of old; that it should be almost universally denied, ridiculed, and exploded, as mere frenzy; and [that] all who dare avow it still [are] branded with the names of madmen and enthusiasts! This is "that falling away" which was to come—that general apostasy of all orders and degrees of men, which we even now find to have overspread the earth. "Run to and fro in the streets of Jerusalem, and see if you can find a man," a man that loveth the Lord his God with all his heart, and serveth him with all his strength. How does our own land mourn (that we look no farther) under the overflowings of ungodliness! What villainies of every kind are committed day by day; yea, too often with impunity, by those who sin with a high hand, and glory in their shame! Who can reckon up the oaths, curses, profaneness, blasphemies; the lying, slandering, evil-speaking; the Sabbath-breaking, gluttony, drunkenness, revenge; the whoredoms, adulteries, and various uncleanness; the frauds, injustice, oppression, extortion, which overspread our land as a flood?

11. And even among those who have kept themselves pure from those grosser abominations; how much anger and pride, how much sloth and idleness, how much softness and effeminacy, how much luxury and self-indulgence, how much covetousness and ambition, how much thirst of praise, how much love of the world, how much fear of man, is to be found! Meanwhile, how little of true religion! For where is he that loveth either God or his neighbor, as he hath given us commandment? On the one hand are those who have not so much as the form of godliness; on the other, those who have the form only: there stands the open, there the painted, sepulcher. So that, in very deed, whosoever were earnestly to behold any public gathering together of the people (I fear those in our churches are not to be excepted) might easily perceive "that the one part were Sadducees, and the other Pharisees": the one having almost as little concern about religion as if there were "no resurrection, neither angel nor spirit"; and the other making it a mere lifeless form, a dull round of external performances, without either true faith, or the love of God, or joy in the Holy Ghost!

12. Would to God I could except us of this place! "Brethren, my heart's desire, and prayer to God for you is that ye may be saved" from this overflowing of ungodliness; and that here may its proud waves be stayed! But is it so indeed? God knoweth, yea, and our own conscience, it is not. We have not kept ourselves pure. Corrupt are we also and abominable; and few are there that understand any more, few that worship God in spirit and in truth. We, too, are "a generation that set not our hearts aright, and whose spirit cleaveth not steadfastly unto God." He hath appointed us indeed to be "the salt of the earth: but if the salt hath lost its savor, it is thenceforth good for nothing but to be cast out, and to be trodden underfoot of men."

13. And "shall I not visit for these things, saith the Lord? Shall not my soul be avenged on such a nation as this?" Yea, we know not how soon he may say to the sword, "Sword, go through this land! He hath given us long space to repent. He lets us alone this year also. But he warns and awakens us by thunder. His judgments are abroad in the earth, and we have all reason to expect that heaviest of all, even that he "should come unto us quickly, and remove our candlestick out of its place, except we repent and do the first works"; unless we return to the principles of the Reformation, the truth and simplicity of the gospel. Perhaps we are now resisting the last effort of divine grace to save us. Perhaps we have well-nigh "filled up the measure of our iniquities" by rejecting the counsel of God against ourselves, and casting out his messengers.

14. O God, "in the midst of wrath, remember mercy"! Be glorified in our reformation, not in our destruction! Let us "hear the rod, and him that appointed it!" Now that thy "judgments are abroad in the earth," let the inhabitants of the world "learn righteousness!"

15. My brethren, it is high time for us to awake out of sleep before the "great trumpet of the Lord be blown," and our land become a field of blood. O may we speedily see the things that make for our peace,

before they are hid from our eyes! "Turn thou us, O good Lord, and let thine anger cease from us. O Lord, look down from heaven, behold and visit this vine"; and cause us to know "the time of our visitation." "Help us, O God of our salvation, for the glory of thy name! O deliver us, and be merciful to our sins, for thy name's sake." And so will we not go back from thee. O let us live, and we shall call upon thy name. Turn us again, O Lord God of Hosts! Show the light of thy countenance, and we shall be whole."

"Now unto him that is able to do exceeding abundantly above all that we can ask or think, according to the power that worketh in us, unto him be glory in the church by Christ Jesus throughout all ages, world without end. Amen!"

Lesson 5—The Almost Christian
and The Altogether Christian

You almost persuade me to become a Christian.

Acts 26:28; NKJV

I did go thus far for many years, as many of this place can testify; using diligence to eschew all evil, and to have a conscience void of offence; redeeming the time; buying up every opportunity of doing all good to all men; constantly and carefully using all the public and all the private means of grace; endeavoring after a steady seriousness of behavior, at all times, and in all places; and, God is my record, before whom I stand, doing all this in sincerity; having a real design to serve God; a hearty desire to do his will in all things; to please him who had called me to "fight the good fight," and to "lay hold of eternal life." Yet my own conscience beareth me witness in the Holy Ghost, that all this time I was but almost a Christian.

John Wesley, The Almost Christian, §I.13

OUR STARTING POINT

We consider ourselves to be "good people," yet being "good" is not the biblical requirement for salvation. There are many good people who seem to be "Christian" on the outside, but lack a true experience of faith on the inside—an experience that results in deep and evident love of God and neighbor. What is required of us is an experience of faith in Jesus Christ.

READING

Read daily the reflection and prayer about every Christian's call to love. *The Almost Christian* (1741) was written a few years after Wesley's experience of assurance at Aldersgate. Wesley describes in this sermon the difference between those who have a form of godliness and those who have genuine faith, which is acted out in love.

Day 1   Scan *The Almost Christian.* Scan Lesson 5.
Day 2   Read Part I up to §I.10. What is heathen honesty?
Day 3   Finish reading Part I, §§I.11-13. Why can Wesley speak so decisively about the "almost Christian"?
Day 4   Read all of Part II. What three things are required for the "altogether Christian"?
Day 5   Read Matt. 5:44-47.
Day 6   Read Matt. 22:34-40. Reread the lesson and answer the questions at the end.
Day 7   Rest

REFLECTION

Woe to you, teachers of the law and Pharisees, you hypocrites! You clean the outside of the cup and dish, but inside they are full of greed and self-indulgence. Blind Pharisee! First clean the inside of the cup and dish, and then the outside also will be clean. Woe to you, teachers of the law and Pharisees, you hypocrites! You are like white-washed tombs, which look beautiful on the outside but on the inside are full of dead men's bones and everything unclean. In the same way, on the outside you appear to people as righteous, but on the inside you are full of hypocrisy and wickedness.

Matt. 23:25-28; NIV

PRAYER

O God, Revealer of My Heart,

Sometimes I am not sure if I am a real Christian. I want to love you and follow you in all of your ways, but it is hard! There are times when I wonder if I have faith and if I truly love my neighbor as I should. Sometimes I am not even sure who my neighbor is! I do believe; help me overcome my unbelief. Amen.

Prayer concerns for this week:

Daily Reflections

Day 1   Scan *The Almost Christian*. Scan Lesson 5.

Meaning for me:

Day 2   Read Part I up to §I.10. What is heathen honesty?

Meaning for me:

Day 3   Finish reading Part I, §§I.11-13. Why can Wesley speak so decisively about the "almost Christian"?

Meaning for me:

Day 4   Read all of Part II. What three things are required for the "altogether Christian"?

Meaning for me:

Day 5   Read Matt. 5:44-47.

Meaning for me:

Day 6   Read Matt. 22:34-40. Reread the lesson and answer the questions at the end.

Meaning for me:

Form Without Faith

As Wesley grew in grace, he noticed that many people around him had "the form of godliness" (*The Almost Christian*, §I.7) but lacked the "belief that is born of God" (§II.3). From his own personal experience he knew it was possible to be a sincere person who has all the outward signs of a Christian—avoiding evil, doing good, and using the means of grace—yet not have *faith of the heart*. And, as his own spiritual life developed, he began to understand the importance of acting out that faith in love in his own daily life.

Wesley came to see a clear distinction between what he described as an "almost Christian" and an "altogether Christian." He became particularly critical of fellow university colleagues who seemed to follow rules and rituals of the Christian tradition, but lacked an inward affective experience of faith that was expressed in "works by love" (§II.6). He saw that they were nominally Christian but did not demonstrate the inward love of God. He expressed this distinction in his sermons, which was not popular with his colleagues. He was ultimately barred from many Anglican pulpits, in part due to his criticism of their external forms of religion without the spiritual power of personal faith.

Distinction Between Almost and Altogether Christians

At first glance, the distinction between "altogether" and "almost" Christians seems harsh. Yet, when we examine the ways in which Wesley differentiated between the two, we see that he was merely following the example set by Jesus.

Jesus criticized Scribes and Pharisees for having the form of godliness, but no love for their neighbor. Jesus said they were going through the motions of religious behavior for show, and not for the love of God or people. Jesus remarked that some of those who seemed to be righteous on the outside were lacking love in action from their hearts. They did not live out a life of love, faith, and service to others. In *The Almost Christian*, Wesley described his own observations, similar to those that had been made by Jesus Christ.

What Is an "Almost Christian"?

Wesley found in Scripture that Jesus had high expectations even for being an "almost Christian"! An "almost Christian" does nothing that the Gospel forbids. This person avoids evil, does good, and uses the means of grace, such as prayer, fasting, taking communion, and searching the Scriptures (see Lesson 8). Wesley asks the question, "Is it possible to go this far without being a real Christian?" (§I.11) Wesley's answer is affirmative, and he acknowledges that, for many years, he himself was an "almost Christian." Such people act piously and, according to Wesley, they may also be very sincere. They have an inward "principle of religion."

But "principle" is not enough. There needs to be one more thing—"*a love of God that engrosses the whole heart as takes up all the affections, as fills the entire capacity of the soul*" (§II.1). This is the source of love from which all actions flow.

But mark this: There will be terrible times in the last days. People will be lovers of themselves, lovers of money, boastful, proud, abusive, disobedient to their parents, ungrateful, unholy, without love, unforgiving, slanderous, without self-control, brutal, not lovers of the good, treacherous, rash, conceited, lovers of pleasure rather than lovers of God—**having a form of godliness but denying its power**.

2 Tim. 3:3-5, *NIV*

A second thing implied in the being almost a Christian, is, the having a form of godliness; of that godliness which is prescribed in the gospel of Christ; the having the outside of a real Christian. Accordingly, the almost Christian does nothing which the gospel forbids.

John Wesley, *The Almost Christian*, §I.4

[Jesus said] For I tell you that unless your righteousness surpasses that of the Pharisees and the teachers of the law, you will certainly not enter the kingdom of heaven.

Matt. 5:20; *NIV*

Then Jesus said to the crowds and to his disciples: "The teachers of the law and the Pharisees sit in Moses' seat. So you must obey them and do everything they tell you. But do not do what they do, for they do not practice what they preach. They tie up heavy loads and put them on men's shoulders, but they themselves are not willing to lift a finger to move them."

Matt. 23:1-4; *NIV*

[Jesus said] "Why do you call me, 'Lord, Lord,' and do not do what I say?"

Luke 6:46, *NIV*

What is more, I [Paul] consider everything a loss compared to the surpassing greatness of knowing Christ Jesus my Lord, for whose sake I have lost all things.

Phil. 3:8; *NIV*

What Is an "Altogether Christian"?

An "altogether" or "real" Christian has a faith that believes on the name of Jesus Christ—personal forgiveness of sins, an assurance of God's pardon, and a new birth experience, which result in love of both God and neighbor (see Lesson 7 on The New Birth). This is "faith of the heart." The person has a faith that works itself out in love and is, therefore, a true Christian both inside and out.

An "altogether Christian" experiences an inward transformation, which can occur in a moment or over many years. This marked inner change is demonstrated by the way we live our daily lives, and is often lived out in service to others. Do we serve out of a sense of duty or guilt, or do we serve out of gratitude, with a faithful heart? When we serve out of duty we will burn out and become overwhelmed. When we serve out of gratitude in response to what God has done for us and the joy that bubbles up in our lives, we have a source of strength for that service in our delight in knowing Jesus Christ.

Wesley best described this faith of the heart in a series of questions (§II.9), including the following:

"Do good designs and good desires make a Christian? By no means, unless they are brought to good effect. "Hell is paved," saith one, "with good intentions." The great question of all, then, still remains. Is the love of God shed abroad in your heart?" That is, have you experienced a personal, life-changing conversion?

How Do We Respond?

If you could not answer in the affirmative to the list of Wesley's questions in §II.9, you may be in spiritual turmoil. Yet, it is when we wrestle with these questions and even may come to a point of despair about our current condition that we are freed up to surrender all; then we can truly rely on the power of God.

Are We Growing in Grace?

Wesley came to realize that we should always be growing and maturing in response to God's grace. This faith is a gradual process, similar to an infant learning to crawl. Such growth in holy living can be described as the "gradual work of God" in the soul.[2]

To become an "altogether Christian" we must respond to God's grace. We are accountable for how we react to God's unmerited free gift of grace. The love of God is not an excuse for a form of self-indulgence. Rather, God's love is ultimately seen in God's love for humanity as demonstrated when Jesus freely gave of himself in a self-emptying form of love on the cross. When we grow in grace, we see that we, too, are called to empty our soul of "me" and ask God to replace it with God's self-giving love. This is what it means to live out a life of love of God and neighbor.

Acting Out Our Faith in Love

In today's society and context there is often little concern for following biblical truths in terms of morals and lifestyle. Often we see outward religious behavior, such as going to church, but we do

NOTES, REFLECTIONS, AND QUESTIONS

Christians. . . . must begin to live more like Jesus Christ.[1]
Mahatma Gandhi

How can we sinners know
our sins on earth forgiven?
How can my gracious Savior show
my name inscribed in heaven?

What we have felt and seen,
with confidence we tell,
and publish to the ends of earth
the signs infallible.

We who in Christ believe
that he for us hath died,
we all his unknown peace receive
and feel his blood applied.

We by his Spirit prove
and know the things of God,
The things which freely of his love
He hath on us bestowed;

His Spirit to us he gave,
And dwells in us, we know;
The witness in ourselves we have,
And all its fruits we show.

Charles Wesley, "How Can We Sinners Know" (1749)—*UM Hymnal #372; AME Hymnal #264*

All to Jesus, I surrender,
All to him I freely give.
I will ever love and trust him,
In his presence daily live.

I surrender all, I surrender all,
All to thee my blessed Savior,
I surrender all.

J. W. Van Deventer, "All to Jesus, I Surrender" (1896)—*United Methodist Hymnal, #354; African Methodist Episcopal Church Hymnal, #251*

Your attitude should be the same as that of Christ Jesus: Who, being in very nature God, did not consider equality with God something to be grasped but made himself nothing, taking the very nature of a servant, being made in human likeness. And being found in appearance as a man, he humbled himself and became obedient to death.

Phil. 2: 5-8, *NIV*

not see a lifestyle that is congruent with the inward faith and practice of being a Christian. Frequently, we do not hold ourselves or others accountable to biblical truths, opting instead for "tolerance" of others.

The Gospels have no record that Jesus ever used the word "tolerance," though Jesus is the very one who came to stand in solidarity with the poor, the outcast, and the marginalized. He stood shoulder to shoulder with sinners, yet he also spoke the truth in love.

Too often we distort the biblical sense of freedom. Freedom is valued in itself as an inalienable right that is centered in choice of self-will and determination. Yet biblical freedom is centered around Jesus Christ. In biblical freedom, we are all freed from slavery to sin due to the life, death, and resurrection of Jesus Christ. Christ freed us so that we may willingly and freely become self-giving servants of the living God. Wesley sees biblical freedom in the assurance of an experience with Jesus Christ, and the adoption of a life of service and love to God and neighbor. This is what it means to be an "altogether" Christian!

NOTES, REFLECTIONS, AND QUESTIONS

Then we will no longer be infants, tossed back and forth by the waves, and blown here and there by every wind of teaching and by the cunning and craftiness of men in their deceitful scheming. Instead, **speaking the truth in love**, we will in all things grow up into him who is the Head, that is, Christ. From him the whole body, joined and held together by every supporting ligament, grows and builds itself up in love, as each part does its work.

Eph. 4:14-16; *NIV*

Make us of one heart and mind,
gentle, courteous, and kind,
lowly, meek, in thought and word,
altogether like our Lord.

Let us for each other care,
each the other's burdens bear;
to thy church the pattern give,
show how true believers live.

Charles Wesley, "Jesus, Lord, We Look to Thee" (1749)—*UM Hymnal #562*

RESPONDING FAITHFULLY

Do you agree with Wesley that people often have an outside form of godliness without its power? Why?

_____

_____

_____

_____

Wesley sets the bar high for being an "Almost Christian." Do you measure up to that standard?

_____

_____

_____

_____

Is the love of God shed abroad in your heart (see §2.9)?

_____

_____

_____

_____

What additional steps would help you grow in grace?

Do you know a person who, for you, is an example of an "altogether Christian"? Describe.

LEARNING MORE

Read other parts of Wesley's writing which describe the "altogether Christian":
- *The More Excellent Way.*

The following books may be of interest:
- Randy L. Maddox, *Responsible Grace: John Wesley's Practical Theology* (pp. 141-191).
- Theodore Runyon, *The New Creation: John Wesley's Theology Today*, Chapter 5.

LOOKING AHEAD

Next Lesson. Justification—the forgiveness of sins. How are we made right before a just and holy God?

Teacher Helps provides follow-up questions that may be useful in class discussions.

END NOTES

[1] Quoted in E. Stanley Jones, *Gandhi: Portrayal of a Friend*, p. 51.
[2] John Wesley, *The Repentance of Believers*, §I.20.

Reading for Lesson 5. The Almost Christian (1741)

Preached at St. Mary's, Oxford, before the University, on July 25, 1741.

Almost thou persuadest me to be a Christian (Acts 26:28; *KJV*).

Introduction

And many there are who go thus far: ever since the Christian religion was in the world, there have been many in every age and nation who were almost persuaded to be Christians. But seeing it avails nothing before God to go *only thus far*, it highly imports us to consider,

First, what is implied in being *almost*; [and]

Secondly, what is being *altogether*, a Christian.

I.

1. Now, in the being *almost a Christian* is implied, first, heathen honesty. No one, I suppose, will make any question of this, especially, since by heathen honesty here I mean, not that which is recommended in the writings of their philosophers only, but such as the common heathens expected one of another, and many of them actually practiced. By the rules of this they were taught that they ought not to be unjust; not to take away their neighbor's goods, either by robbery or theft; not to oppress the poor, neither to use extortion toward any; not to cheat or overreach either the poor or rich, in whatsoever commerce they had with them; to defraud no man of his right; and, if it were possible, to owe no man anything.

2. Again: the common heathens allowed that some regard was to be paid to truth, as well as to justice. And, accordingly, they not only [held] him in abomination who was forsworn, who called God to witness to a lie; but him also who was known to be a slanderer of his neighbor, who falsely accused any man. And indeed, little better did they esteem willful liars of any sort, accounting them the disgrace of humankind, and the pests of society.

3. Yet again: there was a sort of love and assistance which they expected one from another. They expected whatever assistance any one could give another, without prejudice to himself. And this they extended not only to those little offices of humanity which are performed without any expense or labor, but likewise to the feeding the hungry, if they had food to spare; the clothing the naked with their own superfluous raiment; and, in general, the giving, to any that needed, such things as they needed not themselves. Thus far, in the lowest account of it, heathen honesty went; the first thing implied in the being *almost a Christian*.

4. A second thing implied in the being *almost a Christian* is the having a form of godliness, of that godliness which is prescribed in the gospel of Christ—the having the *outside of a real Christian*. Accordingly, the almost Christian does nothing which the gospel forbids. He taketh not the name of God in vain; he blesseth and curseth not; he sweareth not at all, but his communication is yea, yea; nay, nay. He profanes not the day of the Lord, nor suffers it to be profaned, even by the stranger that is within his gates. He not only avoids all actual adultery, fornication, and uncleanness, but every word or look that either directly or indirectly tends thereto; nay, and all idle words, abstaining both from detraction, backbiting, talebearing, evil-speaking, and from "all foolish talking and jesting"—*eutrapelia*, a kind of virtue in the heathen moralist's account—briefly, from all conversation that is not "good to the use of edifying," and that, consequently, "grieves the Holy Spirit of God, whereby we are sealed to the day of redemption."

5. He abstains from "wine wherein is excess"; from reveling and gluttony. He avoids, as much as in him lies, all strife and contention, continually endeavoring to live peaceably with all men. And, if he suffer wrong, he avengeth not himself, neither returns evil for evil. He is no railer, no brawler, no scoffer, either at the faults or infirmities of his neighbor. He does not willingly wrong, hurt, or grieve any man; but in all things acts and speaks by that plain rule, "Whatsoever thou wouldest not he should do unto thee, that do not thou to another."

6. And in doing good, he does not confine himself to cheap and easy offices of kindness, but labors and suffers for the profit of many, that by all means he may help some. In spite of toil or pain, "whatsoever his hand findeth to do, he doeth it with his might"; whether it be for his friends, or for his enemies; for the evil, or for the good. For being "not slothful" in this, or in any "business," as he "hath opportunity" he doeth "good," all manner of good, "to all men"; and to their souls as well as their bodies. He reproves the wicked, instructs the ignorant, confirms the wavering, quickens the good, and comforts the afflicted. He labors to

awaken those that sleep; to lead those whom God hath already awakened to the "fountain opened for sin and for uncleanness," that they may wash therein and be clean; and to stir up those who are saved through faith, to adorn the gospel of Christ in all things.

7. He that hath the form of godliness uses also the means of grace; yea, all of them, and at all opportunities. He constantly frequents the house of God; and that, not as the manner of some is, who come into the presence of the Most High—either loaded with gold and costly apparel, or in all the gaudy vanity of dress; and thereby either by their unseasonable civilities to each other, or the impertinent gaiety of their behavior—[and] disclaim all pretensions to the form as well as to the power of godliness. Would to God there were none, even among ourselves, who fall under the same condemnation! Who come into this house, it may be, gazing about, or with all the signs of the most listless, careless indifference, though sometimes they may *seem* to use a prayer to God for his blessing on what they are entering upon; who, during that awful service, are either asleep or reclined in the most convenient posture for it; or, as though they supposed God was asleep, talking with one another, or looking round, as utterly void of employment. Neither let these be accused of the form of godliness. No; he who has even this, behaves with seriousness and attention in every part of that solemn service. More especially, when he approaches the table of the Lord, it is not with a light or careless behavior, but with an air, gesture, and deportment which speaks nothing else but "God be merciful to me a sinner!"

8. To this, if we add the constant use of family prayer, by those who are masters of families, and the setting times apart for private addresses to God, with a daily seriousness of behavior—he who uniformly practices this outward religion has the form of godliness. There needs but one thing more in order to* his being *almost a Christian*, and that is, sincerity.

9. By sincerity I mean, a real, inward principle of religion, from whence these outward actions flow. And, indeed, if we have not this, we have not heathen honesty; no, not so much of it as will answer the demand of a heathen, Epicurean poet.[1] Even this poor wretch, in his sober intervals, is able to testify,

Oderunt peccare boni, virtutis amore;
Oderunt peccare mali, formidine poenae.

[Good men avoid sin from the love of virtue;
Wicked men avoid sin from a fear of punishment.]

So that, if a man only abstains from doing evil in order to avoid punishment—*Non pasces in cruce corvos* [Thou shalt not be hanged], saith the pagan—there, "thou hast thy reward." But even he will not allow such a harmless man as this to be so much as a *good heathen*. If, then, any man, from the same motive—viz., to avoid punishment, to avoid the loss of his friends, or his gain, or his reputation—should not only abstain from doing evil, but also do ever so much good; yea, and use all the means of grace; yet we could not with any propriety say, this man is even *almost a Christian*. If he has no better principle in his heart, he is only a hypocrite altogether.

10. Sincerity, therefore, is necessarily implied in the being *almost a Christian*; a real design to serve God, a hearty desire to do his will. It is necessarily implied that a man have a sincere view of pleasing God in all things: in all his conversation; in all his actions; in all he does or leaves undone. This design, if any man be *almost a Christian*, runs through the whole tenor of his life. This is the moving principle, both in his doing good, his abstaining from evil, and his using the ordinances of God.

11. But here it will probably be inquired, "Is it possible that any man living should go so far as this, and, nevertheless, be *only almost a Christian*? What more than this can be implied in the being *a Christian altogether*?" I answer, first, that it is possible to go thus far, and yet be but *almost a Christian*; I learn, not only from the oracles of God, but also from the sure testimony of experience.

12. Brethren, great is "my boldness toward you in this behalf." And "forgive me this wrong" if I declare my own folly upon the house-top, for yours and the gospel's sake. Suffer me, then, to speak freely of myself, even as of another man. I am content to be abased so ye may be exalted, and to be yet more vile for the glory of my Lord.

13. I did go thus far for many years, as many of this place can testify—using diligence to eschew all evil, and to have a conscience void of offence; redeeming the time, buying up every opportunity of doing all good

---

[1] Ed: Horace, *Epistles*, I.16.

to all men; constantly and carefully using all the public and all the private means of grace; endeavoring after a steady seriousness of behavior, at all times, and in all places; and, God is my record, before whom I stand, doing all this in sincerity—having a real design to serve God, a hearty desire to do his will in all things, to please him who had called me to "fight the good fight," and to "lay hold of eternal life." Yet my own conscience beareth me witness in the Holy Ghost, that all this time I was but *almost a Christian*.

II.

1. If it be inquired, "What more than this is implied in the being *altogether a Christian?*" I answer first, the love of God. For thus saith his Word, "Thou shalt love the Lord thy God with all thy heart, and with all thy soul, and with all thy mind, and with all thy strength." Such a love of God is this as engrosses the whole heart, as takes up all the affections, as fills the entire capacity of the soul and employs the utmost extent of all its faculties. He that thus loves the Lord his God, his spirit continually "rejoiceth in God his Savior." His delight is in the Lord, *his* Lord and his all, to whom "in everything he giveth thanks." All *his* "desire is unto God, and to the remembrance of his name." His heart is ever crying out, "Whom have I in heaven but thee? And there is none upon earth that I desire beside thee." Indeed, what can he desire beside God? Not the world, or the things of the world: for he is "crucified to the world, and the world crucified to him." He is crucified to "the desire of the flesh, the desire of the eye, and the pride of life." Yea, he is dead to pride of every kind: for "love is not puffed up," but "he that dwelling in love, dwelleth in God, and God in him," is less than nothing in his own eyes.

2. The second thing implied in the being *altogether a Christian* is the love of our neighbor. For thus said our Lord in the following words: "Thou shalt love thy neighbor as thyself." If any man ask, "Who is my neighbor?" we reply, "Every man in the world; every child of his who is the Father of the spirits of all flesh." Nor may we in any wise except our enemies, or the enemies of God and their own souls. But every Christian loveth these also as himself, yea, "as Christ loved us." He that would more fully understand what manner of love this is, may consider St. Paul's description of it. It is "long-suffering and kind." It "envieth not." It is not rash or hasty in judging. It "is not puffed up"; but maketh him that loves, the least, the servant of all. Love "doth not behave itself unseemly," but becometh "all things to all men." She "seeketh not her own"; but only the good of others, that they may be saved. "Love is not provoked." It casteth out wrath, which he who hath is wanting in love. "It thinketh no evil. It rejoiceth not in iniquity, but rejoiceth in the truth. It covereth all things, believeth all things, hopeth all things, endureth all things."

3. There is yet one thing more that may be separately considered, though it cannot actually be separate from the preceding, which is implied in the being *altogether a Christian*; and that is the ground of all, even faith. Very excellent things are spoken of this throughout the oracles of God. "Everyone," saith the beloved disciple, "that believeth is born of God." "To as many as received him, gave he power to become the sons of God. Even to them that believe on his name." And "this is the victory that overcometh the world, even our faith." Yea, our Lord himself declares, "He that believeth in the Son hath everlasting life; and cometh not into condemnation, but is passed from death unto life."

4. But here let no man deceive his own soul. It is diligently to be noted, "the faith which bringeth not forth repentance," and love, and all good works, is not that "right living faith," which is here spoken of, but a dead and devilish one. For, even the devils believe that Christ was born of a virgin: that he wrought all kinds of miracles, declaring himself very God: that, for our sakes, he suffered a most painful death, to redeem us from death everlasting; that he rose again the third day: that he ascended into heaven, and sitteth at the right hand of the Father and at the end of the world shall come again to judge both the quick and the dead. These articles of our faith the devils believe, and so they believe all that is written in the Old and New Testament. And yet for all this faith, they be but devils. They remain still in their damnable estate lacking the very true Christian faith." [Homily on the Salvation of Man.]

5. "The right and true Christian faith is" (to go on in the words of our own Church), "not only to believe that Holy Scripture and the articles of our faith are true, but also to have a sure trust and confidence to be saved from everlasting damnation by Christ." It is a "sure trust and confidence" which a man hath in God, "that, by the merits of Christ, his sins are forgiven, and he reconciled to the favor of God"; "whereof doth follow a loving heart to obey his commandments."

6. Now, whosoever has this faith which "purifies the heart" (by the power of God, who dwelleth therein) from pride, anger, desire, from "all unrighteousness," from "all filthiness of flesh and spirit"; which fills it with

love stronger than death, both to God and to all mankind; love that doeth the works of God, glorying to spend and to be spent for all men, and that endureth with joy, not only the reproach of Christ, the being mocked, despised, and hated of all men, but whatsoever the wisdom of God permits the malice of men or devils to inflict—whosoever has this faith thus "working by love" is not *almost only*, but *altogether*, a Christian.

7. But who are the living witnesses of these things? I beseech you, brethren, as in the presence of that God before whom "hell and destruction are without a covering—how much more the hearts of the children of men?"—that each of you would ask his own heart, "Am I of that number? Do I so far practice justice, mercy, and truth, as even the rules of heathen honesty require? If so, have I the very *outside* of a Christian—the form of godliness? Do I abstain from evil—from whatsoever is forbidden in the written Word of God? Do I, whatever good my hand findeth to do, do it with my might? Do I seriously use all the ordinances of God at all opportunities? And is all this done with a sincere design and desire to please God in all things?"

8. Are not many of you conscious that you never came thus far; that you have not been even *almost a Christian*; that you have not come up to the standard of heathen honesty—at least, not to the form of Christian godliness? Much less hath God seen sincerity in you, a real design of pleasing him in all things. You never so much as intended to devote all your words and works—your business, studies, diversions—to his glory. You never even designed or desired that whatsoever you did should be done "in the name of the Lord Jesus," and as such should be "a spiritual sacrifice, acceptable to God through Christ."

9. But, supposing you had, do good designs and good desires make a Christian? By no means, unless they are brought to good effect. "Hell is paved," saith one, "with good intentions." The great question of all, then, still remains. Is the love of God shed abroad in your heart? Can you cry out, "My God, and my all"? Do you desire nothing but him? Are you happy in God? Is he your glory, your delight, your crown of rejoicing? And is this commandment written in your heart, "That he who loveth God love his brother also"? Do you then love your neighbor as yourself? Do you love every man, even your enemies, even the enemies of God, as your own soul? as Christ loved you? Yea, dost thou believe that Christ loved thee, and gave himself for thee? Hast thou faith in his blood? Believest thou the Lamb of God hath taken away *thy* sins, and cast them as a stone into the depth of the sea? that he hath blotted out the handwriting that was against *thee*, taking it out of the way, nailing it to his cross? Hast *thou* indeed redemption through his blood, even the remission of *thy* sins? And doth his Spirit bear witness with *thy* spirit that thou art a child of God?

10. The God and Father of our Lord Jesus Christ, who now standeth in the midst of us, knoweth that, if any man die without this faith and this love, good it were for him that he had never been born. Awake, then, thou that sleepest, and call upon thy God: call in the day when he may be found. Let him not rest, till he make his "goodness to pass before thee"; till he "proclaim unto thee the name of the Lord"—"the Lord, the Lord God, merciful and gracious, long-suffering, and abundant in goodness and truth—keeping mercy for thousands, forgiving iniquity, and transgression, and sin." Let no man persuade thee, by vain words, to rest short of this prize of thy high calling. But cry unto him day and night, who, "while we were without strength, died for the ungodly," until thou knowest in whom thou hast believed, and canst say, "My Lord, and my God!" Remember "always to pray and not to faint," till thou also canst lift up thy hand unto heaven and declare to him that liveth for ever and ever, "Lord, thou knowest all things, thou knowest that I love thee."

11. May we all thus experience what it is to be, not almost only; but altogether Christians! Being justified freely by his grace, through the redemption that is in Jesus; knowing we have peace with God through Jesus Christ; rejoicing in hope of the glory of God; and having the love of God shed abroad in our hearts, by the Holy Ghost given unto us!

Lesson 6–Justification: The Forgiveness of Sin

To one who without works trusts him who justifies the ungodly,
such faith is reckoned as righteousness.

Rom. 4:5; NRSV

To him that is justified or forgiven, God "will not impute sin" to his condemnation.
He will not condemn him on that account, either in this world or in that which is to come.
His sins, all his past sins, in thought, word, and deed, are covered, are blotted out, shall not be
remembered or mentioned against him, any more than if they had not been. God will not
inflict on that sinner what he deserved to suffer, because the Son of his love hath suffered for him.
And from the time we are "accepted through the Beloved," "reconciled to God through his blood,"
he loves, and blesses, and watches over us for good, even as if we had never sinned.

John Wesley, Justification by Faith, §II.5

OUR STARTING POINT

If, on the one hand, we feel that we are far away from God or, on the other, we consider ourselves to be "good," religious people—in whatever spiritual condition we are in—we are all sinners in need of God's grace. Grace gives us the opportunity to begin to turn toward God; then, we are in a position where we can receive God's forgiveness, release from our guilt, and pardon for our sins.

READING

Read daily the reflection and prayer and turn your attention to:

Day 1   Scan the sermon Justification by Faith (1746); then, reread the introduction. Scan Lesson 6.

Day 2   Read the Introduction and Part I. What has knowledge of one's own sin to do with justification?

Day 3   Read Part II, §§II.1-5. What is the nature of justification?

Day 4   Read Part III, §§III.1-6. What sorts of people are justified?

Day 5   Read Part IV, §§IV.1-9. On what condition is one justified?

Day 6   Read Romans 4 and Hebrews 11. Reread the lesson and answer the questions at the end.

Day 7   Rest.

REFLECTION

For by grace you have been saved through faith, and this is not your own doing; it is the gift of God—not the result of works—so that no one may boast.

Eph. 2:8-9; NRSV

Therefore, since we are justified by faith, we have peace with God through our Lord Jesus Christ, though whom we have obtained access to this grace in which we stand; and we boast in our hope of sharing the glory of God.

Rom. 5: 1-2; NRSV

PRAYER

O Great Redeemer and Healer of my soul,

We have acknowledged to you from the depths of our minds and hearts our sorrow at the state of our sin, especially separation from you O God. Great Savior, we have let sin come into our lives and so we call upon your mercy and overflowing grace to forgive our sins against you, in thought, word, and deed. Strengthen your gifts to us of faith, hope, and love. Be our rock and fortress against all storms and temptations. Enable and empower us to return to your way of salvation. Amen.

Prayer concerns for this week:

Daily Reflections

Day 1   Scan the sermon *Justification by Faith*; then, reread the introduction. Scan Lesson 6.

Meaning for me:

Day 2   Read the Introduction and Part I. What has knowledge of one's own sin to do with justification?

Meaning for me:

Day 3   Read Part II, §§II.1-5. What is the nature of justification?

Meaning for me:

Day 4   Read Part III, §§III.1-6. What sorts of people are justified?

Meaning for me:

Day 5   Read Part IV, §§IV.1-9. On what condition is one justified?

Meaning for me:

Day 6   Read Romans 4 and Hebrews 11. Reread the lesson and answer the questions at the end.

Meaning for me:

Toward Justification

Justification describes how we as sinners can be made right before God; literally, it means "declared to be blameless," as in a court of law. How can we as imperfect vessels be declared blameless before a perfect, holy God?

Journey in Grace. As noted, Wesley taught that the way to salvation was a journey—a continuous, life-long process, enabled and empowered by "grace upon grace"—"a gradual work of God."[1] It begins with prevenient grace, given to everyone.

Awakening. God has placed within every heart the ability to respond to God's love for us. Prevenient grace awakens us, in a spiritual sense, to the need for healing. Apathy is replaced by a conviction of sinfulness and knowledge that the needed healing cannot come from within ourselves. In preaching, Wesley often reminded people of the consequences of the decisions we make in this life. Moreover, Wesley taught that all Christians need "continual awakenings to remaining sin within the Christian life."[2] (See Lesson 4.)

Repentance. Nurtured by the Holy Spirit, serious pilgrims on the Way of Salvation *cooperate* with God's prevenient grace. This leads to repentance, which Wesley characterized as knowing oneself as a sinner, that is, knowing one's "total ungodliness, of [one's] utter inability to think, speak, or do good" (*Justification by Faith*, §IV.6). Repentance is personally acknowledging one's personal need: *I* am a sinner; there is no health in *me*. Personal repentance is more than an affirmation—it is a thorough conviction of sin: a deep sense of the [lack] of all good, and the presence of all evil" (§IV.2).

Wesley also believed that repentance, where possible, was accompanied by a literal "turning oneself around" with an active change of both heart and life. In this active sense, repentance is continuous in one's Christian journey.[3] (Note that this activity on our part is only possible due to grace.) Increasingly, as we turn from evil ways, we are gradually empowered to think and do only the good. In turning around, we take on a position from which we can receive more of God's grace.

Faith Not Good Works. Along with other Protestant leaders, Wesley believed justification came by faith and faith alone; that is, faith is the one and only condition for justification. Even faith comes by God's grace. However, there were many (e.g., the Quietists) in the eighteenth century who thought that one should not attempt "good works" or practice the means of grace until one had assurance of justification. Wesley agreed (§III.5-6) that actions "good and profitable to men" are not "good" in themselves or in the sight of God. Wesley taught that works are only "good" if they "spring out of a true and living faith" (§III.5); that is, if they are "done as God hath willed and commanded them to be done" (§III.6).

However, Wesley did acknowledge and value the changes that occur in those who have repented prior to justification. He commends those who cease from doing evil and intend to do good. He calls such efforts "bring[ing] forth fruits meet for repentance."[4]

My God, my God, to thee I cry,
Thee only would I know;
Thy purifying blood apply,
And wash me white as snow.

Tell me again my peace is made,
And bid the sinner live;
The debt's discharged, the ransom's paid,
My Father must forgive.

Behold, for me the victim bleeds,
His wounds are opened wide;
For me the blood of sprinkling pleads,
And speaks me justified.

Charles Wesley, "My God, To Thee
I Cry" (1740)—AME Hymnal #278

*Look for no peace within, till you are at peace with God;
which cannot be without "fruits meet for repentance."*
John Wesley, *The Wilderness State*, §III.3

The Key Question

Can we gain God's favor by doing good works, or is it the receiving of God's favor that gives us the power to do good works?

'Tis finished! the Messiah dies,
cut off for sins, but not his own.
Accomplished is the sacrifice,
the great redeeming work is done.

'Tis finished! All my guilt and pain,
I want no sacrifice beside;
for me, for me the Lamb is slain;
'tis finished! I am justified.

Charles Wesley, "'Tis Finished! the Messiah
Dies" (1740)—UM Hymnal #282

These acts of devotion, mercy, and justice are not *means to* salvation, but they do help to open us up to receive God's justifying grace.

Justification

Justifying Grace. God's overflowing grace offers a divine response to our repentance. God's response is called "justification," and the enabling power to experience it is called "justifying grace." Justification, at its root, is "pardon, the forgiveness of sins" (§II.5).[5] We are justified freely by God's grace, through the redemption that is in Jesus Christ [Rom. 3:24]. Only God can justify—only God in Christ can save.

Personal Relationship with God. Justification is the act of God that brings us into a proper relationship.[6] In justification, we are liberated from the power of guilt as well as sin, and we are restored to a right relationship with God.[7] Having turned around, we are in the posture to make such a relationship possible. Our proper personal relationship to God begins to restore us to right relationship with others and, indeed, with all creation. Thus, justification is an essential step towards recovering the image of God we were meant to have.

Forgiveness of Sins. Christian faith is reliance on the sacrifice of Christ, given for us, with the full confidence that through Jesus, our sins are forgiven and we are reconciled by God. "Being 'justified by faith,' [believers] have the peace of God ruling in their hearts—flowing from a continual sense of his pardoning mercy—and 'the answer of a good conscience toward God.'"[8]

Salvation. Wesley defined *salvation* as the entire work of justification (including the new birth; see Lesson 7). He expresses it this way:

> *The salvation which is through faith, even in the present world [is] a salvation from sin, and the consequences of sin, both often expressed in the word <u>justification</u>; which, taken in the largest sense, implies a deliverance from guilt and punishment, by the atonement of Christ actually applied to the soul of the sinner now believing on him, and a deliverance from the power of sin, through Christ formed in his heart. So that he who is thus justified, or saved by faith, is indeed <u>born again</u>. He is <u>born again of the Spirit</u> unto a new life.*[9]

Faith. We are justified by grace through faith. As noted, the one and only condition for receiving justification is faith (§IV.5).[10] Faith is not only assent but hearty trust. This faith is the divine evidence and conviction of things not seen (Heb. 11:1) and "a sure trust and confidence that Christ died for *my* sins, that he loved *me*, and gave himself for *me*" (§IV.2). Faith brings good works; indeed, fruits of living faith include "happiness (peace) and holiness (power)."[11] Wesley calls faith "the life of the soul."[12]

Wesleyans frequently used expressions such as the "blood of Jesus" and the "Lamb of God." Use of these terms is illustrated in the hymns of Charles Wesley included with this lesson. Christ was the unique and special sacrifice of God, and freely given by God,

Bold shall I stand in thy great day,
For who aught to my charge shall lay?
Fully absolved through these I am,
From sin and fear, from guilt and shame,

The holy, meek, unspotted Lamb,
Who from the Father's bosom came,
Who died for me, even me, to atone,
Now for my Lord and God I own.

Lord, I believe thy precious blood,
Which at the mercy-seat of God
For ever doth for sinners plead,
For me, even for my soul, was shed.

Jesu, be endless praise to thee,
Whose boundless mercy hath for me,
For me and all thy hands have made,
An everlasting ransom paid.

Nicolaus L. von Zinzendorf (translated by John Wesley), "Jesu, Thy Blood and Righteousness"— *1889 Hymnal* #190 (vs. 2-4,8)

But I looked on salvation, not as an attainment through one's efforts, but as an obtainment through grace.[13]
E. Stanley Jones, 1948

Let us plead for faith alone,
faith which by our works is shown;
God it is who justifies,
only faith the grace applies.

Active faith that lives within,
conquers hell and death and sin,
hallows whom it first made whole,
forms the Savior in the soul.

Let us for this faith contend,
sure salvation is the end;
heaven already is begun,
everlasting life is won.

Only let us persevere
till we see our Lord appear,
never from the Rock remove,
saved by faith which works by love.

Charles Wesley, "Let Us Plead for Faith Alone" (1740); *UM Hymnal* #385

on the cross in the earthshaking battle of Jesus Christ against all the forces of evil we could imagine. That sacrifice was a victory for our redemption, as demonstrated in Christ's resurrection from the dead. Thus, "shedding Jesus' blood for me" is a personal claim in faith of God's promises in Christ—our sins *are* forgiven. We *are* redeemed. In this way, the blood of Jesus purifies each of us. We are ready for something new.

New Birth and Assurance. Wesley understood salvation to include both the gradual process of spiritual growth and specific moments of decision and spiritual clarity, when God's grace becomes real to us. At the moment of justification, the believer experiences a new birth, being born again of God.[14] This experience of the Holy Spirit makes moral change possible in our lives. With Justification and New Birth comes an assurance of God's pardon. (The new birth and assurance are the subjects of the next lesson, Lesson 7.)

NOTES, REFLECTIONS, AND QUESTIONS

And can it be that I should gain
an interest in the Savior's blood!
Died he for me? who caused his pain!
For me? who him to death pursued?

Amazing love! How can it be
that thou, my God, shouldst die for me?
Amazing love! How can it be
that thou, my God, shouldst die for me?

Charles Wesley, "And Can It Be that I Should Gain" (1739)—*UM Hymnal #363; AME Hymnal #459; Free Methodist Ch. & The Wesleyan Ch. Hymnal #273; Ch. of Nazarene Hymnal #225*

RESPONDING FAITHFULLY

It is tempting to try to *attain* faith by our good works rather than trusting in God. How can we increasingly rely on God's grace?

Do you agree that faith is the one and only condition for justification as forgiveness of sins? In what way?

Can you remember a time when you repented and turned toward God? (What was it like?)

What difference do repentance, faith, and justification make in your life? Do you need to affirm or reaffirm these now?

_____

_____

_____

_____

_____

_____

_____

_____

LEARNING MORE

The following sermons by Wesley also speak of repentance, faith, and justification:

- *Salvation by Faith*
- *The Scripture Way of Salvation*
- *The Repentance of Believers*.

The following books outline Wesley's full theology:

- Randy L. Maddox, *Responsible Grace: John Wesley's Practical Theology*
- Kenneth J. Collins, *The Scripture Way of Salvation: The Heart of John Wesley's Theology*

LOOKING AHEAD

Next Lesson. New Birth—the beginning of a life in sanctification, growing in holiness.

Teacher Helps provides follow-up questions that may be useful in class discussions.

END NOTES

[1] John Wesley, *Salvation By Faith*, §3; and *The Repentance of Believers*, §I.20.

[2] Randy L. Maddox, op. cit., p. 161.

[3] John Wesley, *The Scripture Way of Salvation*, §III.6.

[4] *The Scripture Way of Salvation*, §III.2.

[5] In *Salvation By Faith*, §II.5, Wesley also notes that, in Romans (e.g., 5:9), Paul speaks of a future justification, which has its focus on the final victory of Christ when he comes again. At the final judgment, justifying grace again comes into play for the believer.

[6] As used by Paul in the New Testament letters, "justify" is the verb form of the Greek word for "righteous."

[7] Kenneth J. Collins, *The Scripture Way of Salvation: The Heart of John Wesley's Theology*, pp. 90-91.

[8] John Wesley, *The First Fruits of the Spirit*, §II.2.

[9] John Wesley, *Salvation by Faith*, §II.7. Compare *The Law Established Through Faith I*, §III.2: " . . . salvation from the guilt of sin, [Paul] commonly terms justification."

[10] See also *The Scripture Way of Salvation*, §III.1; and Wesley's (probably last) sermon, *On Faith*.

[11] Collins, op. cit., p. 75.

[12] John Wesley, *Awake Thou Sleepest*, §I.11.

[13] *The Repentance of Believers*, §III.2.

[14] E. Stanley Jones, *Gandhi: Portrayal of a Friend*, p. 61.

Reading for Lesson 6. Justification By Faith (1746)

To him that worketh not, but believeth on him that justifieth the ungodly,
his faith is counted to him for righteousness (Rom. 4:5).

Introduction

1. How a sinner may be justified before God, the Lord and Judge of all, is a question of no common importance to every child of man. It contains the foundation of all our hope, inasmuch as while we are at enmity with God there can be no true peace, no solid joy, either in time or in eternity. What peace can there be, while our own heart condemns us; and much more, he that is "greater than our heart, and knoweth all things"? What solid joy, either in this world or that to come, while "the wrath of God abideth on us"?

2. And yet how little hath this important question been understood! What confused notions have many had concerning it! Indeed, not only confused, but often utterly false; contrary to the truth, as light to darkness; notions absolutely inconsistent with the oracles of God, and with the whole analogy of faith. And hence, erring concerning the very foundation, they could not possibly build thereon; at least, not "gold, silver, or precious stones," which would endure when "tried as by fire" but only "hay and stubble," neither acceptable to God nor profitable to man.

3. In order to [do] justice, in far as in me lies, to the vast importance of the subject, to save those that seek the truth in sincerity from "vain jangling" and "strife of words," to clear the confusedness of thought into which so many have already been led thereby, and to give them true and just conceptions of this great mystery of godliness, I shall endeavor to show,

First, what is the general ground of this whole doctrine of justification;
Secondly, what justification is;
Thirdly, who they are that are justified; and,
Fourthly, on what terms they are justified.

I.

I am, first, to show what is the general ground of this whole doctrine of justification.

1. In the image of God was man made: holy as he that created him is holy; merciful as the Author of all is merciful; perfect as his Father in heaven is perfect. As God is love, so man, dwelling in love, dwelt in God, and God in him. God made him to be an "image of his own eternity," an incorruptible picture of the God of glory. He was accordingly pure, as God is pure, from every spot of sin. He knew not evil in any kind or degree, but was inwardly and outwardly sinless and undefiled. He "loved the Lord his God with all his heart, and with all his mind, and soul, and strength."

2. To man thus upright and perfect, God gave a perfect law, to which he required full and perfect obedience. He required full obedience in every point, and this to be performed without any intermission, from the moment man became a living soul till the time of his trial should be ended. No allowance was made for any falling short. As, indeed, there was no need of any man being altogether equal to the task assigned, and thoroughly furnished for every good word and work.

3. To the entire law of love which was written in his heart (against which, perhaps, he could not sin directly), it seemed good to the sovereign wisdom of God to superadd one positive law: "Thou shalt not eat of the fruit of the tree that groweth in the midst of the garden"; annexing that penalty thereto, "In the day thou eatest thereof, thou shalt surely die."

4. Such, then, was the state of man in paradise. By the free, unmerited love of God, he was holy and happy; he knew, loved, enjoyed God, which is, in substance, life everlasting. And in this life of love, he was to continue for ever, if he continued to obey God in all things; but, if he disobeyed him in any, he was to forfeit all. "In that day," said God, "thou shalt surely die."

5. Man did disobey God. He "ate of the tree of which God commanded him, saying, Thou shalt not eat of it." And in that day he was condemned by the righteous judgment of God. Then also the sentence whereof he was warned before began to take place upon him. For the moment he tasted that fruit, he died. His soul died, was separated from God; separate from whom the soul has no more life than the body has when separate from the soul. His body, likewise, became corruptible and mortal; so that death then took hold on this also. And being already dead in spirit, dead to God, dead in sin, he hastened on to death everlasting; to the destruction both of body and soul, in the fire never to be quenched

6. Thus "by one man sin entered into the world, and death by sin. And so death passed upon all men," as being contained in him who was the common father and representative of us all. Thus, "through the offence of one," all are dead, dead to God, dead in sin, dwelling in a corruptible, mortal body, shortly to be dissolved, and under the sentence of death eternal. For as, "by one man's disobedience," all "were made sinners"; so, by that offence of one, "judgment came upon all men to condemnation" (Rom. 5:12ff).

7. In this state we were, even all mankind, when "God so loved the world, that he gave his only-begotten Son, to the end we might not perish, but have everlasting life." In the fullness of time he was made man, another common head of mankind, a second general parent and representative of the whole human race. And as such it was that "he bore our griefs," the Lord "laying upon him the iniquities of us all." Then was he "wounded for our transgressions, and bruised for our iniquities." "He made his soul an offering for sin." He poured out his blood for the transgressors. He "bare our sins in his own body on the tree," that "by his stripes we might be healed." And "by that one oblation of himself once offered," he hath "redeemed me and all mankind"; having thereby "made a full, perfect, and sufficient sacrifice and satisfaction for the sins of the whole world."

8. In consideration of this, that the Son of God hath "tasted death for every man," God hath now "reconciled the world to himself, not imputing to them their" former "trespasses." And thus, "as by the offence of one judgment came upon all men to condemnation, even so by the righteousness of one the free gift came upon all men unto justification." So that, for the sake of his well-beloved Son, of what he hath done and suffered for us, God now vouchsafes, on one only condition (which himself also enables us to perform), both to remit the punishment due to our sins, to reinstate us in his favor, and to restore our dead souls to spiritual life, as the earnest of life eternal.

9. This, therefore, is the general ground of the whole doctrine of justification. By the sin of the first Adam, who was not only the father, but likewise the representative of us all, we all "fell short of the favor of God"; we all became children of wrath; or, as the Apostle expresses it, "judgment came upon all men to condemnation." Even so, by the sacrifice for sin made by the second Adam, as the representative of us all, God is so far reconciled to all the world that he hath given them a new covenant. The plain condition whereof being once fulfilled, "there is no more condemnation" for us, but "we are justified freely by his grace through the redemption that is in Jesus Christ."

II.

1. But what is it to be "justified? What is "justification? This was the second thing which I proposed to show. And it is evident, from what has been already observed, that it is not the being made actually just and righteous. This is "sanctification"; which is, indeed, in some degree, the immediate *fruit* of justification, but, nevertheless, is a distinct gift of God, and of a totally different nature. The one implies what God *does for us* through his Son; the other, what he *works in us* by his Spirit. So that, although some rare instances may be found wherein the term "justified" or "justification" is used in so wide a sense as to include "sanctification" also yet, in general use, they are sufficiently distinguished from each other, both by St. Paul and the other inspired writers.

2. Neither is that far-fetched conceit, that justification is the clearing us from accusation, particularly that of Satan, easily provable from any clear text of Holy Writ. In the whole scriptural account of this matter, as above laid down, neither that accuser nor his accusation appears to be at all taken in. It can not indeed be denied that he is the "accuser" of men, emphatically so called. But it does in nowise appear that the great Apostle hath any reference to this, more or less, in all he hath written touching justification, either to the Romans or the Galatians.

3. It is also far easier to take for granted, than to prove from any clear Scripture testimony, that justification is the clearing us from the accusation brought against us by *the law*: At least, if this forced, unnatural way of speaking mean either more or less than this, that, whereas we have transgressed the law of God, and thereby deserved the damnation of hell, God does not inflict on those who are justified the punishment which they had deserved.

4. Least of all does justification imply that God is *deceived* in those whom he justifies; that he thinks them to be what, in fact, they are not; that he accounts them to be otherwise than they are. It does by no means imply that God judges concerning us contrary to the real nature of things; that he esteems us better than we really are, or believes us righteous when we are unrighteous. Surely no. The judgment of the all-wise God is always according to truth. Neither can it ever consist with his unerring wisdom to think that I am innocent, to judge that I am righteous or holy, because another is so. He can no more, in this manner, confound me with Christ than with David or Abraham. Let any man to whom God hath given understanding, weigh this without prejudice; and he cannot but perceive that such a notion of justification is neither reconcilable to reason nor Scripture.

5. The plain scriptural notion of justification is pardon, the forgiveness of sins. It is that act of God the Father, whereby, for the sake of the propitiation made by the blood of his Son, he "showeth forth his righteousness (or mercy) by the remission of the sins that are past." This is the easy, natural account of it given by St. Paul throughout this whole Epistle [of Romans]. So he explains it himself, more particularly in this and in the following chapter. Thus, in the next verses but one to the text, "Blessed are they," saith he, "whose iniquities are forgiven, and whose sins are covered. Blessed is the man to whom the Lord will not impute sin." To him that is justified or forgiven, God "will not impute sin" to his condemnation. He will not condemn him on that account, either in this world or in that which is to come. His sins, all his past sins, in thought, word, and deed, are "covered," are blotted out, shall not be remembered or mentioned against him, any more than if they had not been. God will not inflict on that sinner what he deserved to suffer, because the Son of his love hath suffered for him. And from the time we are "accepted through the Beloved," "reconciled to God through his blood," he loves, and blesses, and watches over us for good, even as if we had never sinned.

> Indeed the Apostle in one place seems to extend the meaning of the word much farther, where he says, "Not the hearers of the law, but the doers of the law, shall be justified." Here he appears to refer our justification to the sentence of the great day. And so our Lord himself unquestionably doth, when he says, "By thy words thou shalt be justified"; proving thereby that "for every idle word men shall speak, they shall give an account in the day of judgment." But perhaps we can hardly produce another instance of St. Paul's using the word in that distant sense. In the general tenor of his writings, it is evident he doth not; and least of all in the text before us, which undeniably speaks, not of those who have already "finished their course," but of those who are now just "setting out," just beginning to "run the race which is set before them."

III.

1. But this is the third thing which was to be considered, namely, who are they that are justified? And the Apostle tells us expressly, the ungodly: "he" (that is, God) "justifieth the ungodly"; the ungodly of every kind and degree, and none but the ungodly. As "they that are righteous need no repentance," so they need no forgiveness. It is only sinners that have any occasion for pardon: it is sin alone which admits of being forgiven. Forgiveness, therefore, has an immediate reference to sin, and, in this respect, to nothing else. It is our "unrighteousness" to which the pardoning God is "merciful"; it is our "iniquity" which he "remembereth no more."

2. This seems not to be at all considered by those who so vehemently contend that a man must be sanctified, that is, holy, before he can be justified; especially by such of them as affirm that universal holiness or obedience must precede justification (unless they mean that justification at the last day, which is wholly out of the present question). So far from it that the very supposition is not only flatly impossible (for where there is no love of God, there is no holiness, and there is no love of God but from a sense of his loving us), but also grossly, intrinsically absurd, contradictory to itself. For it is not a *saint* but a *sinner* that is *forgiven*, and under the notion of a sinner. God *justifieth* not the godly, but the *ungodly*; not those that are holy already, but the unholy. Upon what condition he doeth this will be considered quickly; but whatever it is, it cannot be holiness. To assert this, is to say the Lamb of God takes away only those sins which were taken away before.

3. Does then the good Shepherd seek and save only those that are found already? No: He seeks and saves that which is lost. He pardons those who need his pardoning mercy. He saves from the guilt of sin (and, at the same time, from the power), sinners of every kind, of every degree: men who, till then, were altogether ungodly; in whom the love of the Father was not; and, consequently, in whom dwelt no good thing, no good or truly Christian temper, but all such as were evil and abominable: pride, anger, love of the world—the genuine fruits of that "carnal mind" which is "enmity against God."

4. These who are sick, the burden of whose sins is intolerable, are they that need a physician; these who are guilty, who groan under the wrath of God, are they that need a pardon. These who are "condemned already," not only by God, but also by their own conscience, as by a thousand witnesses, of all their ungodliness, both in thought, and word, and work, cry aloud for him that "justifieth the ungodly," through the "redemption that is in Jesus"—the ungodly and "him that worketh not"; that worketh not, before he is justified, anything that is good, that is truly virtuous or holy, but only evil continually. For his heart is necessarily, essentially evil, till the love of God is shed abroad therein. And while the tree is corrupt, so are the fruits; "for an evil tree cannot bring forth good fruit."

> 5. If it be objected, "Nay, but a man, before he is justified, may feed the hungry, or clothe the naked, and these are good works"; the answer is easy: he *may* do these, even before he is justified; and these are, in one sense,

"good works"; they are "good and profitable to men." But it does not follow that they are, strictly speaking, good in themselves, or good in the sight of God. All truly "good works" (to use the words of our Church) "follow after justification"; and they are therefore good and "acceptable to God in Christ," because they "spring out of a true and living faith." By a parity of reason, all "works done before justification are not good," in the Christian sense, "forasmuch as they spring not of faith in Jesus Christ" (though from some kind of faith in God they may spring); "yea, rather, for that they are not done as God hath willed and commanded them to be done, we doubt not" (how strange soever it may appear to some) "but they have the nature of sin."

6. Perhaps those who doubt of this have not duly considered the weighty reason which is here assigned, why no works done before justification can be truly and properly good. The argument runs thus—

No works are good which are not done as God hath willed and commanded them to be done.

But no works done before justification are done as God hath willed and commanded them to be done.

Therefore, no works done before justification are good.

The first proposition is self-evident; and the second, that no works done before justification are done as God hath willed and commanded them to be done, will appear equally plain and undeniable, if we only consider God hath willed and commanded that "all our works" should "be done in charity" (*en agape*); in love, in that love to God which produces love to all mankind. But none of our works can be done in this love while the love of the Father (of God as our Father) is not in us; and this love can not be in us till we receive the "Spirit of adoption, crying in our hearts, Abba, Father." If, therefore, God doth not "justify the ungodly," and him that (in this sense) "worketh not," then hath Christ died in vain; then, notwithstanding his death, can no flesh living be justified.

IV.

1. But on what terms, then, is he justified who is altogether "ungodly," and till that time "worketh not"? On one alone, which is faith. He "believeth in him that justifieth the ungodly," and "he that believeth is not condemned"; yea, he is "passed from death unto life." For "the righteousness (or mercy) of God is by faith of Jesus Christ unto all and upon all them that believe . . . whom God hath set forth to be a propitiation through faith in his blood" that "he might be just, and" (consistently with his justice) "the justifier of him which believeth in Jesus . . . . Therefore we conclude that a man is justified by faith without the deeds of the law"; without previous obedience to the moral law, which, indeed, he could not, till now, perform. That it is the moral law, and that alone, which is here intended, appears evidently from the words that follow: "Do we then make void the law through faith? God forbid! Yea, we establish the law." What law do we establish by faith? Not the ritual law; not the ceremonial law of Moses. In nowise; but the great, unchangeable law of love, the holy love of God and of our neighbor.

2. Faith in general is a divine, supernatural "*elegchos*," "evidence" or conviction, "of things not seen," not discoverable by our bodily senses, as being either past, future, or spiritual. Justifying faith implies, not only a divine evidence or conviction that "God was in Christ, reconciling the world unto himself"; but a sure trust and confidence that Christ died for *my* sins, that he loved *me*, and gave himself for *me*. And at what time soever a sinner thus believes, be it in early childhood, in the strength of his years, or when he is old and hoary-haired, God justifieth that ungodly one. God, for the sake of his Son, pardoneth and absolveth him who had in him, till then, no good thing. Repentance, indeed, God had given him before. But that repentance was neither more nor less than a deep sense of the want of all good, and the presence of all evil. And whatever good he hath, or doeth, from that hour when he first believes in God through Christ, faith does not *find*, but *bring*. This is the fruit of faith. First the tree is good, and then the fruit is good also.

3. I cannot describe the nature of this faith better than in the words of our own Church: "The only instrument of salvation" (whereof justification is one branch) "is faith; that is, a sure trust and confidence that God both hath and will forgive our sins, that he hath accepted us again into his favor, for the merits of Christ's death and Passion. But here we must take heed that we do not halt with God, through an inconstant, wavering faith. Peter, coming to Christ upon the water, because he fainted in faith, was in danger of drowning; so we, if we begin to waver or doubt, it is to be feared that we should sink as Peter did, not into the water, but into the bottomless pit of hell-fire. ([*Homilies*,] Second Sermon on the Passion).

"Therefore, have a sure and constant faith, not only that the death of Christ is available for all the world, but that he hath made a full and sufficient sacrifice for *thee*, a perfect cleansing of *thy* sins, so that thou mayest say, with the Apostle, he loved *thee*, and gave himself for *thee*. For this is to make Christ *thine own*, and to apply his merits unto *thyself* ([*Homilies*,] Sermon on the Sacrament, First Part).

4. By affirming that this faith is the term or *condition* of justification, I mean, first, that there is no justification without it. "He that believeth not is condemned already"; and so long as he believeth not, that condemnation cannot be removed, but "the wrath of God abideth on him." As "there is no other name given

under heaven," than that of Jesus of Nazareth, no other merit whereby a condemned sinner can ever be saved from the guilt of sin; so there is no other way of obtaining a share in his merit than "by faith in his name." So that as long as we are without this faith, we are "strangers to the covenant of promise," we are "aliens from the commonwealth of Israel," and "without God in the world." Whatsoever virtues (so called) a man may have—I speak of those unto whom the gospel is preached; for "what have I to do to judge them that are without?"—whatsoever good works (so accounted) he may do, it profiteth not; he is still a "child of wrath," still under the curse, till he believes in Jesus.

5. Faith, therefore, is the *necessary* condition of justification; yea, and the *only necessary* condition thereof. This is the second point carefully to be observed: that the very moment God giveth faith (for "it is the gift of God") to the "ungodly" that "worketh not," that "faith is counted to him for righteousness." He hath no righteousness at all, antecedent to this, not so much as negative righteousness, or innocence. But "faith is imputed to him for righteousness" the very moment that he believeth. Not that God (as was observed before) thinketh him to be what he is not. But as "he made Christ to be sin for us"—that is, treated him as a sinner, punished him for our sins—so he counteth us righteous from the time we believe in him; that is, he doth not punish us for our sins, yea, treats us as though we were guiltless and righteous.

6. Surely the difficulty of assenting to this proposition, that "faith is the "only condition" of justification," must arise from not understanding it. We mean thereby thus much, that it is the only thing without which none is justified; the only thing that is immediately, indispensably, absolutely requisite in order to pardon. As, on the one hand, though a man should have everything else without faith, yet he cannot be justified; so, on the other, though he be supposed to want everything else, yet if he hath faith, he cannot but be justified. For suppose a sinner of any kind or degree, in a full sense of his total ungodliness, of his utter inability to think, speak, or do good, and his absolute meetness for hell-fire; suppose, I say, this sinner, helpless and hopeless, casts himself wholly on the mercy of God in Christ (which indeed he cannot do but by the grace of God), who can doubt but he is forgiven in that moment? Who will affirm that any more is *indispensably required* before that sinner can be justified?

Now, if there ever was one such instance from the beginning of the world (and have there not been, and are there not, ten thousand times ten thousand?), it plainly follows that faith is, in the above sense, the sole condition of justification.

7. It does not become poor, guilty, sinful worms, who receive whatsoever blessings they enjoy (from the least drop of water that cools our tongue, to the immense riches of glory in eternity), of grace, of mere favor, and not of debt, to ask of God the reasons of his conduct. It is not meet for us to call him in question "who giveth account to none of his ways"; to demand, "Why didst thou make faith the condition, the only condition, of justification? Wherefore didst thou decree, "He that believeth, and he only, shall be saved"? This is the very point on which Saint Paul so strongly insists in the ninth chapter of this Epistle, viz., that the terms of pardon and acceptance must depend, not on us, but "on him that calleth us"; that there is no "unrighteousness with God," in fixing his own terms, not according to ours, but his own good pleasure; who may justly say, "I will have mercy on whom I will have mercy"; namely, on him who believeth in Jesus. "So then it is not of him that willeth, nor of him that runneth," to choose the condition on which he shall find acceptance "but of God that showeth mercy," that accepteth none at all but of his own free love, his unmerited goodness. "Therefore hath he mercy on whom he will have mercy," viz., on those who believe on the Son of his love; "and whom he will," that is, those who believe not, "he hardeneth," leaves at last to the hardness of their hearts.

8. One reason, however, we may humbly conceive, of God's fixing this condition of justification—"if thou believest in the Lord Jesus Christ, thou shalt be saved"—was to "hide pride from man." Pride had already destroyed the very angels of God, had cast down "a third part of the stars of heaven." It was likewise in great measure owing to this, when the tempter said, "Ye shall be as gods," that Adam fell from his own steadfastness and brought sin and death into the world. It was therefore an instance of wisdom worthy of God to appoint such a condition of reconciliation for him and all his posterity as might effectually humble, might abase them to the dust. And such is faith. It is peculiarly fitted for this end: For he that cometh unto God by this faith must fix his eye singly on his own wickedness, on his guilt and helplessness, without having the least regard to any supposed good in himself, to any virtue or righteousness whatsoever. He must come as a *mere sinner* inwardly and outwardly, self-destroyed and self-condemned, bringing nothing to God but ungodliness only, pleading nothing of his own but sin and misery. Thus it is, and thus alone, when his "mouth is stopped," and he stands utterly "guilty before" God, that he can "look unto Jesus," as the whole and sole "propitiation for his sins." Thus only can he be "found in him," and receive the "righteousness which is of God by faith."

9. Thou ungodly one, who hearest or readest these words! thou vile, helpless, miserable sinner! I charge thee before God, the Judge of all, go straight unto him, with all thy ungodliness. Take heed thou destroy not thy own soul by pleading thy righteousness, more or less. Go as altogether ungodly, guilty, lost, destroyed, deserving and dropping into hell; and thou shalt then find favor in his sight, and know that he justifieth the ungodly. As such thou shalt be brought unto the "blood of sprinkling," as an undone, helpless, damned sinner. Thus "look unto Jesus"! There is "the Lamb of God who taketh away *thy* sins"! Plead thou no works, no righteousness of thine own! No humility, contrition, sincerity! In no wise. That were, in very deed, to deny the Lord that bought thee. No. Plead thou, singly, the blood of the covenant, the ransom paid for thy proud, stubborn, sinful soul. Who art thou that now seest and feelest both thine inward and outward ungodliness? Thou art the man! I want thee for my Lord! I challenge *thee* for a child of God by faith! The Lord hath need of thee. Thou who feelest thou art just fit for hell, art just fit to advance his glory; the glory of his free grace, justifying the ungodly and him that worketh not. O come quickly! Believe in the Lord Jesus; and *thou*, even *thou*, art reconciled to God.

Lesson 7–Spiritual Rebirth

You must be born again.

John 3:7b; *NIV*

The new birth . . . is that great change which God works in the soul when he brings it into life: when he raises it from the death of sin to the life of righteousness. It is the change wrought in the whole soul by the almighty Spirit of God when it is 'created anew in Christ Jesus', when it is 'renewed after the image of God', 'in righteousness and true holiness', when the love of the world is changed into the love of God, pride into humility, passion into meekness; hatred, envy, malice, into a sincere, tender, disinterested love for all mankind.

John Wesley, *The New Birth*, §II.5

OUR STARTING POINT

Every person—all humankind—is bound by sin, spiritually dead to God, and far removed from God's image. This entire corruption of our human nature is the reason why we need the new birth. Everyone who comes into this world must be born again by the Spirit of God.

READING

Read daily the reflection and prayer about the new creation that we can experience if we receive Christ and are reconciled to God.

The New Birth, published in 1760, was the written expression of a theme—being born again—on which Wesley preached over sixty times during a twenty-year period, indicating the significance of this subject among early Methodists.

Day 1   Scan *The New Birth* in its entirety and read thoroughly the Introduction. Read about the relationship of the new birth to justification. Scan Lesson 7.
Day 2   Read Part I, §§I.1-4. Why we must be born again.
Day 3   Read Part II, §§II.1-5. How we can be born again.
Day 4   Read Part III, §§III.1-3. Why is it necessary that we should be born again?
Day 5   Read §§IV.1-3. The new birth is not the same as baptism.
Day 6   Read §IV.4. You must be born again. Reread the lesson and answer the questions at the end.
Day 7   Rest.

REFLECTION

If anyone is in Christ, the new creation has come: the old has gone, the new is here! All this is from God, who reconciled us to himself through Christ and gave us the ministry of reconciliation . . . . We implore you on Christ's behalf: be reconciled to God.

2 Cor. 5:17-19, 20b; *TNIV*

PRAYER

Pray daily before study:
We live in a broken world, O God, and my sinfulness has convinced me of my own complicity in that brokenness. Grant me, I pray, a "contrite heart," so that the remembrance of my sins will distress me. Then I will be aware of my need for spiritual rebirth—for the work of your transforming Spirit. Humbly, I ask you to make me a new person in Christ, holy and righteous, and to give me your promised assurance that my sins have been forgiven, through the death and resurrection of our Savior, Jesus Christ. Amen.

Prayer concerns for this week:

Daily Reflections

Day 1   Scan *The New Birth* in its entirety and read thoroughly the Introduction. Read about the relationship of the new birth to justification. Scan Lesson 7.

Meaning for me:

Day 2   Read Part I, §§I.1-4. Why we must be born again.

Meaning for me:

Day 3   Read Part II, §§II.1-5. How we can be born again.

Meaning for me:

Day 4   Read Part III, §§III.1-3. Why is it necessary that we should be born again?

Meaning for me:

Day 5   Read §§IV.1-3. The new birth is not the same as baptism.

Meaning for me:

Day 6   Read §IV.4. You must be born again. Reread the lesson and answer the questions at the end.

Meaning for me:

What is the New Birth?

The new birth is an important biblical concept that became an essential component of Wesley's Way of Salvation. But what is it? When we acknowledge by faith God's acceptance of us in justification, we also receive the new birth—the transforming work of God.

Justification is what God does *for* us through the death of Jesus Christ (pardon and forgiveness of sins), while the new birth is what God does *in* us by the Holy Spirit (restoring a right relationship with God and others). This regenerative action is when the image of God begins to be reconstructed in our lives, a real change that signifies we are moving from being a nominal or "almost Christian" to being an "altogether Christian" (see Lesson 5). Like the metamorphosis of a caterpillar to a butterfly, "the new creation has come. The old is gone, the new is here!" (2 Cor. 5:17) "As soon as [someone] is born of God, there is a total change" (*The New Birth*, §II.4). God is renewing our fallen nature, giving us power over sin.

The new birth is both an experience of the Holy Spirit and the beginning of a moral character change in our life. Experientially, the new birth is the gateway through which salvation comes into our consciousness. We become "alive to God through Jesus Christ."[1] We have intimate fellowship with God "by a kind of *spiritual respiration*" through prayer and praise—so natural that it's like breathing! Wesley wrote that "God is continually breathing, as it were, upon [our] soul, and [our] soul is breathing unto God" (§II.4).

Morally, the new birth indicates that the Spirit has implanted seeds of virtue (love, joy, peace, patience, kindness, etc.), growing in the soil of God's love, so that as those seeds grow, they will choke out the old life of sin.

Necessity of the New Birth. Is it necessary to receive the new birth? Wesley certainly thought so. The new birth is necessary, he asserted, in order to live a holy life, since it is only through the Spirit's action that we have the power to overcome sin. It is also necessary in order to experience deep happiness, since without the Spirit's revitalization, our life's circumstances will be dominated by attitudes of pride, self-will, "malice, hatred, envy, jealousy, [and] revenge, [which] create a present hell" in the soul (§III.3).

Some regular church-goers may wish to claim that they have always been "real Christians" and that they have known of "no time when [they] had need of such a change" (*The Witness of the Spirit*, I, §II.5). This may be particularly the case for someone who believes that he or she was "born again when I was baptized." Wesley addresses that argument directly, declaring that the new birth is *not* the same thing as baptism. Whether or not one is "baptized or unbaptized, you must be born again," since "the new birth is absolutely necessary in order to [receive] eternal salvation." Indeed, someone may "go to church twice a day, go to the Lord's table every week, say ever so many prayers in private; hear ever so many sermons…read ever so many good books—still you

NOTES, REFLECTIONS, AND QUESTIONS

You have been born again, not of perishable seed, but of imperishable, through the living and enduring Word of God.

1 Peter 1:23; *TNIV*

Jesus replied, "Very truly, I tell you, no one can see the kingdom of God, without being born again."

John 3:3; *TNIV*

The Scriptures describe the being born of God, which must precede the witness that we are his children, as a vast and mighty change . . . . But what knoweth [the nominal Christian] of any such change as this? . . . . This is a language which he does not understand. He tells you he always was a Christian. He knows no time when he had need of such a change. By this also, if he give himself leave to think, may he know that he is not born of the Spirit; that he has never yet known God, but has mistaken the voice of nature for the voice of God.

John Wesley, *The Witness of the Spirit*, I, §II.5

must be born again. None of these things will stand in the place of the new birth." (*The New Birth*, §§III.2, IV.4)

An Event That Begins a Process

The new birth can be compared to falling in love: you know when it has happened, and you may even be able to pinpoint the date and time. Your emotions and your actions have changed, and there is a quality of relationship that exists that was not there previously. But also like any committed relationship, our life with God must be continually nurtured. The new birth denotes when we start to experience a personal and intimate relationship with God, but it is not a one-time event; it is the beginning of the Spirit's everyday revival of the soul.

A person "is born of God in a short time, if not in a moment. But it is by slow degrees that he afterward grows up to the measure of the full stature of Christ" (§IV.3). The new birth is "only our *birth* as Christians. What it brings is a new vitality and responsiveness to God, but not yet a completed transformation of our character."[2]

In the new birth, the Holy Spirit "adopts" us into God's family and we become heirs of eternal salvation. Thus, our salvation is a present encounter with God. We should never rest in the memory of past spiritual experiences, but rather should encourage God's Spirit to be living and active in our hearts.

Assurance of Salvation

When he finally trusted in Christ, John Wesley recorded in his *Journal*: "I felt my heart strangely warmed . . . and an assurance was given me, that [Christ] had taken away *my* sins, even *mine*." He had stepped over the line—from endless striving and joyless "faith in faith"—to "faith itself, from aspiration to assurance."[3] This "blessed assurance" (in the words of Methodist hymn writer Fanny Crosby) is also known as the "witness of the Spirit."

It is the "spirit of adoption" that makes us aware that we have been accepted as God's children—"heirs of salvation." Charles Wesley, whose own spiritual rebirth was at about the same time as his brother's, asked a crucial question: "How can we sinners know our sins on earth forgiven?" (The hymn based on this question is provided at the right.)

The Wesley brothers determined through their own experience that God has given all believers the privilege of knowing that they are God's children. There are two ways by which Christians can have such a knowledge, such an assurance of their salvation: (1) objectively, by an examination of the conduct of their lives; and (2) subjectively, by what they "have felt and seen." That is, believers receive an internal peace in which they "feel his [Christ's] blood applied." This "inward impression on the soul"[4] is when God, figuratively speaking, stamps the hot wax of the Holy Spirit on one's heart. We can know we are forgiven inwardly when we can answer positively the question: Is my heart changed? And we

NOTES, REFLECTIONS, AND QUESTIONS

How precious did that grace appear, the hour I first believed.

John Newton, "Amazing Grace" (1779)

Let us draw near to God with a sincere heart in full assurance of faith.

Heb. 10:22; *TNIV*

Wesley's Experience of Assurance

*About a quarter before nine . . . I felt my heart strangely warmed. I felt I did trust in Christ, Christ alone for salvation; And an assurance was given me, that he had taken away **my** sins, even **mine**, and saved **me** from the law of sin and death.*

John Wesley, *Journal*, May 24, 1738

Blessed assurance, Jesus is mine! O what a foretaste of glory divine!

Heir of salvation, purchase of God, Born of his Spirit, washed in his blood.

Fanny Crosby, "Blessed Assurance" (1873)— UM Hymnal #369

How can we sinners know Our sins on earth forgiven? How can my gracious Savior show My name inscribed in heaven?

What we have felt and seen, With confidence we tell, And publish to the ends of earth The signs infallible.

We who in Christ believe That he for us hath died, We all his unknown peace receive, And feel his blood applied.

Our nature's turned, our mind Transformed in all its powers, And both the witnesses are joined, The Spirit of God with ours.

Charles Wesley, "How Can We Sinners Know" (1749)—UM Hymnal #372; AME Hymnal #264

can know we are forgiven outwardly when we can answer positively the analogous question: Is my life changed?

Spreading the Good News

John Wesley's life certainly changed after his Aldersgate experience of being assured of God's forgiveness. Within two years of being a defeated, discouraged, and disillusioned religious man who was trying to find his way via his own power, Wesley had become the acknowledged leader of a nationwide spiritual revival that continued to grow dramatically for the next half century. Like Wesley, after we become a "new creation" in which God "reconciles us to himself through Christ," then we, too, are summoned to a "ministry of reconciliation"—sharing the message of the good news with others. We are called to become "Christ's ambassadors" (2 Cor. 5:17-18,20; TNIV).

NOTES, REFLECTIONS, AND QUESTIONS

You have received a spirit of adoption. When we cry, "Abba! Father!" it is that very Spirit bearing witness with our spirit that we are children of God.

Romans 8:15b-16; NRSV

How does [God] "bear witness with our spirit that we are the children of God"? It is hard to find words in the language of men to explain the "deep things of God." . . . But perhaps one might say [that] the testimony of the Spirit is an inward impression on the soul, whereby the Spirit of God directly "witnesses to my spirit that I am a child of God"; that Jesus Christ hath loved me, and given himself for me; that all my sins are blotted out, and I, even I, am reconciled to God.

John Wesley, *The Witness of the Spirit,* I, §I.7

RESPONDING FAITHFULLY

What would it be like to have a relationship with God characterized by "spiritual respiration"?

_____

_____

_____

_____

_____

Are your spiritual experiences from the past still alive in the present?

_____

_____

_____

_____

_____

If sharing the message of the new birth with others became a priority for your faith community, how would you act differently? What would a church look like if its members were all sharing the "ministry of reconciliation"?

_____

_____

_____

_____

_____

_____

Do you agree or disagree with Wesley's assessment that "the new birth is absolutely necessary in order to [receive] eternal salvation"? Why?

_____

_____

_____

_____

_____

_____

LEARNING MORE

The following sermons by Wesley refer to the new birth and the assurance of salvation.
- *The Marks of the New Birth*
- *The Witness of the Spirit, I*

The following books describe Wesley's concept of the new birth:
- Kenneth J. Collins, *The Scripture Way of Salvation*
- Kenneth J. Collins and John H. Tyson, Editors, *Conversion in the Wesleyan Tradition*, especially the article "Conversion and Baptism in Wesleyan Spirituality" by T. A. Campbell.

LOOKING AHEAD

Next Lesson. The Means of Grace—developing habits of holiness in our lives.

Teacher Helps provides follow-up questions that may be useful in class discussions.

END NOTES

[1] Being "alive to God" (Eph 2:5) is a common expression in Wesley's other sermons. See, for example: *Awake Thou Sleepest* (§I.11); *The Righteousness of Faith* (§II.1), *The Witness of the Spirit* I (§I.5); *The Witness of Our Own Spirit* (§19); *Upon the Lord's Sermon on the Mount XI* (§I.5); *The Nature of Enthusiasm* (§2); *The Scripture Way of Salvation* (§I.8); *In What Sense Are We To Leave the World* (§16); and *On Zeal* (§II.10).
[2] Randy L. Maddox, *Responsible Grace: John Wesley's Practical Theology.* Nashville: Kingswood Books, Abingdon Press, 1994, p. 177.
[3] Albert C. Outler, Editor, *John Wesley: A Representative Collection of His Writings.* New York: Oxford University Press, 1964, p. 14.
[4] John Wesley, *The Witness of the Spirit, I,* §I.7.

Reading for Lesson 7. The New Birth (1760)

Ye must be born again (John 3:7).

Introduction

1. If any doctrines within the whole compass of Christianity may be properly termed fundamental, they are doubtless these two—the doctrine of justification, and that of the new birth: The former relating to that great work which God does for us, in forgiving our sins; the latter, to the great work which God does *in us,* in renewing our fallen nature. In order of *time,* neither of these is before the other: in the moment we are justified by the grace of God, through the redemption that is in Jesus, we are also "born of the Spirit"; but in order of *thinking,* as it is termed, justification precedes the new birth. We first conceive his wrath to be turned away, and then his Spirit to work in our hearts.

2. How great importance then must it be of, to every child of man, thoroughly to understand these fundamental doctrines! From a full conviction of this, many excellent men have wrote very largely concerning justification, explaining every point relating thereto, and opening the Scriptures which treat upon it. Many likewise have written on the new birth: And some of them largely enough; but yet not so clearly as might have been desired, nor so deeply and accurately; having either given a dark, abstruse account of it, or a slight and superficial one. Therefore a full, and at the same time a clear, account of the new birth, seems to be wanting still; such as may enable us to give a satisfactory answer to these three questions:

I. First, Why must we be born again? What is the foundation of this doctrine of the new birth?

II. Secondly, How must we be born again? What is the nature of the new birth? and,

III. Thirdly, Wherefore must we be born again? To what end is it necessary?

IV. These questions, by the assistance of God, I shall briefly and plainly answer; and then subjoin a few inferences which will naturally follow.

I.

1. And, first, Why must we be born again? What is the foundation of this doctrine? The foundation of it lies near as deep as the creation of the world; in the scriptural account whereof we read, "And God," the three-one God, "said, Let us make man in our image, after our likeness. So God created man in his own image, in the image of God created he him": (Gen. 1:26, 27)—not barely* in his *natural image,* a picture of his own immortality; a spiritual being, endued with understanding, freedom of will, and various affections; nor merely in his *political image,* the governor of this lower world, having "dominion over the fishes of the sea, and over the fowl of the air, and over the cattle, and over all the earth"—but chiefly in his *moral image;* which, according to the Apostle, is "righteousness and true holiness" (Eph. 4:24)—in this image of God was man made. "God is love"—accordingly, man at his creation was full of love; which was the sole principle of all his tempers, thoughts, words, and actions. God is full of justice, mercy, and truth; so was man as he came from the hands of his Creator. God is spotless purity; and so man was in the beginning pure from every sinful blot; otherwise God could not have pronounced him, as well as all the other works of his hands, "very good" (Gen. 1:31). This he could not have been, had he not been pure from sin, and filled with righteousness and true holiness. For there is no medium: if we suppose an intelligent creature not to love God, not to be righteous and holy, we necessarily suppose him not to be good at all; much less to be "very good."

2. But, although man was made in the image of God, yet he was not made immutable. This would have been inconsistent with that state of trial in which God was pleased to place him. He was therefore created able to stand, and yet liable to fall. And this God himself apprized him of, and gave him a solemn warning against it. Nevertheless, man did not abide in honor. He fell from his high estate. He "ate of the tree whereof the Lord had commanded him, 'Thou shalt not eat thereof.'" By this willful act of disobedience to his Creator, this flat rebellion against his Sovereign, he openly declared that he would no longer have God to rule over him; that he would be governed by his own will, and not the will of him that created him; and that he would not seek his happiness in God, but in the world, in the works of his hands. Now, God had told him before, "In the day that thou eatest" of that fruit, "thou shalt surely die." And the word of the Lord cannot be broken. Accordingly, in that day he did die. He died to God—the most dreadful of all deaths. He lost the life of God. He was separated from him, in union with whom his spiritual life consisted. The body dies when it is separated from the soul; the soul, when it is separated from God. But this separation from God, Adam sustained in the day, the hour, he ate of the forbidden fruit. And of this he gave immediate proof; presently showing by his behavior that the love of God was

extinguished in his soul, which was now "alienated from the life of God." Instead of this, he was now under the power of servile fear, so that he fled from the presence of the Lord. Yea, so little did he retain even of the knowledge of him who filleth heaven and earth, that he endeavored to "hide himself from the Lord God among the trees of the garden" (Gen. 3:8). So had he lost both the knowledge and the love of God, without which the image of God would not subsist. Of this, therefore, he was deprived at the same time, and became unholy as well as unhappy. In the room of this, he had sunk into pride and self-will, the very image of the devil; and into sensual appetites and desires, the image of the beasts that perish.

3. If it be said, "Nay, but that threatening, 'In the day that thou eatest thereof, thou shalt surely die,' refers to temporal death, and that alone, to the death of the body only"; the answer is plain: to affirm this is flatly and palpably to make God a liar; to aver that the God of truth positively affirmed a thing contrary to truth. For it is evident, Adam did not *die* in this sense, "in the day that he ate thereof." He lived, in the sense opposite to this death, above nine hundred years after. So that this cannot possibly be understood of the death of the body, without impeaching the veracity of God. It must therefore be understood of spiritual death, the loss of the life and image of God.

4. And in Adam all died, all human kind, all the children of men who were then in Adam's loins. The natural consequence of this is, that everyone descended from him comes into the world spiritually dead, dead to God, wholly dead in sin; entirely void of the life of God; void of the image of God, of all that righteousness and holiness wherein Adam was created. Instead of this, every man born into the world now bears the image of the devil in pride and self-will; the image of the beast, in sensual appetites and desires. This, then, is the foundation of the new birth—the entire corruption of our nature. Hence it is, that being born in sin, we must be "born again." Hence everyone that is born of a woman must be born of the Spirit of God.

II.

1. But how must a man be born again? What is the nature of the new birth? This is the second question. And a question it is of the highest moment that can be conceived. We ought not, therefore, in so weighty a concern, to be content with a slight inquiry; but to examine it with all possible care, and to ponder it in our hearts, till we fully understand this important point, and clearly see how we are to be born again.

2. Not that we are to expect any minute, philosophical account of the manner how this is done. Our Lord sufficiently guards us against any such expectation, by the words immediately following the text; wherein he reminds Nicodemus of as indisputable a fact as any in the whole compass of nature, which, notwithstanding, the wisest man under the sun is not able fully to explain. "The wind bloweth where it listeth"—not by thy power or wisdom; "and thou hearest the sound thereof"—thou art absolutely assured, beyond all doubt, that it doth blow; "but thou canst not tell whence it cometh, neither whither it goeth"—the precise manner how it begins and ends, rises and falls, no man can tell. "So is everyone that is born of the Spirit"—thou mayest be as absolutely assured of the fact, as of the blowing of the wind; but the precise manner how it is done, how the Holy Spirit works this in the soul, neither thou nor the wisest of the children of men is able to explain.

3. However, it suffices for every rational and Christian purpose that, without descending into curious, critical inquiries, we can give a plain scriptural account of the nature of the new birth. This will satisfy every reasonable man, who desires only the salvation of his soul. The expression, "being born again," was not first used by our Lord in his conversation with Nicodemus: It was well known before that time, and was in common use among the Jews when our Savior appeared among them. When an adult heathen was convinced that the Jewish religion was of God, and desired to join therein, it was the custom to baptize him first, before he was admitted to circumcision. And when he was baptized, he was said to be born again; by which they meant that he who was before a child of the devil was now adopted into the family of God, and accounted one of his children. This expression, therefore, which Nicodemus, being "a teacher in Israel," ought to have understood well, our Lord uses in conversing with him; only in a stronger sense than he was accustomed to. And this might be the reason of his asking, "How can these things be? They cannot be literally—a man cannot "enter a second time into his mother's womb, and be born"—but they may spiritually. A man may be born from above, born of God, born of the Spirit, in a manner which bears a very near analogy to the natural birth.

4. Before a child is born into the world he has eyes, but sees not; he has ears, but does not hear. He has a very imperfect use of any other sense. He has no knowledge of any of the things of the world, nor any natural understanding. To that manner of existence which he then has, we do not even give the name of life. It is then only when a man is born that we say he begins to live. For as soon as he is born, he begins to see the light, and the various objects with which he is encompassed. His ears are then opened, and he hears the sounds which successively strike upon them. At the same time, all the other organs of sense begin to be

exercised upon their proper objects. He likewise breathes, and lives in a manner wholly different from what he did before. How exactly does the parallel hold in all these instances! While a man is in a mere natural state, before he is born of God, he has, in a spiritual sense, eyes and sees not; a thick impenetrable veil lies upon them; he has ears, but hears not; he is utterly deaf to what he is most of all concerned to hear. His other spiritual senses are all locked up: He is in the same condition as if he had them not. Hence he has no knowledge of God; no intercourse* with him; he is not at all acquainted with him. He has no true knowledge of the things of God, either of spiritual or eternal things; therefore, though he is a living man, he is a dead Christian. But as soon as he is born of God, there is a total change in all these particulars. The "eyes of his understanding are opened" (such is the language of the great Apostle); and, He who of old "commanded light to shine out of darkness shining on his heart, he sees the light of the glory of God," his glorious love, "in the face of Jesus Christ." His ears being opened, he is now capable of hearing the inward voice of God, saying, "Be of good cheer; thy sins are forgiven thee"; "go and sin no more."

> This is the purport of what God speaks to his heart; although perhaps not in these very words. He is now ready to hear whatsoever "He that teacheth man knowledge" is pleased, from time to time, to reveal to him. He "feels in his heart," to use the language of our Church, "the mighty working of the Spirit of God"; not in a gross, carnal sense as the men of the world stupidly and willfully misunderstand the expression; though they have been told again and again, we mean thereby neither more nor less than this. He feels, is inwardly sensible of, the graces which the Spirit of God works in his heart. He feels, he is conscious of, a "peace which passeth all understanding." He many times feels such a joy in God as is "unspeakable, and full of glory." He feels "the love of God shed abroad in his heart by the Holy Ghost which is given unto him"; and all his spiritual senses are then exercised to discern spiritual good and evil.

By the use of these, he is daily increasing in the knowledge of God, of Jesus Christ whom he hath sent and to all the things pertaining to his inward kingdom. And now he may properly be said to live: God having quickened him by his Spirit, he is alive to God through Jesus Christ. He lives a life which the world knoweth not of, a "life which is hid with Christ in God." God is continually breathing, as it were, upon his soul; and his soul is breathing unto God. Grace is descending into his heart; and prayer and praise ascending to heaven: And by this intercourse between God and man, this fellowship with the Father and the Son, as by a kind of spiritual respiration, the life of God in the soul is sustained; and the child of God grows up, till he comes to the "full measure of the stature of Christ."

5. From hence it manifestly appears, what is the nature of the new birth. It is that great change which God works in the soul when he brings it into life; when he raises it from the death of sin to the life of righteousness. It is the change wrought in the whole soul by the almighty Spirit of God when it is "created anew in Christ Jesus"; when it is "renewed after the image of God, in righteousness and true holiness"; when the love of the world is changed into the love of God; pride into humility; passion into meekness; hatred, envy, malice, into a sincere, tender, disinterested* love for all mankind. In a word, it is that change whereby the earthly, sensual, devilish mind is turned into the "mind which was in Christ Jesus." This is the nature of the new birth: "So is everyone that is born of the Spirit."

III.

1. It is not difficult for any who has considered these things, to see the necessity of the new birth, and to answer the third question, Wherefore, to what ends is it necessary that we should be born again? It is very easily discerned that this is necessary, first, in order to [have] holiness. For what is holiness according to the oracles of God? Not a bare external religion, a round of outward duties, how many soever they be, and how exactly soever performed. No: gospel holiness is no less than the image of God stamped upon the heart; it is no other than the whole mind which was in Christ Jesus; it consists of all heavenly affections and tempers mingled together in one. It implies such a continual, thankful love to him who hath not withheld from us his Son, his only Son, as makes it natural, and in a manner necessary to us, to love every child of man; as fills us "with bowels* of mercies, kindness, gentleness, long-suffering." It is such a love of God as teaches us to be blameless in all manner of conversation; as enables us to present our souls and bodies, all we are and all we have, all our thoughts, words, and actions, a continual sacrifice to God, acceptable through Christ Jesus. Now, this holiness can have no existence till we are renewed in the image of our mind. It cannot commence in the soul till that change be wrought; till, by the power of the Highest overshadowing us, we are "brought from darkness to light, from the power of Satan unto God"; that is, till we are born again; which, therefore, is absolutely necessary in order to [have] holiness.

2. But "without holiness no man shall see the Lord," shall see the face of God in glory. Of consequence, the new birth is absolutely necessary in order to [receive] eternal salvation. Men may indeed flatter themselves (so desperately wicked and so deceitful is the heart of man!) that they may live in their sins till they come to the last gasp, and yet afterward live with God; and thousands do really believe that they have found a broad way which leadeth not to destruction.

> "What danger," say they, "can a woman be in that is so *harmless* and so *virtuous*? What fear is there that so *honest* a man, one of so strict *morality*, should miss of heaven; especially if, over and above all this, they constantly attend on church and sacrament? One of these will ask with all assurance, "What! Shall not I do as well as my neighbors?" Yes as well as your unholy neighbors; as well as your neighbors that die in their sins! For you will all drop into the pit together, into the nethermost hell! You will all lie together in the lake of fire; "the lake of fire burning with brimstone." Then, at length, you will see (but God grant you may see it before!) the necessity of holiness in order to [see] glory; and, consequently, of the new birth, since none can be holy, except he be born again.

3. For the same reason, except he be born again, none can be happy even in this world. For it is not possible, in the nature of things, that a man should be happy who is not holy. Even the poor, ungodly poet could tell us, *Nemo malus felix*: "no wicked man is happy." The reason is plain. All unholy tempers are uneasy tempers. Not only malice, hatred, envy, jealousy, revenge, create a present hell in the breast; but even the softer passions, if not kept within due bounds, give a thousand times more pain than pleasure. Even "hope," when "deferred" (and how often must this be the case!), "maketh the heart sick"; and every desire which is not according to the will of God is liable to "pierce" us "through with many sorrows." And all those general sources of sin—pride, self-will, and idolatry—are, in the same proportion as they prevail, general sources of misery. Therefore, as long as these reign in any soul, happiness has no place there. But they must reign till the bent of our nature is changed, that is, till we are born again; consequently, the new birth is absolutely necessary in order to [experience] happiness in this world, as well as in the world to come.

IV.

I proposed in the last place to subjoin a few inferences, which naturally follow from the preceding observations.

1. And, first, it follows that baptism is not the new birth. They are not one and the same thing. Many indeed seem to imagine that they are just the same; at least, they speak as if they thought so; but I do not know that this opinion is publicly avowed by any denomination of Christians whatever. Certainly it is not by any within these kingdoms, whether of the Established Church, or dissenting from it. The judgment of the latter is clearly declared in their larger Catechism: Q[163] "What are the parts of a sacrament? Ans. The parts of a sacrament are two: the one an outward and sensible sign; the other, and inward and spiritual grace, thereby signified; and Q[165] What is baptism? Ans. Baptism is a sacrament, wherein Christ hath ordained the washing with water, to be a sign and seal of regeneration by his Spirit." Here it is manifest—baptism, the sign, is spoken of as distinct from regeneration, the thing signified.

> In the Church Catechism likewise, the judgment of our Church is declared with the utmost clearness: "What meanest thou by this word, sacrament? Ans. I mean an outward and visible sign of an inward and spiritual grace. Q. What is the outward part or form in baptism? Ans. Water, wherein the person is baptized, in the name of the Father, Son, and Holy Ghost. Q. What is the inward part, or thing signified? Ans. A death unto sin, and a new birth unto righteousness." Nothing, therefore, is plainer than that, according to the Church of England, baptism is not the new birth.

> But indeed the reason of the thing is so clear and evident, as not to need any other authority. For what can be more plain, that the one is an external, the other an internal work?—that the one is a visible, the other an invisible thing, and therefore wholly different from each other?—the one being an act of man, purifying the body; the other a change wrought by God in the soul: so that the former is just as distinguishable from the latter, as the soul from the body, or water from the Holy Ghost.

2. From the preceding reflections we may, secondly, observe that as the new birth is not the same thing with baptism, so it does not always accompany baptism: they do not constantly go together. A man may possibly be "born of water," and yet not be "born of the Spirit." There may sometimes be the outward sign, where there is not the inward grace. I do not now speak with regard to infants. It is certain our Church supposes that all who are baptized in their infancy are at the same time born again; and it is allowed that the whole Office for the Baptism of Infants proceeds upon this supposition. Nor is it an objection of any weight against this, that we cannot comprehend how this work can be wrought in infants. For neither can we comprehend how it

is wrought in a person of riper years. But whatever be the case with infants, it is sure all of riper years who are baptized are not at the same time born again. "The tree is known by its fruits"; and thereby it appears too plain to be denied, that divers of those who were children of the devil before they were baptized continue the same after baptism: "for the works of their father they do." They continue servants of sin, without any pretence either to inward or outward holiness.

3. A third inference, which we may draw from what has been observed, is that the new birth is not the same with sanctification. This is indeed taken for granted by many; particularly by an eminent writer, in his late treatise on "The Nature and Grounds of Christian Regeneration." To waive several other weighty objections which might be made to that tract, this is a palpable one. It all along speaks of regeneration as a progressive work, carried on in the soul by slow degrees, from the time of our first turning to God. This is undeniably true of sanctification; but of regeneration, the new birth, it is not true. This is a part of sanctification, not the whole; it is the gate of it, the entrance into it. When we are born again, then our sanctification, our inward and outward holiness, begins; and thenceforward we are gradually to "grow up in him who is our head." This expression of the Apostle admirably illustrates the difference between one and the other, and farther points out the exact analogy there is between natural and spiritual things. A child is born of a woman in a moment, or at least in a very short time: Afterward he gradually and slowly grows, till he attains to the stature of a man. In like manner, a child is born of God in a short time, if not in a moment. But it is by slow degrees that he afterward grows up to the measure of the full stature of Christ. The same relation, therefore, which there is between our natural birth and our growth, there is also between our new birth and our sanctification.

4. One point more we may learn from the preceding observations. But it is a point of so great importance, as may excuse the considering it the more carefully, and prosecuting it at some length. What must one who loves the souls of men, and is grieved that any of them should perish, say to one whom he sees living in sabbath-breaking, drunkenness, or any other willful sin? What can he say, if the foregoing observations are true, but, "You must be born again?" "No," says a zealous man, "that cannot be. How can you talk so uncharitably to the man? Has he not been baptized already? He cannot be born again now." Can he not be born again? Do you affirm this? Then he cannot be saved. Though he be as old as Nicodemus was, yet "except he be born again, he cannot see the kingdom of God."

> Therefore in saying, "He cannot be born again," you in effect deliver him over to damnation. And where lies the uncharitableness now?—on my side, or on yours? I say, he may be born again, and so become an heir of salvation. You say, "He cannot be born again": And if so, he must inevitably perish! So you utterly block up his way to salvation, and send him to hell, out of mere charity!

But perhaps the sinner himself, to whom in real charity we say, "You must be born again," has been taught to say, "I defy your new doctrine; I need not be born again: I was born again when I was baptized. What! Would you have me deny my baptism? I answer, first, There is nothing under heaven which can excuse a lie; otherwise I should say to an open sinner, if you have been baptized, do not own it. For how highly does this aggravate your guilt! How will it increase your damnation!

> Was you devoted to God at eight days old, and have you been all these years devoting yourself to the devil? Was you, even before you had the use of reason, consecrated to God the Father, the Son, and the Holy Ghost? And have you, ever since you had the use of it, been flying in the face of God, and consecrating yourself to Satan? Does the abomination of desolation—the love of the world, pride, anger, lust, foolish desire, and a whole train of vile affections—stand where it ought not? Have you set up all these accursed things in that soul which was once a temple of the Holy Ghost; set apart for a "habitation of God, through the Spirit"; yea, solemnly given up to him? And do you glory in this, that you once belonged to God? O be ashamed! Blush! Hide yourself in the earth! Never boast more of what ought to fill you with confusion, to make you ashamed before God and man!

I answer, secondly, you have already denied your baptism; and that in the most effectual manner. You have denied it a thousand and a thousand times; and you do so still, day by day. For in your baptism you renounced the devil and all his works. Whenever, therefore, you give place to him again, whenever you do any of the works of the devil, then you deny your baptism. Therefore you deny it by every willful sin; by every act of uncleanness, drunkenness, or revenge; by every obscene or profane word; by every oath that comes out of your mouth. Every time you profane the day of the Lord, you thereby deny your baptism; yea, every time you do anything to another which you would not he should do to you.

I answer, thirdly, be you baptized or unbaptized, "you must be born again"; otherwise it is not possible you should be inwardly holy; and without inward as well as outward holiness, you cannot be happy, even in this world, much less in the world to come.

Do you say, "Nay, but I do no harm to any man; I am honest and just in all my dealings; I do not curse, or take the Lord's name in vain; I do not profane the Lord's day; I am no drunkard; I do not slander my neighbor, nor live in any willful sin?" If this be so, it were much to be wished that all men went as far as you do. But you must go farther yet, or you cannot be saved: still, "you must be born again."

Do you add, "I do go farther yet; for I not only do no harm, but do all the good I can?" I doubt that fact; I fear you have had a thousand opportunities of doing good which you have suffered to pass by unimproved, and for which therefore you are accountable to God. But if you had improved them all, if you really had done all the good you possibly could to all men, yet this does not at all alter the case; still, "you must be born again." Without this nothing will do any good to your poor, sinful, polluted soul. "Nay, but I constantly attend all the ordinances of God: I keep to my church and sacrament." It is well you do: but all this will not keep you from hell, except you be born again. Go to church twice a day; go to the Lord's table every week; say ever so many prayers in private; hear ever so many good sermons, excellent sermons, the best that ever were preached; read ever so many good books; still, "you must be born again." None of these things will stand in the place of the new birth; no, nor anything under heaven.

Let this therefore, if you have not already experienced this inward work of God, be your continual prayer: "Lord, add this to all thy blessings—let me be born again! Deny whatever thou pleasest, but deny not this; let me be 'born from above!' Take away whatsoever seemeth thee good—reputation, fortune, friends, health— only give me this, to be born of the Spirit, to be received among the children of God! Let me be born, 'not of corruptible seed, but incorruptible, by the Word of God, which liveth and abideth for ever'; and then let me daily 'grow in grace, and in the knowledge of our Lord and Savior Jesus Christ!'"

Lesson 8—Channels of God's Grace

Ever since the days of your ancestors you have turned aside from
my statutes and have not kept them. Return to me, and I will return to you.

Mal. 3:7; *NIV*

The whole body of Christians [agree] that Christ had ordained certain outward means for conveying
his grace into the souls [of all people] . . . By "means of grace" I understand outward signs,
words, or actions ordained of God, and appointed to this end, to be the ordinary channels
whereby he might convey . . . preventing, justifying, or sanctifying grace.

John Wesley, *The Means of Grace*, §§I.1, II.1

OUR STARTING POINT

Grace is a free gift from God. Grace is not earned as a result of good works on our part, but rather it is freely given by a loving God. Yet, instead of waiting quietly upon God to act, there are things that we can do—actions which were instituted by Christ—that can become channels for God's free grace. Training in these habits of holiness brings us into a closer relationship with Jesus Christ.

READING

Use daily the Scripture verse and prayer as a means to channel God's divine grace. Written in 1746, Wesley preached *The Means of Grace* in order to help believers understand that we have God-given methods for receiving divine grace. This sermon was written in direct opposition to Wesley's mentors, the Moravians, who believed that one was to wait quietly for God to act in one's life.

Day 1   Scan *The Means of Grace* in its entirety. Scan Lesson 8.

Day 2   Read Part I, §§I.1-6. The outward means of grace.

Day 3   Read Part II, §§II.1-8. What are the means of grace?

Day 4   Read Part III, §§III.1-12. How do we wait for God's grace?

Day 5   Read Part IV, §§IV.1-6. Objections to the use of the means of grace.

Day 6   Read Part V, §§V.1-4. Order and manner in using the means of grace. Reread the lesson and answer the questions at the end.

Day 7   Rest.

REFLECTION

Though by this time you ought to be teachers, you need someone to teach you again the basic elements of the oracles of God. You need milk, not solid food; for everyone who lives on milk, being still an infant, is unskilled in the word of righteousness. But solid food is for the mature, for those whose faculties have been trained by practice to distinguish good from evil.

Heb. 5:12-14; *NIV*

PRAYER

Pray daily before study:

O God, my Creator and Redeemer,

I acknowledge that everything I am, everything I do and everything I have is by your grace. In fact, I know my very life is a free gift from you. Thank you for the way you have entered my life and turned me toward you. I want to continue to grow in my walk with you. Help me to use your means of grace daily, especially our conversation in prayer, Scripture, and the Lord's Supper, so that I may become more like your Son, who willingly gave up his life in order to bring me back to you. I lift up this prayer to you in his name. Amen.

Prayer concerns for this week:

Daily Reflections

Day 1   Scan *The Means of Grace* in its entirety. Scan Lesson 8.

Meaning for me:

Day 2   Read Part I, §§I.1-6. The outward means of grace.

Meaning for me:

Day 3   Read Part II, §§II.1-8. What are the means of grace?

Meaning for me:

Day 4   Read Part III, §§III.1-12. How do we wait for God's grace?

Meaning for me:

Day 5   Read Part IV, §§IV.1-6. Objections to the use of the means of grace.

Meaning for me:

Day 6   Read Part V, §§V.1-4. Order and manner in using the means of grace. Reread the lesson and answer the questions at the end.

Meaning for me:

Means of Grace Distinguished from Quietism

As we saw in Lesson 1, Wesley was deeply influenced by a group of German Christians called Moravians. He appreciated their steadfast and deeply personal faith in God. However, Wesley did not agree with the Moravian practice of waiting quietly for God to act in their lives. This manner of waiting is called "quietism." Wesley wanted to use the means God had provided in order to enable him to grow in grace.

While waiting for God to act in his life, Wesley was already in the habit of reading Scripture regularly, praying daily, taking communion, and visiting those in prison, thanks to his participation in the "Holy Club." Wesley realized that these holy habits, to which this group of men kept each other accountable, were actually means of grace. The regular meeting with the group was in itself also a means of grace. Thus, he had *not* been waiting quietly for God to act in his life; rather, he had been using the means of grace, which were instituted by Christ, as channels through which God conveyed grace to him.

The means of grace are ordinary ways that God uses to provide divine grace. Wesley realized that faith is mediated by the agency of the Holy Spirit, and the Holy Spirit uses the means of grace, which were modeled and begun by Jesus Christ. In short, we can participate in the divine life while we wait for God to act in our lives. The way we participate is by practicing holy habits in the daily use of the means of grace in the renewal of the image of God in our lives.

A Spirit-Filled Life

The methodical practices of the Holy Club had sustained Wesley since the time he had been at Oxford. Over the years, he realized that these methods were the only ways to sustain and grow in a spirit-filled life. Christ meets us where we are through the means of grace. They enable a person to grow in discipleship.

These same means of grace that bring us to the point of justification and new birth also help us to grow in holiness (also called sanctification; see Lesson 9).

Wesley talked about the means of grace differently at various times. Sometimes he distinguished:

- Instituted and prudential means of grace
- Acts of piety and acts of mercy.

What Are the Means of Grace?

The means of grace are specific channels through which God conveys divine grace to God's people. The *instituted* means of grace, also known as ordinary means of grace, are those practices commanded by Jesus Christ in the Scriptures for his disciples.

Wesley consistently named prayer, searching the Scriptures, and partaking in the Lord's Supper as the primary examples of the instituted means of grace. Sometimes he added fasting (which he

NOTES, REFLECTIONS, AND QUESTIONS

And let the peace of Christ rule in your hearts, to which indeed you were called in the one body. And be thankful. Let the word of Christ dwell in you richly; teach and admonish one another in all wisdom; and with gratitude in your hearts sing psalms, hymns, and spiritual songs to God. And whatever you do, in word and deed, do everything in the name of the Lord Jesus, giving thanks to God the Father through him.

Col. 3:15-17; *NIV*

Wesley's theology is a theology of grace. No matter where we are in our spiritual life, we got there by grace and we can go on in grace. The call of the Christian is the call to grow.[1]

Steve Harper, *The Way to Heaven*

I want a principle within
of watchful, godly fear,
a sensibility of sin,
a pain to feel it near.

I want the first approach to feel
of pride or wrong desire,
to catch the wandering of my will,
and quench the kindling fire.

From thee that I no more may stray,
no more thy goodness grieve,
grant me the filial awe, I pray,
the tender conscience give.

Quick as the apple of an eye,
O God, my conscience make;
awake my soul when sin is nigh,
and keep it still awake.

Charles Wesley, "I Want a Principle Within"
(1749)—*UM Hymnal* #410; *Free Methodist Ch. & The Wesleyan Ch. Hymnal* #344

There is a kind of order, wherein God himself is generally pleased to use these means in bringing a sinner to salvation. A stupid, senseless wretch is going on in his own way, not having God in all his thoughts, when God comes upon him unawares, perhaps by an awakening sermon or conversation, perhaps by some awful providence, or, it may be, an immediate stroke of his convincing Spirit, without any outward means at all. Having now a desire to flee from the wrath to come, he purposely goes to hear how it may be done. If he finds a preacher who speaks to the heart, he is amazed, and begins searching the Scriptures, whether these things are so. The more he hears and reads, the more convinced he is; and the more he meditates thereon day and night.

John Wesley, *The Means of Grace*, §V.1

did at least once a week) and fellowship in Christian community (which the Holy Club provided). The latter practice is also known as "Christian Conferencing." Small group accountability was critical to his own spiritual growth, the success of the Methodist revival, and, ultimately, it will be essential if the church is to experience similar revival today.

Wesley was quick to point out that though these practices are vital, since Christ enacted them, God can still act however God pleases in conveying divine grace. God can convey grace to people who do not use these means of grace at all. "There is no inherent power in the means of grace themselves, Jesus Christ is the only saving power; however, if Christ instituted these as divine means of grace, why not use them?" (*The Means of Grace*, §II.3). God meets us where we are in the faithful practice of the means of grace. The means of grace are practices where we *expect* to meet God.

Prudential Means of Grace

There are also non-instituted means of grace or "prudential" means of grace that can help us grow in grace or holiness. While the instituted means were modeled by Jesus Christ, there are other practices that are also helpful towards spiritual growth. These prudential means vary from culture to culture and person to person. Wesley would often include journaling and acts of mercy, such as visiting those who are sick and in prison, in this category. These means are called "prudential" because, as we use them, we find we encounter God's grace; thus, it is "prudent"—appropriate, sensible, and expedient—for us to engage in these means. They can be any practice that brings us into a closer relationship with God.

Acts of Piety and Acts of Mercy

Wesley sometimes distinguished the means of grace as acts of piety, which are focused on our relationship with God, and acts of mercy, which are focused on our relationship with neighbor. The acts of piety include the instituted means of grace. Acts of mercy are to help relieve the distress of our neighbors. Of course, they are more than a means of grace—they are acts of love. To love our neighbor is also to show love to God. For Wesley, the love of a neighbor is active, not passive.

Traditionalist and Enthusiast

Early Methodists accused the Anglican church of Wesley's day of having nothing more than a "dead formalism." In return, some of the Methodists were accused of being "enthusiasts," due to the exuberance that others observed in their new life in Christ. Sometimes the new enthusiasm seemed extreme in demonstrating assurance of salvation or experience of the new birth. New believers in Christ who were still excited about their experience in the faith could feel there was no longer a need for the traditional

Sent by my Lord, on you I call;
The invitation is to all.
Come all the world! Come, sinner thou!
All things in Christ are ready now.

Come, all ye souls by sin oppressed,
Ye restless wanderers after rest;
Ye poor, and maimed, and halt, and blind,
In Christ a hearty welcome find.

This is the time, no more delay!
This is the Lord's accepted day.
Come thou, this moment, at his call,
And live for him who died for all.

Charles Wesley, "Come, Sinners, to the Gospel Feast" (1747)—*UM Hymnal #616; AME Hymnal #234*

things of the church, such as the frequent sacramental practice of communion.

Wesley, however, envisioned the two combined. He clearly saw the need for both the tradition of the Anglican church and the enthusiasm of the new birth in Christ. For Wesley, this was not an either/or situation, but a both/and situation. He had an unmistakable vision of how the traditional means of grace brought about the zeal of the new birth and subsequent growth in holiness. Part of the sermon, *The Means of Grace*, encouraged spirit-filled Christians to remain faithful to all of the means of grace, as they provide a continued channel and meeting place for God's grace (§§V.1-4).

Works and Grace

It is important not to confuse the means of grace with works. These means are not an end unto themselves, nor are they a way of buying God's pardon. Rather, they offer us a way of growing in our spiritual journey, and they offer us a helpful way to allow the Holy Spirit to work in our lives.

For Wesley, the means of grace offer a way of combining theology with practical daily living. They allow us to live a life of loving God and loving neighbor, that is, obeying Jesus' double commandment of love. The means of grace give us a method that forms and shapes us as Christian disciples. These spiritual disciplines are structures that assist us in growing in our restoration to the image of God, that perfect image in which we were each originally made. They are practices that we use in order to become more mature in Christ.

NOTES, REFLECTIONS, AND QUESTIONS

For I received from the Lord what I also passed on to you: The Lord Jesus, on the night he was betrayed, took bread, and when he had given thanks, he broke it and said, "This is my body, which is for you; do this in remembrance of me." In the same way, after supper he took the cup, saying, "This cup is the new covenant in my blood; ***do this, whenever you drink it, in remembrance of me.***" For whenever you eat this bread and drink this cup, you proclaim the Lord's death until he comes.

1 Cor. 11:23-26; *NIV*

Grace is not opposed to effort, it is opposed to earning.[2]
Dallas Willard, *The Great Omission*

They [the new believers] devoted themselves to the apostles' teaching and to the fellowship, to the breaking of bread and to prayer.

Acts 2:42; *NIV*

RESPONDING FAITHFULLY

What means of grace, both instituted and prudential, are part of your daily or weekly routine?

_____

_____

Share a time when you might have grown in faith as a result of using one of the means of grace.

_____

_____

_____

How would small group accountability provide you personal support for encouraging one another to be more faithful in your practice of the means of grace?

_____

_____

_____

How can your church more faithfully practice the means of grace?

How do you think your faith community could be transformed if everyone daily practiced at least one of the means of grace? Which one can you add now?

LEARNING MORE

Read other Wesley sermons which discuss the means of grace such as:

- *The Wilderness State*
- *On Visiting the Sick*
- *The Duty of Constant Communion.*

See also:

- Henry H. Knight III, *The Presence of God in the Christian Life: John Wesley and the Means of Grace*
- Steve Harper, *The Way to Heaven: The Gospel According to John Wesley.*

LOOKING AHEAD

Next Lesson. Sanctification—a process of growth in holiness, empowered by the Holy Spirit.

Teacher Helps provides follow-up questions that may be useful in class discussions.

END NOTES

[1] Steve Harper, *The Way to Heaven: The Gospel According to John Wesley.* Grand Rapids: Zondervan, 1983, p. 67.
[2] Dallas Willard, *The Great Omission: Reclaiming Jesus' Essential Teachings on Discipleship.* San Francisco: Harper, 2006, p. 61.

Reading for Lesson 8. The Means of Grace (1746)

Ye are gone away from mine ordinances, and have not kept them (Mal. 3:7).

Introduction

I.   Are there any ordinances now, since life and immortality were brought to light by the gospel?
II. Are there any means of grace?
III. All who desire the grace of God are to wait for it in the means which he hath ordained.
IV. As plainly as God hath pointed out the means, men have objected against it.

I.

1. But are there any *ordinances* now, since life and immortality were brought to light by the gospel? Are there, under the Christian dispensation, any *means* ordained of God as the usual channels of his grace? This question could never have been proposed in the apostolic church, unless by one who openly avowed himself to be a heathen, the whole body of Christians being agreed that Christ had ordained certain outward means for conveying his grace into the souls of men. Their constant practice set this beyond all dispute; for so long as "all that believed were together, and had all things common" (Acts 2:44), "they continued steadfastly in the teaching of the apostles, and in the breaking of bread, and in prayers" (Acts 2:42).

2. But in process of time, when "the love of many waxed cold," some began to mistake the *means* for the *end*, and to place religion rather in doing those outward works, than in a heart renewed after the image of God. They forgot that "the end of" every "commandment is love, out of a pure heart," with "faith unfeigned": the loving the Lord their God with all their heart, and their neighbor as themselves; and the being purified from pride, anger, and evil desire, by a "faith of the operation of God." Others seemed to imagine that though religion did not principally consist in these outward means, yet there was something in them wherewith God was well pleased, something that would still make them acceptable in his sight, though they were not exact in the weightier matters of the law, in justice, mercy, and the love of God.

3. It is evident, in those who abused them thus, they did not conduce to the end for which they were ordained. Rather, the things which should have been for their health, were to them an occasion of falling. They were so far from receiving any blessing therein, that they only drew down a curse upon their head; so far from growing more heavenly in heart and life, that they were two-fold more the children of hell than before. Others, clearly perceiving that these means did not convey the grace of God to those children of the devil, began, from this particular case, to draw a general conclusion—that they were not means of conveying the grace of God.

4. Yet the number of those who *abused* the ordinances of God, was far greater than of those who *despised* them, till certain men arose, not only of great understanding (sometimes joined with considerable learning), but who likewise appeared to be men of love, experimentally acquainted with true, inward religion. Some of these were burning and shining lights, persons famous in their generations, and such as had well deserved of the church of Christ, for standing in the gap against the overflowings of ungodliness.

It cannot be supposed that these holy and venerable men intended any more, at first, than to show that outward religion is nothing worth, without the religion of the heart; that "God is a Spirit, and they who worship him must worship him in spirit and in truth"; that, therefore, external worship is lost labor without a heart devoted to God; that the outward ordinances of God then profit much, when they advance inward holiness, but, when they advance it not, are unprofitable and void, are lighter than vanity; yea, that when they are used, as it were *in the place* of this, they are an utter abomination to the Lord.

5. Yet is it not strange, if some of these, being strongly convinced of that horrid profanation of the ordinances of God, which had spread itself over the whole church, and well-nigh driven true religion out of the world—in their fervent zeal for the glory of God, and the recovery of souls from that fatal delusion—spake as if outward religion were *absolutely nothing*, as if it had *no* place in the religion of Christ. It is not surprising at all, if they should not always have expressed themselves with sufficient caution; so that unwary hearers might believe they condemned all outward means as altogether unprofitable, and as not designed of God to be the ordinary channels of conveying his grace into the souls of men.

Nay, it is not impossible, some of these holy men did, at length, themselves fall into this opinion; in particular those who, not by choice, but by the providence of God, were cut off from all these ordinances; perhaps wandering up and down, having no certain abiding-place, or dwelling in dens and caves of the earth. These, experiencing the grace of God in themselves, though they were deprived of all outward means, might infer that the same grace would be given to them who of set purpose abstained from them.

6. And experience shows how easily this notion spreads, and insinuates itself into the minds of men; especially of those who are thoroughly awakened out of the sleep of death, and begin to feel the weight of their sins a burden too heavy to be borne. These are usually impatient of their present state; and, trying every way to escape from it, they are always ready to catch at any new thing, any new proposal of ease or happiness. They have probably tried most outward means, and found no ease in them—it may be, more and more of remorse, and fear, and sorrow, and condemnation. It is easy, therefore, to persuade these that it is better for them to abstain from all those means. They are already weary of striving (as it seems) in vain, of laboring in the fire; and are therefore glad of any pretence to cast aside that wherein their soul had no pleasure, to give over the painful strife, and sink down into an indolent inactivity.

II.

1. In the following discourse, I propose to examine at large whether there are any means of grace.

By "means of grace" I understand outward signs, words, or actions, ordained of God, and appointed for this end, to be the ordinary channels whereby he might convey to men, preventing, justifying, or sanctifying grace.

I use this expression, "means of grace," because I know none better; and because it has been generally used in the Christian church for many ages—in particular by our own Church, which directs us to bless God both for the "means of grace and hope of glory"; and teaches us that a sacrament is "an outward sign of inward *grace*, and a *means* whereby we receive the same."

The chief of these means are prayer, whether in secret or with the great congregation; searching the Scriptures (which implies reading, hearing, and meditating thereon); and receiving the Lord's Supper, eating bread and drinking wine in remembrance of him—and these we believe to be ordained of God, as the ordinary channels of conveying his grace to the souls of men.

2. But we allow that the whole value of the means depends on their actual subservience to the end of religion; that, consequently, all these means, when separate from the end, are less than nothing and vanity; that if they do not actually conduce to the knowledge and love of God, they are not acceptable in his sight; yea, rather, they are an abomination before him, a stink in his nostrils; he is weary to bear them. Above all, if they are used as a kind of *commutation* for the religion they were designed to subserve, it is not easy to find words for the enormous folly and wickedness of thus turning God's arms against himself; of keeping Christianity out of the heart by those very means which were ordained for the bringing it in.

3. We allow, likewise, that all outward means whatever, if separate from the Spirit of God, cannot profit at all, cannot conduce, in any degree, either to the knowledge or love of God. Without controversy, the help that is done upon earth, He doeth it himself. It is he alone who, by his own almighty power, worketh in us what is pleasing in his sight; and all outward things, unless he work in them and by them, are mere weak and beggarly elements. Whosoever, therefore, imagines there is any intrinsic power in any means whatsoever, does greatly err, not knowing the Scriptures, neither the power of God. We know that there is no inherent power in the words that are spoken in prayer, in the letter of Scripture read, the sound thereof heard, or the bread and wine received in the Lord's Supper; but that it is God alone who is the Giver of every good gift, the Author of all grace; that the whole power is of him, whereby, through any of these, there is any blessing conveyed to our soul. We know, likewise, that he is able to give the same grace, though there were no means on the face of the earth. In this sense, we may affirm that, with regard to God, there is no such thing as means; seeing he is equally able to work whatsoever pleaseth him, by any, or by none at all.

4. We allow further that the use of all means whatever will never atone for one sin; that it is the blood of Christ alone, whereby any sinner can be reconciled to God; there being no other propitiation for our sins, no other fountain for sin and uncleanness. Every believer in Christ is deeply convinced that there is no *merit* but in him; that there is no *merit* in any of his own works; not in uttering the prayer, or searching the Scripture, or hearing the Word of God, or eating of that bread and drinking of that cup. So that if no more be intended by the expression some have used, "Christ is the only means of grace," than this—that he is the only *meritorious cause* of it—it cannot be gainsaid by any who know the grace of God.

5. Yet once more: We allow, though it is a melancholy truth, that a large proportion of those who are called Christians do to this day abuse the means of grace to the destruction of their souls. This is doubtless the case with all those who rest content in the form of godliness, without the power. Either they fondly presume they are Christians already, because they do thus and thus—although Christ was never yet revealed in their hearts, nor the love of God shed abroad therein—or else they suppose they shall infallibly be so, barely because they use

these means; idly dreaming (though perhaps hardly conscious thereof), either that there is some kind of *power* therein, whereby, sooner or later (they know not when), they shall certainly be made holy; or that there is a sort of *merit* in using them, which will surely move God to give them holiness or accept them without it.

6. So little do they understand that great foundation of the whole Christian building, "By grace are ye saved." Ye are saved from your sins, from the guilt and power thereof, ye are restored to the favor and image of God, not for any works, merits, or deservings of yours, but by the free *grace*, the mere mercy of God, through the merits of his well-beloved Son. Ye are thus saved, not by any power, wisdom, or strength which is in you, or in any other creature, but merely through the grace or power of the Holy Ghost, which worketh all in all.

7. But the main question remains: "We know this salvation is the gift and the work of God, but how" (may one say who is convinced he hath it not) "may I attain thereto?" If you say, "Believe, and thou shalt be saved!" he answers, "True; but how shall I believe?" You reply, "Wait upon God." "Well, but how am I to wait? In the means of grace, or out of them? Am I to wait for the grace of God which bringeth salvation by using these means, or by laying them aside?"

8. It cannot possibly be conceived that the Word of God should give no direction in so important a point; or that the Son of God, who came down from heaven for us men and for our salvation, should have left us undetermined with regard to a question wherein our salvation is so nearly concerned.

And, in fact, he hath not left us undetermined; he hath shown us the way wherein we should go. We have only to consult the oracles of God, to inquire what is written there; and, if we simply abide by their decision, there can no possible doubt remain.

III.

1. According to this, according to the decision of Holy Writ, all who desire the grace of God are to wait for it in the means which he hath ordained; in using, not in laying them aside.

And, first, all who desire the grace of God are to wait for it in the way of *prayer*. This is the express direction of our Lord himself. In his Sermon upon the Mount, after explaining at large wherein religion consists, and describing the main branches of it, he adds, "Ask, and it shall be given you; seek, and ye shall find; knock, and it shall be opened unto you: for everyone that asketh, receiveth; and he that seeketh, findeth; and to him that knocketh, it shall be opened" (Matt. 7:7-8). Here we are in the plainest manner directed to ask in order to, or as a means of, receiving; to seek in order to find the grace of God, the pearl of great price; and to knock, to continue asking and seeking, if we would enter into his kingdom.

2. That no doubt might remain, our Lord labors this point in a more peculiar manner. He appeals to every man's own heart: "What man is there of you, who, if his son ask bread, will give him a stone? Or, if he ask a fish, will he give him a serpent? If ye then, being evil, know how to give good gifts unto your children, how much more shall your Father which is in heaven"—the Father of angels and men, the Father of the spirits of all flesh— "give good things to them that ask him" (Matt. 7:9-11)? Or, as he expresses himself on another occasion, including all good things in one, "How much more shall your heavenly Father give the Holy Spirit to them that ask him" (Luke 11:13)? It should be particularly observed here that the persons directed to ask had not then received the Holy Spirit. Nevertheless, our Lord directs them to use this means, and promises that it should be effectual; that upon asking they should receive the Holy Spirit from him whose mercy is over all his works.

3. The absolute necessity of using this means, if we would receive any gift from God, yet further appears from that remarkable passage which immediately precedes these words: "And he said unto them," whom he had just been teaching how to pray, "Which of you shall have a friend, and shall go unto him at midnight, and shall say unto him, 'Friend, lend me three loaves.' And he from within shall answer, 'Trouble me not; I cannot rise and give thee.' I say unto you, though he will not rise and give him, because he is his friend, yet because of his importunity he will rise, and give him as many as he needeth. And I say unto you, 'Ask, and it shall be given you'" (Luke 11:5,7-9). "Though he will not give him, because he is his friend, yet because of his importunity he will rise and give him as many as he needeth." How could our blessed Lord more plainly declare that we may receive of God, by this means, by importunately asking, what otherwise we should not receive at all?

4. "He spake also another parable, to this end, that men ought always to pray, and not to faint," till through this means they should receive of God whatsoever petition they asked of him. "There was in a city a judge which feared not God, neither regarded man. And there was a widow in that city, and she came unto him, saying, 'Avenge me of my adversary.' And he would not for a while; but afterward he said within himself, though I fear not God, nor regard man, yet because this widow troubleth me, I will avenge her, lest, by her continual coming, she weary me" (Luke 18:1-5). The application of this our Lord himself hath made: "Hear what the unjust judge saith!" Because she continues to ask, because she will take no denial, therefore I will avenge her. "And shall not

God avenge his own elect, which cry day and night unto him? I tell you he will avenge them speedily," if they pray and faint not.

5. A direction, equally full and express, to wait for the blessings of God in private prayer, together with a positive promise that, by this means, we shall obtain the request of our lips, he hath given us in those well-known words: "Enter into thy closet, and, when thou hast shut thy door, pray to thy Father which is in secret; and thy Father, which seeth in secret, shall reward thee openly" (Matt. 6:6).

6. If it be possible for any direction to be more clear, it is that which God hath given us by the Apostle with regard to prayer of every kind, public and private, and the blessing annexed thereto: "If any of you lack wisdom, let him ask of God that giveth to all men liberally"—if they ask; otherwise "ye have not, because ye ask not" (James 4:2)—"and upbraideth not; and it shall be given him" (James 1:5).

If it be objected, "But this is no direction to unbelievers, to them who know not the pardoning grace of God; for the Apostle adds, 'But let him ask in faith'; otherwise, 'let him not think that he shall receive anything of the Lord.'" I answer, the meaning of the word *faith*, in this place, is fixed by the Apostle himself, as if it were on purpose to obviate this objection, in the words immediately following: "Let him ask in faith, nothing wavering," nothing doubting, *meden dikrinomenos*. Not doubting God heareth his prayer, and will fulfill the desire of his heart.

The gross, blasphemous absurdity of supposing *faith*, in this place, to be taken in the full Christian meaning appears hence: it is supposing the Holy Ghost to direct a man who knows he has not this faith (which is here termed *wisdom*) to ask it of God, with a positive promise that "it shall be given him"; and then immediately to subjoin that it shall not be given him, unless he have it before he asks for it! But who can bear such a supposition? From this Scripture, therefore, as well as those cited above, we must infer that all who desire the grace of God are to wait for it in the way of prayer.

7. Secondly, all who desire the grace of God are to wait for it in searching the Scriptures. Our Lord's direction with regard to the use of this means is likewise plain and clear. "Search the Scriptures," saith he to the unbelieving Jews, "for they testify of me" (John 5:39). And for this very end did he direct them to search the Scriptures, that they might *believe in him*.

The objection that "this is not a command, but only an assertion, that they did search the Scriptures," is shamelessly false. I desire those who urge it, to let us know how a command can be more clearly expressed, than in those terms, *Ereunate tas graphas*. It is as peremptory as so many words can make it.

And what a blessing from God attends the use of this means, appears from what is recorded concerning the Bereans; who—after hearing St. Paul, "searched the Scriptures daily, whether those things were so. Therefore many of them believed"—found the grace of God, in the way which he had ordained (Acts 17:11, 12).

It is probable, indeed, that in some of those who had "received the word with all readiness of mind," "faith came," as the same Apostle speaks, "by hearing," and was only confirmed by *reading* the Scriptures. But it was observed above that under the general term of searching the Scriptures, both hearing, reading, and meditating are contained.

8. And that this is a means whereby God not only gives, but also confirms and increases, true wisdom, we learn from the words of St. Paul to Timothy: "From a child thou hast known the Holy Scriptures, which are able to make thee wise unto salvation through faith which is in Christ Jesus" (2 Tim. 3:15). The same truth (namely, that this is the great means God has ordained for conveying his manifold grace to man) is delivered, in the fullest manner that can be conceived, in the words which immediately follow: "All Scripture is given by inspiration of God." Consequently, all Scripture is infallibly true; "and is profitable for doctrine, for reproof, for correction, for instruction in righteousness"; to the end "that the man of God may be perfect, thoroughly furnished unto all good works" (2 Tim. 3:16-17).

9. It should be observed that this is spoken primarily and directly of the Scriptures which Timothy had known from a child; which must have been those of the Old Testament, for the New was not then wrote. How far then was St. Paul (though he was "not a whit behind the very chief of the apostles," nor, therefore, I presume, behind any man now upon earth) from making light of the Old Testament! Behold this, lest ye one day "wonder and perish," ye who make so small account of one half of the oracles of God! Yea, and that half of which the Holy Ghost expressly declares that it is "profitable," as a means ordained of God, for this very thing, "for doctrine, for reproof, for correction, for instruction in righteousness"; to the end, "the man of God may be perfect, thoroughly furnished unto all good works."

10. Nor is this profitable only for the men of God, for those who walk already in the light of his countenance; but also for those who are yet in darkness, seeking him whom they know not. Thus St. Peter, "We have also a more sure word of prophecy"—literally, "And we have the prophetic word more sure"; *Kai echomen bebaioteron ton prophetikon logon*—confirmed by our being "eye-witnesses of his Majesty," and "hearing the voice

which came from the excellent glory"; unto which (prophetic word; so he styles the Holy Scriptures) "ye do well that ye take heed, as unto a light that shineth in a dark place, until the day dawn, and the day-star arise in your hearts" (2 Pet. 1:19). Let all, therefore, who desire that day to dawn upon their hearts, wait for it in searching the Scriptures.

11. Thirdly, all who desire an increase of the grace of God are to wait for it in partaking of the Lord's Supper. For this also is a direction [he] himself hath given: "The same night in which he was betrayed, he took bread, and brake it, and said, Take, eat; this is my body" (that is, the sacred sign of my body). "This do in remembrance of me. Likewise, he took the cup, saying, This cup is the new testament," or covenant, "in my blood" (the sacred sign of that covenant): "this do ye in remembrance of me." "For as often as ye eat this bread, and drink this cup, ye do show forth the Lord's death till he come" (1 Cor. 11:23-26). Ye openly exhibit the same by these visible signs, before God, and angels, and men; ye manifest your solemn remembrance of his death, till he cometh in the clouds of heaven.

Only "let a man" first "examine himself," whether he understand the nature and design of this holy institution, and whether he really desire to be himself made conformable to the death of Christ; and so, nothing doubting, "let him eat of that bread, and drink of that cup" (1 Cor. 11:28).

Here, then, the direction first given by our Lord is expressly repeated by the Apostle: "Let him eat; let him drink" (*esthieto, pineto*—both in the imperative mood); words not implying a bare permission only, but a clear, explicit command; a command to all those either who already are filled with peace and joy in believing, or who can truly say, "The remembrance of our sins is grievous unto us; the burden of them is intolerable."

12. And that this is also an ordinary, stated means of receiving the grace of God, is evident from those words of the Apostle which occur in the preceding chapter: "The cup of blessing which we bless, is it not the communion" (or *communication*) "of the blood of Christ? The bread which we break, is it not the communion of the body of Christ" (1 Cor. 10:16)? Is not the eating of that bread, and the drinking of that cup, the outward, visible means, whereby God conveys into our souls all that spiritual grace, that righteousness, and peace, and joy in the Holy Ghost, which were purchased by the body of Christ once broken and the blood of Christ once shed for us? Let all, therefore, who truly desire the grace of God, eat of that bread and drink of that cup.

IV.

1. But as plainly as God hath pointed out the way wherein he will be inquired after, innumerable are the objections which men, wise in their own eyes, have, from time to time, raised against it. It may be needful to consider a few of these; not because they are of weight in themselves, but because they have so often been used, especially of late years, to turn the lame out of the way; yea, to trouble and subvert those who did run well, till Satan appeared as an angel of light. The first and chief of these is, "You cannot use these means (as you call them) without *trusting* in them." I pray, where is this written? I expect you should show me plain Scripture for your assertion; otherwise, I dare not receive it, because I am not convinced that you are wiser than God.

If it really had been as you assert, it is certain Christ must have known it. And if he had known it, he would surely have warned us; he would have revealed it long ago. Therefore, because he has not, because there is no tittle of this in the whole revelation of Jesus Christ, I am as fully assured your assertion is false as that this revelation is of God.

"However, leave them off for a short time, to see whether you trusted in them or no." So I am to disobey God, in order to know whether I trust in obeying him! And do you avow this advice? Do you deliberately teach to "do evil, that good may come?" O tremble at the sentence of God against such teachers! Their "damnation is just."

"Nay, if you are troubled when you leave them off, it is plain you trusted in them." By no means. If I am troubled when I willfully disobey God, it is plain his Spirit is still striving with me; but if I am not troubled at willful sin, it is plain I am given up to a reprobate mind.

But what do you mean by "*trusting* in them?"—looking for the blessing of God therein? Believing that if I wait in this way, I shall attain what otherwise I should not? So I do. And so I will, God being my helper, even to my life's end. By the grace of God I will *thus* trust in them, till the day of my death; that is, I will believe that whatever God hath promised, he is faithful also to perform. And seeing he hath promised to bless me in this way, I *trust* it shall be according to his Word.

2. It has been, secondly, objected, "This is seeking salvation by works." Do you know the meaning of the expression you use? What is seeking salvation by works? In the writings of St. Paul, it means, either seeking to be saved by observing the ritual works of the Mosaic law; or expecting salvation for the sake of our own works,

by the merit of our own righteousness. But how is either of these implied in my waiting in the way God has ordained, and expecting that he will meet me there because he has promised so to do?

I do expect that he will fulfill his Word, that he will meet and bless me in this way. Yet not for the sake of any works which I have done, nor for the merit of my righteousness; but merely through the merits, and sufferings, and love of his Son, in whom he is always well pleased.

3. It has been vehemently objected, thirdly, "that Christ is the only means of grace." I answer, this is mere playing upon words. Explain your term, and the objection vanishes away. When we say, "Prayer is a means of grace," we understand a channel through which the grace of God is conveyed. When you say, "Christ is the means of grace," you understand the sole price and purchaser of it; or that "no man cometh unto the Father, but through him." And who denies it? But this is utterly wide of the question.

4. "But does not the Scripture" (it has been objected, fourthly) "direct us to *wait* for salvation? Does not David say, 'My soul waiteth upon God, for of him cometh my salvation?' And does not Isaiah teach us the same thing, saying, 'O Lord, we have waited for thee'?" All this cannot be denied. Seeing it is the gift of God, we are undoubtedly to *wait* on him for salvation. But how shall we wait? If God himself has appointed a way, can you find a better way of waiting for him? But that he hath appointed a way hath been shown at large, and also what that way is. The very words of the Prophet which you cite put this out of the question. For the whole sentence runs thus—"In the way of thy judgments" (or ordinances), "O Lord, have we waited for thee" (Isa. 26:8). And in the very same way did David wait, as his own words abundantly testify: "I have waited for thy saving health, O Lord, and have kept thy law. Teach me, O Lord, the way of thy statutes, and I shall to keep it unto the end."

5. "Yea," say some, "but God has appointed another way: stand still and see the salvation of God.'" Let us examine the Scriptures to which you refer. The first of them, with the context, runs thus—

And when Pharaoh drew nigh, the children of Israel lifted up their eyes; and they were sore afraid. And they said unto Moses, Because there were no graves in Egypt, hast thou taken us away to die in the wilderness? And Moses said unto the people, Fear ye not; stand still, and see the salvation of the Lord. And the Lord said unto Moses, Speak unto the children of Israel that they go forward. But lift thou up thy rod, and stretch out thine hand over the sea, and divide it. And the children of Israel shall go on dry ground through the midst of the sea" (Exod. 14:10ff).

This was the *salvation of God*, which they *stood still* to see, by *marching forward* with all their might! The other passage, wherein this expression occurs stands thus:

There came some that told Jehoshaphat, saying, 'There cometh a great multitude against thee, from beyond the sea.' And Jehoshaphat feared, and set himself to seek the Lord, and proclaimed a fast throughout all Judah. And Judah gathered themselves together to ask help of the Lord: Even out of all the cities they came to seek the Lord. And Jehoshaphat stood in the congregation, in the house of the Lord . . . . . Then upon Jahaziel came the Spirit of the Lord. And he said, 'Be not dismayed by reason of this great multitude. Tomorrow go ye down against them; ye shall not need to fight in this battle. Set yourselves: stand ye still, and see the salvation of the Lord.' And they rose early in the morning, and went forth. And when they began to sing and to praise, the Lord set ambushments against the children of Moab, Ammon, and mount Seir, . . . and everyone helped to destroy another (2 Chron. 20:2ff).

Such was the salvation which the children of Judah saw. But how does all this prove that we ought not to wait for the grace of God in the means which he hath ordained?

6. I shall mention but one objection more, which, indeed, does not properly belong to this head; nevertheless, because it has been so frequently urged, I may not wholly pass it by. "Does not St. Paul say, 'If ye be dead with Christ, why are ye subject to *ordinances*' (Col. 2:20)? Therefore a Christian, one that is dead with Christ, need not use the ordinances any more."

So you say, "If I am a Christian, I am not subject to the ordinances of Christ!" Surely, by the absurdity of this, you must see at the first glance that the ordinances here mentioned cannot be the ordinances of Christ! That they must needs be the Jewish ordinances, to which it is certain a Christian is no longer subject. And the same undeniably appears from the words immediately following, "Touch not, taste not, handle not"; all evidently referring to the ancient ordinances of the Jewish law. So that this objection is the weakest of all. And, in spite of all, that great truth must stand unshaken—that all who desire the grace of God, are to wait for it in the means which he hath ordained.

V.

1. But this being allowed—that all who desire the grace of God are to wait for it in the means he hath ordained—it may still be inquired, how those means should be used, both as to the *order* and the *manner* of using them. With regard to the former, we may observe, there is a kind of order, wherein God himself is

generally pleased to use these means in bringing a sinner to salvation. A stupid, senseless wretch is going on in his own way, not having God in all his thoughts, when God comes upon him unawares, perhaps by an awakening sermon or conversation, perhaps by some awful providence, or, it may be, an immediate stroke of his convincing Spirit, without any outward means at all.

Having now a desire to flee from the wrath to come, he purposely goes to *hear* how it may be done. If he finds a preacher who speaks to the heart, he is amazed, and begins searching the Scriptures, whether these things are so. The more he *hears* and *reads*, the more convinced he is; and the more he *meditates* thereon day and night. Perhaps he finds some other book which explains and enforces what he has heard and read in Scripture. And by all these means, the arrows of conviction sink deeper into his soul. He begins also to *talk* of the things of God, which are ever uppermost in his thoughts; yea, and to talk with God, to *pray* to him, although through fear and shame he scarce knows what to say. But whether he can speak or no, he cannot but pray, were it only in "groans which cannot be uttered."

Yet, being in doubt, whether "the high and lofty One that inhabiteth eternity" will regard such a sinner as him, he wants to pray with those who know God, with the faithful, in the great congregation. But here he observes others go up to the table of the Lord. He considers, "Christ has said, 'Do this!' How is it that I do not? I am too great a sinner. I am not fit. I am not worthy." After struggling with these scruples a while, he breaks through. And thus he continues in God's way—in hearing, reading, meditating, praying, and partaking of the Lord's Supper—till God, in the manner that pleases him, speaks to his heart, "Thy faith hath saved thee. Go in peace."

2. By observing this order of God, we may learn what means to recommend to any particular soul. If any of these will reach a stupid, careless sinner, it is probably *hearing* or *conversation*. To such, therefore, we might recommend these, if he has ever any thought about salvation. To one who begins to feel the weight of his sins, not only hearing the Word of God, but reading it too, and perhaps other *serious books*, may be a means of deeper conviction. May you not advise him also to *meditate* on what he reads, that it may have its full force upon his heart? Yea, and to *speak* thereof, and not be ashamed, particularly among those who walk in the same path. When trouble and heaviness take hold upon him, should you not then earnestly exhort him to pour out his soul before God, "always to pray and not to faint." And when he feels the worthlessness of his own prayers, are you not to work together with God, and remind him of going up into the house of the Lord, and praying with all them that fear him? But if he does this, the *dying word* of his Lord will soon be brought to his remembrance: a plain intimation that this is the time when we should second the motions of the blessed Spirit. And thus may we lead him, step by step, through all the means which God has ordained; not according to our own will, but just as the providence and the Spirit of God go before and open the way.

3. Yet, as we find no command in Holy Writ for any particular order to be observed herein, so neither do the providence and the Spirit of God adhere to any without variation; but the means into which different men are led, and in which they find the blessing of God, are varied, transposed, and combined together a thousand different ways. Yet still our wisdom is to follow the leadings of his providence and his Spirit; to be guided herein (more especially as to the means wherein we ourselves seek the grace of God), partly by his outward providence, giving us the opportunity of using sometimes one means, sometimes another, partly by our experience, which it is whereby his free Spirit is pleased most to work in our heart. And in the meantime, the sure and general rule for all who groan for the salvation of God is this—whenever opportunity serves, use all the means which God has ordained; for who knows in which God will meet thee with the grace that bringeth salvation?

4. As to the *manner* of using them, whereon indeed it wholly depends whether they should convey any grace at all to the user; it behooves us, first, always to retain a lively sense that God is above all means. Have a care, therefore, of limiting the Almighty. He doeth whatsoever and whensoever it pleaseth him. He can convey his grace, either in or out of any of the means which he hath appointed. Perhaps he will. "Who hath known the mind of the Lord? Or who hath been his counselor?" Look then every moment for his appearing! Be it at the hour you are employed in his ordinances; or before, or after that hour; or when you are hindered therefrom: He is not hindered. He is always ready, always able, always willing to save. "It is the Lord: Let him do what seemeth him good!"

Secondly, before you use any means, let it be deeply impressed on your soul—there is no *power* in this. It is, in itself, a poor, dead, empty thing. Separate from God, it is a dry leaf, a shadow. Neither is there any *merit* in my using this; nothing intrinsically pleasing to God, nothing whereby I deserve any favor at his hands, no, not a drop of water to cool my tongue. But because God bids, therefore I do; because he directs me to wait in this way, therefore here I wait for his free mercy, whereof cometh my salvation.

Settle this in your heart, that the *opus operatum*, the mere *work done*, profiteth nothing; that there is no *power* to save but in the Spirit of God, no *merit*, but in the blood of Christ; that, consequently, even what God ordains conveys no grace to the soul if you trust not in him alone. On the other hand, he that does truly trust in him, cannot fall short of the grace of God, even though he were cut off from every outward ordinance, though he were shut up in the center of the earth.

Thirdly, in using all means, seek God alone. In and through every outward thing, look singly to the *power* of his Spirit; and the *merits* of his Son. Beware you do not stick in the *work* itself; if you do, it is all lost labor. Nothing short of God can satisfy your soul. Therefore, eye him in all, through all, and above all.

Remember, also, to use all means, *as means*; as ordained, not for their own sake, but in order to [have] the renewal of your soul in righteousness and true holiness. If, therefore, they actually tend to this, well; but if not, they are dung and dross.

Lastly, after you have used any of these, take care how you value yourself thereon, how you congratulate yourself as having done some great thing. This is turning all into poison. Think, "If God was not there, what does this avail? Have I not been adding sin to sin? How long, O Lord! Save, or I perish! O lay not this sin to my charge!" If God was there, if his love flowed into your heart, you have forgot, as it were, the outward work. You see, you know, you feel, God is all in all. Be abased. Sink down before him. Give him all the praise. "Let God in all things be glorified through Christ Jesus." Let all your bones cry out, "My song shall be always of the loving-kindness of the Lord; with my mouth will I ever be telling of thy truth, from one generation to another!"

Lesson 9–Sanctification: Growing In Holiness

Circumcision is that of the heart, in the spirit, and not in the letter.

Rom 2:29; *KJV*

[Circumcision of the heart] is that habitual disposition of soul which, in the Sacred Writings, is termed holiness; and which directly implies, the being cleansed from sin, "from all filthiness both of flesh and spirit"; and, by consequence, the being endued with those virtues which were also in Christ Jesus; the being so "renewed in the spirit of our mind," as to be "perfect as our Father in heaven is perfect". . . . .
    To be more particular, circumcision of heart implies humility, faith, hope, and charity.

John Wesley, *The Circumcision of the Heart*; §I.1-2

Take away our bent to sinning . . . set our hearts at liberty.

Charles Wesley, "Love Divine, All Loves Excelling" (1747)

OUR STARTING POINT

If justification and the new birth mark the beginning of our Christian journey, how do we move forward? How do we grow as Christians? Sanctification describes a grace-empowered process in which believers are enabled to grow in their love of God and neighbor. Sanctification describes *how* we grow in holiness.

READING

Read daily the reflection and prayer about every Christian's calling to holiness. *The Circumcision of the Heart* (1733) discusses what it means to be holy or sanctified. It also points those who have experienced the new birth toward the qualities that Christians should increasingly come to exhibit as they are being sanctified.

Day 1   Read Introduction and scan the rest of the sermon. Being a Christian involves having a changed heart. Scan Lesson 9.

Day 2   Read §§I.1-I.8. Humility and faith are two marks of the circumcision of the heart.

Day 3   Read §§I.9-I.10. Hope—having an assurance that one is a child of God—is a third mark of the circumcision of the heart.

Day 4   Read §§I.11-I.13. Love is the final mark of the circumcision of the heart.

Day 5   Read §§II.1-II.4. A person whose heart has been circumcised has humility and faith.

Day 6   Read §§II.5-II.10. A person whose heart has been circumcised has hope and love. Reread the lesson and answer the questions at the end.

Day 7   Rest.

REFLECTION

As obedient children, do not conform to the evil desires you had when you lived in ignorance. But just as he who called you is holy, so be holy in all you do; for it is written: "Be holy, because I am holy."

1 Peter 1:14-16; *TNIV*

PRAYER

Lord Jesus,

Your love for me is incredible. I know that I have done nothing to deserve it. I rejoice that I have new hope because you intercede with your Father on my behalf. I am thankful that your righteousness is applied to my life and, by your death on the cross, I am forgiven of my sins and cleansed from all unrighteousness. Yet, I know that you are not content only to forgive me. I know that you want to change me and mold me so that I become more and more like you. Help me, Lord, to participate in this renewal and cleansing of my soul. Amen.

Prayer concerns for this week:

Daily Reflections

Day 1   Read the Introduction and scan the rest of the sermon. Being a Christian involves having a changed heart. Scan Lesson 9.

Meaning for me:

Day 2   Read §§I.1-I.8. Humility and faith are two marks of the circumcision of the heart.

Meaning for me:

Day 3   Read §§I.9-I.10. Hope—having an assurance that one is a child of God—is a third mark of the circumcision of the heart.

Meaning for me:

Day 4   Read §§I.11-I.13. Love is the final mark of the circumcision of the heart.

Meaning for me:

Day 5   Read §§II.1-II.4. A person whose heart has been circumcised has humility and faith.

Meaning for me:

Day 6   Read §§II.5-II.10. A person whose heart has been circumcised has hope and love. Reread the lesson and answer the questions at the end.

Meaning for me:

Sanctification or Growth in Holiness

We have seen throughout this study that one of the orienting themes of John Wesley's understanding of Scripture is that there is one thing needful for humankind, the restoration of sinners to the image of God, which is the essence of salvation. We have seen that humanity is in need of restoration due to the Fall and that God's prevenient grace awakens sinners to their need for forgiveness and repentance. By the merit of Jesus Christ, we are forgiven of our sins and justified in God's sight. Justification leads to the new birth, which is the first step in sanctification.

A Real Change. What *is* sanctification? How are we sanctified? A key to understanding sanctification is being able to distinguish it properly from justification. Wesley summarizes the distinction between the two in his sermon, *Justification by Faith*: "the one [justification] implies what God *does for us* through his Son; the other [sanctification] what he *works in us* by his Spirit."[1] As we noted in Lesson 6, in justification God declares us righteous, or holy, because of Jesus Christ's righteousness. In sanctification, by the power of the Holy Spirit, God actually *makes* us righteous. Justification involves a relative change; sanctification involves a real change.[2]

Sanctification. Sanctification can be described as the process of growing in holiness. Defining sanctification as growth in holiness highlights it as a process that involves transformation of the person who is being sanctified. Those who experience God's forgiveness grow in grace so that they actually become more and more like Christ and less and less chained to sin. Becoming like Christ involves the transformation of our souls so that we love the Lord our God with all of our heart and love our neighbor as ourselves. Wesley summarized God's desire for our sanctification as "a desire for love to be not a transient guest but the constant ruling temper of our soul."[3] Sanctification, like justification, is by grace.

Active Participation. Another key element of sanctification is that individual Christians are active participants in their own transformation. God's justifying grace and the new birth make it *possible* for the Christian to participate in becoming holy. Theologian Randy Maddox has argued that grace makes us response-*able*, so that we *can* respond faithfully and willingly to the work that God is doing in our lives. As a result, we are enabled to cooperate with God's sanctifying grace.

In *The Circumcision of the Heart*, Wesley describes the real change that occurs within Christians as they grow in holiness. Wesley uses the metaphor of circumcision, which usually implies an outward or physical change, to highlight the idea that sanctification, or growth in holiness, is a radical transformation of the heart. Wesley emphasized the importance of becoming holy, as Christ is holy. For Wesley, "If Christ be risen, ye ought then to die unto the world, and to live wholly unto God" (§Intro.1). Sanctification is a real change that happens within the person, not merely a symbolic one.

The Christian life must either wax or wane. It is impossible for the Christian, even if fully sanctified to stand still . . . you must either rise or fall; rise higher or fall lower.[4]
Harald Lindström, *Wesley and Sanctification*

Without God's grace, we cannot be saved; while without our (grace-empowered, but uncoerced) participation, God's grace will not save.[5]

Randy Maddox, *Responsible Grace*

Goal of Sanctification

Becoming Righteous. While sanctification is a life-long process, the goal of sanctification is "a right state of soul," in which each person has been inwardly changed, so that he or she is no longer just declared to be righteous, but has also actually become righteous. The circumcision of the heart is "being so 'renewed in the spirit of our mind,' as to be 'perfect as our Father in heaven is perfect'" (§I.1).

Perfection in Love. Christian perfection is the logical result of Wesley's belief that sanctification is a process of growing in holiness. Christian perfection is loving both God and neighbor fully, to the exclusion of all else. Two other expressions are used for Christian perfection: "entire sanctification" and "perfection in love." We will discuss what Wesley did and did not mean when he talked about Christian perfection in Lesson 12. For now, let us remember that being perfected in the love of God and neighbor is the *goal* of sanctification; it is what Christians hope for and strive to become.

The Heart That Has Been Circumcised

In *The Circumcision of the Heart*, Wesley at times seems simultaneously to talk about the *process* of growing in holiness (sanctification) and the *goal* of Christian perfection. This makes sense because, for Wesley, sanctification is a transformation that should lead to entire sanctification, or perfection in love. The goal is so intimately connected with the process that Wesley often used the same terminology and theology for both.

Charles Wesley's hymn, "Love Divine, All Loves Excelling" (at the right), identifies characteristics of sanctification: the pure, unbounded love of Jesus Christ enters our hearts and dwells within us; the mercies of God in Christ become our crowning glory; the Holy Spirit as the breath of God in Christ fills our entire body ("breast") and soul; we inherit divine joy as a sign of God's faithfulness; we experience at least a taste of "second rest" that we will one day fully experience in heaven; our "bent to sinning" is taken away; and our hearts are freed in the sure confidence and assurance of freedom from the power of sin.

In *The Circumcision of the Heart*, John Wesley described the circumcision of the heart by listing four qualities that a person exhibits due to their heart being circumcised: humility, faith, hope, and love (§I.2). This designation is helpful because Wesley is lifting up characteristics that we should increasingly come to demonstrate as our souls are renewed in the image of our Creator. Practicing these qualities will result in the development of a "holy temper," a habitual pattern of living that culminates in a virtuous and holy life, through grace.

Wesley lists these four qualities in the logical order that he thought the believer would acquire them. Humility (§I.2ff[6]) leads to a recognition of who we really are and the depth of our sin. This leads to repentance and despair in our ability to save

NOTES, REFLECTIONS, AND QUESTIONS
Marks of the Community

In Judaism, physical circumcision was a mark that was also an event; it brought the person into the covenant community. It is a sign that acts—Christians would call it a "sacrament." Christians are marked with the seal of the Holy Spirit:

> And you also were included in Christ when you heard the word of truth, the gospel of your salvation. Having believed, you were marked in him with a seal, the promised Holy Spirit, who is a deposit guaranteeing our inheritance until the redemption of those who are God's possession—to the praise of his glory.
>
> Eph. 1:13-14; *NIV*

In general we may observe, it [circumcision of the heart] is that habitual disposition of soul which, in the Sacred Writings, is termed holiness; and which directly implies, the being cleansed from sin . . . and by consequence, the being endued with those virtues which were also in Christ Jesus.

John Wesley, *The Circumcision of the Heart*, §I.1

May God himself, the God of peace, sanctify you through and through. May your whole spirit, soul and body be kept blameless at the coming of our Lord Jesus Christ. The one who calls you is faithful, and he will do it.

1 Thess. 5:23-24; *NIV*

Love divine, all loves excelling,
joy of heaven, to earth come down;
Fix in us thy humble dwelling;
all thy faithful mercies crown!
Jesus thou art all compassion,
pure, unbounded love thou art;
Visit us with thy salvation;
enter every trembling heart.

Breathe, O breathe thy loving Spirit
into every troubled breast!
Let us all in thee inherit;
let us find that second rest.
Take away our bent to sinning;
Alpha and Omega be;
End of faith, as its beginning,
set our hearts at liberty.

Charles Wesley, "Love Divine, All Loves Excelling" (1747)—*UM Hymnal* #384; *AME Hymnal* #455; *CME Hymnal* #44; *Afr. Amer. Heritage Hymnal* #440; *Free Methodist Ch. & The Wesleyan Ch. Hymnal* #335; *Ch. of Nazarene Hymnal* #507

ourselves. The cleansing provided by humility prepares us to embrace faith in Jesus Christ. Faith (trusting in God's promises through the life, death, and resurrection of Jesus Christ; §I.6ff), leads to hope (§I.9f). Wesley links hope with the witness of the Spirit or assurance (which was discussed in Lesson 7). Faith leads to hope because the Spirit "witnesses in the hearts of believers that they are the children of God" (§I.9). The final quality of the heart that has been circumcised is love (§I.11f). When our hearts have been circumcised so that we fully love both God and neighbor, we will have been made perfect in love.

NOTES, REFLECTIONS, AND QUESTIONS

If thou wilt be perfect, add to all these, charity; add love, and thou hast the circumcision of the heart . . . It is not only the first and great command, but it is all the commandments in one.
John Wesley, *The Circumcision of the Heart*, §I.11

RESPONDING FAITHFULLY

How is the "one thing needful" (recovering the image of God) connected to your growth in holiness?

_____

_____

How is forgiveness of sins (justification) different from sanctification?

_____

_____

In light of Wesley's concept of sanctification, how would you relate to someone who spoke about their salvation as a one-time, static event in the past, (for example: "I was saved on…") and did not speak about their current experience of God?

_____

_____

Do you agree with Harald Lindström that Christian life must either "wax or wane" (p. 100)?

_____

_____

Can you think of any other qualities—in addition to those listed in §I.2—that would be characteristic of someone whose heart has been circumcised? (See Gal. 5:13-23.)

_____

How is your church community growing in holiness?

_____

_____

LEARNING MORE

Read other sermons dealing with sanctification and the process of growth in holiness:
- *Christian Perfection*
- *The Scripture Way of Salvation* (see Lesson 11).

Read parts of:
- Randy L. Maddox, *Responsible Grace: John Wesley's Practical Theology*
- Harald Lindström, *Wesley and Sanctification*.

LOOKING AHEAD

Next Lesson. Catholic Spirit—a Wesleyan view of Christian unity.

Teacher Helps provides follow-up questions that may be useful in class discussions.

END NOTES

[1] John Wesley, *Justification by Faith*, §II.1.

[2] John Wesley, *The Scripture Way of Salvation*, §I.4. This sermon is discussed in Lesson 11.

[3] John Wesley, *On Pleasing All Men*, §II.1. Cited in Randy Maddox, *Responsible Grace.* Nashville: Abingdon, 1994, p. 178.

[4] Harald Lindström, *Wesley and Sanctification.* Wilmore, Kentucky: Francis Asbury, 1980, p. 118.

[5] Maddox, op. cit., p. 19.

[6] The symbol "ff" indicates that the citation continues on two or more pages that follow. The symbol "f" indicates that the citation continues on the next page.

Reading for Lesson 9. The Circumcision of the Heart (1733)

Preached at St. Mary's, Oxford, before the University, on January 1, 1733.

Circumcision is that of the heart, in the spirit, and not in the letter (Rom. 2:29).

Introduction

1. 'Tis the melancholy remark of an excellent man, that he who now preaches the most essential duties of Christianity, runs the hazard of being esteemed, by a great part of his hearers, "a setter forth of new doctrines." Most men have so *lived away* the substance of that religion, the profession whereof they still retain, that no sooner are any of those truths proposed which difference the Spirit of Christ from the spirit of the world, than they cry out, "Thou bringest strange things to our ears; we would know what these things mean"—though he is only preaching to them "Jesus and the resurrection," with the necessary consequence of it. If Christ be risen, ye ought then to die unto the world, and to live wholly unto God.

2. A hard saying this to the natural man, who is alive unto the world, and dead unto God; and one that he will not readily be persuaded to receive as the truth of God, unless it be so qualified in the interpretation as to have neither use nor significance left. He "receiveth not the" words "of the Spirit of God," taken in their plain and obvious meaning. "They are foolishness unto him; neither" indeed "can he know them, because they are spiritually discerned"—they are perceivable only by that spiritual sense which in him was never yet awakened, for want of which he must reject, as idle fancies of men what are both the wisdom and the power of God.

3. That "circumcision is that of the heart, in the spirit, and not in the letter," that the distinguishing mark of a true follower of Christ, of one who is in a state of acceptance with God, is not either outward circumcision or baptism, or any other outward form, but a right state of soul—a mind and spirit renewed after the image of him that created it—is one of those important truths that can only be spiritually discerned. And this the Apostle himself intimates in the next words: "Whose praise is not of men, but of God." As if he had said, "Expect not, whoever thou art, who thus followest thy great Master, that the world, the men who follow him not, will say, 'Well done, good and faithful servant!' Know that the circumcision of the heart, the seal of thy calling, is foolishness with the world. Be content to wait for thy applause till the day of thy Lord's appearing. In that day shalt thou have praise of God in the great assembly of men and angels."

I design:

I. First, particularly to inquire wherein this circumcision of the heart consists; and,

II. Secondly, to mention some reflections that naturally arise from such an inquiry.

I.

1. I am, first, to inquire wherein that circumcision of the heart consists, which will receive the praise of God. In general, we may observe it is that habitual disposition of soul which, in the Sacred Writings, is termed "holiness," and which directly implies the being cleansed from sin, "from all filthiness both of flesh and

spirit"; and, by consequence, the being endued with those virtues which were also in Christ Jesus, the being so "renewed in the image of our mind" as to be "perfect, as our Father in heaven is perfect."

2. To be more particular, circumcision of heart implies humility, faith, hope, and charity. Humility, a right judgment of ourselves, cleanses our minds from those high conceits of our own perfections, from the undue opinions of our own abilities and attainments, which are the genuine fruit of a corrupted nature. This entirely cuts off that vain thought, "I am rich, and wise, and have need of nothing"; and convinces us that we are by nature wretched, and poor, and miserable, and blind, and naked. It convinces us that in our best estate we are, of ourselves, all sin and vanity; that confusion, and ignorance, and error reign over our understanding; that unreasonable, earthly, sensual, devilish passions usurp authority over our will: in a word, that there is no whole part in our soul, that all the foundations of our nature are out of course.

3. At the same time we are convinced that we are not sufficient of ourselves to help ourselves; that, without the Spirit of God, we can do nothing but add sin to sin; that it is he alone who worketh in us by his almighty power, either to will or do that which is good—it being as impossible for us even to think a good thought, without the supernatural assistance of his Spirit, as to create ourselves, or to renew our whole souls in righteousness and true holiness.

4. A sure effect of our having formed this right judgment of the sinfulness and helplessness of our nature, is a disregard of that "honor which cometh of man," which is usually paid to some supposed excellence in us. He who knows himself neither desires nor values the applause which he knows he deserves not.

> It is therefore "a very small thing with him to be judged by man's judgment." He has all reason to think, by comparing what it has said, either for or against him, with what he feels in his own breast, that the world, as well as the god of this world, was "a liar from the beginning." And even as to those who are not of the world; though he would choose, if it were the will of God, that they should account of him as of one desirous to be found a faithful steward of his Lord's goods, if haply this might be a means of enabling him to be of more use to his fellow-servants, yet as this is the one end of his wishing for their approbation, so he does not at all rest upon it. For he is assured that whatever God wills, he can never want instruments to perform; since he is able, even of these stones, to raise up servants to do his pleasure.

5. This is that lowliness of mind which they have learned of Christ who follow his example and tread in his steps. And this knowledge of their disease, whereby they are more and more cleansed from one part of it, pride and vanity, disposes them to embrace, with a willing mind, the second thing implied in circumcision of the heart—that faith which alone is able to make them whole, which is the one medicine given under heaven to heal their sickness.

6. The best guide of the blind, the surest light of them that are in darkness, the most perfect instructor of the foolish, is faith. But it must be such a faith as is "mighty through God, to the pulling down of strongholds," to the overturning all the prejudices of corrupt reason, all the false maxims revered among men, all evil customs and habits, all that "wisdom of the world which is foolishness with God"; as "casteth down imaginations" (reasonings) "and every high thing that exalteth itself against the knowledge of God, and bringeth into captivity every thought to the obedience of Christ."

> 7. "All things are possible to him that" thus "believeth." "The eyes of his understanding being enlightened," he sees what is his calling, even to glorify God, who hath bought him with so high a price, in his body and in his spirit, which now are God's by redemption, as well as by creation. He feels what is "the exceeding greatness of his power," who, as he raised up Christ from the dead, so is able to quicken us, "dead in sin," by his Spirit which dwelleth in us." "This is the victory which overcometh the world, even our faith": that faith, which is not only an unshaken assent to all that God hath revealed in Scripture—and in particular to those important truths, "Jesus Christ came into the world to save sinners"; "He bare our sins in his own body on the tree"; "He is the propitiation for our sins, and not for ours only, but also for the sins of the whole world"—[N.B. The following part of this paragraph is now added to the Sermon formerly preached.] but likewise the revelation of Christ in our hearts: a divine evidence or conviction of his love, his free, unmerited love to me a sinner; a sure confidence in his pardoning mercy, wrought in us by the Holy Ghost; a confidence, whereby every true believer is enabled to bear witness, "I know that my Redeemer liveth," that I have an "advocate with the Father," that "Jesus Christ the righteous" is my Lord, and "the propitiation for my sins"—I know he hath "loved me, and given himself for me." He hath reconciled me, even me, to God; and I "have redemption through his blood, even the forgiveness of sins."

8. Such a faith as this cannot fail to show evidently* the power of him that inspires it, by delivering his children from the yoke of sin, and "purging their consciences from dead works"; by strengthening them so that they are no longer constrained to obey sin in the desires thereof; but instead of yielding their members

unto it, as instruments of unrighteousness," they now "yield themselves" entirely "unto God, as those that are alive from the dead."

9. Those who are thus by faith born of God, have also strong consolation through hope. This [hope] is the next thing which the circumcision of the heart implies—even the testimony of their own spirit with the Spirit which witnesses in their hearts, that they are the children of God. Indeed it is the same Spirit who works in them that clear and cheerful confidence that their heart is upright toward God; that good assurance that they now do, through his grace, the things which are acceptable in his sight; that they are now in the path which leadeth to life, and shall, by the mercy of God, endure therein to the end. It is he who giveth them a lively expectation of receiving all good things at God's hand, a joyous prospect of that crown of glory which is reserved in heaven for them. By this anchor a Christian is kept steady in the midst of the waves of this troublesome world, and preserved from striking upon either of those fatal rocks: presumption or despair. He is neither discouraged by the misconceived severity of his Lord, nor does he despise the richness of his goodness." He neither apprehends the difficulties of the race set before him to be greater than he has strength to conquer, nor expects them to be so little as to yield him the conquest till he has put forth all his strength.

The experience he already has in the Christian warfare, as it assures him his "labor is not in vain," if "whatever his hand findeth to do, he doeth it with his might"; so it forbids his entertaining so vain a thought as that he can otherwise gain any advantage, as that any virtue can be shown, any praise attained, by faint hearts and feeble hands; or, indeed, by any but those who pursue the same course with the great Apostle of the Gentiles: "I," says he, "so run, not as uncertainly; so fight I, not as one that beateth the air. But I keep under my body, and bring it into subjection; lest by any means, when I have preached to others, I myself should be a castaway."

10. By the same discipline is every good soldier of Christ to inure himself to endure hardships. Confirmed and strengthened by this, he will be able not only to renounce the works of darkness, but every appetite too, and every affection which is not subject to the law of God. For "everyone," saith St. John, "who hath this hope, purifieth himself, even as he is pure." It is his daily care, by the grace of God in Christ, and through the blood of the covenant, to purge the inmost recesses of his soul from the lusts that before possessed and defiled it: from uncleanness, and envy, and malice, and wrath; from every passion and temper that is after the flesh, that either springs from or cherishes his native corruption; as well knowing that he whose very body is the temple of God ought to admit into it nothing common or unclean; and that holiness becometh that house for ever, where the Spirit of holiness vouchsafes to dwell.

11. Yet lackest thou one thing, whosoever thou art, that to a deep humility and a steadfast faith, hast joined a lively hope, and thereby in a good measure cleansed thy heart from its inbred pollution. If thou wilt be perfect, add to all these, charity: add love, and thou hast the circumcision of the heart. "Love is the fulfilling of the law, the end of the commandment." Very excellent things are spoken of love; it is the essence, the spirit, the life of all virtue. It is not only the first and great command, but it is all the commandments in one. "Whatsoever things are just, whatsoever things are pure, whatsoever things are amiable" or honorable; "if there be any virtue, if there be any praise," they are all comprised in this one word—love. In this is perfection, and glory, and happiness. The royal law of heaven and earth is this, "Thou shalt love the Lord thy God with all thy heart, and with all thy soul, and with all thy mind, and with all thy strength."

12. Not that this forbids us to love anything besides God: it implies that we love our brother also. Nor yet does it forbid us (as some have strangely imagined) to take pleasure in anything but God.

To suppose this, is to suppose the fountain of holiness is directly the author of sin, since he has inseparably annexed pleasure to the use of those creatures which are necessary to sustain the life he has given us. This, therefore, can never be the meaning of his command.

What the real sense of it is, both our blessed Lord and his apostles tell us too frequently, and too plainly, to be misunderstood. They all with one mouth bear witness that the true meaning of those several declarations—"The Lord thy God is one Lord; thou shalt have no other gods but me"; "Thou shalt love the Lord thy God with all thy strength"; "Thou shalt cleave unto him"; "The desire of thy soul shall be to his name"—is no other than this: the one perfect Good shall be your ultimate end. One thing shall ye desire for its own sake—the fruition of him that is All in All. One happiness shall ye propose to your souls, even an union with him that made them; the having "fellowship with the Father and the Son"; the being joined to the Lord in one Spirit. One design you are to pursue to the end of time—the enjoyment of God in time and in eternity. Desire other things—so far as they tend to this. Love the creature, as it leads to the Creator. But in every step you take, be this the glorious point that terminates your view. Let every affection, and thought, and word, and work, be subordinate to this. Whatever ye desire or fear, whatever ye seek or shun, whatever ye think, speak, or do, be it in order to [have] your happiness in God, the sole end, as well as source, of your being.

13. Have no end, no ultimate end, but God. Thus our Lord: "One thing is needful." And if thine eye be singly fixed on this one thing, "thy whole body shall be full of light." Thus St. Paul: "This one thing I do; I press toward the mark, for the prize of the high calling in Christ Jesus." Thus St. James: "Cleanse your hands, ye sinners, and purify your hearts, ye double-minded." Thus St. John: "Love not the world, neither the things that are in the world…. For all that is in the world, the lust of the flesh, the lust of the eye, and the pride of life, is not of the Father, but is of the world." The seeking happiness in what gratifies either the desire of the flesh, by agreeably striking upon the outward senses—the desire of the eye, of the imagination, by its novelty, greatness, or beauty; or the pride of life, whether by pomp, grandeur, power, or, the usual consequence of them, applause and admiration—"is not of the Father"; cometh not from, neither is approved by, the Father of spirits; "but of the world"; it is the distinguishing mark of those who will not have him to reign over them.

II.

1. Thus have I particularly inquired what that circumcision of the heart is which will obtain the praise of God. I am, in the second place, to mention some reflections that naturally arise from such an inquiry, as a plain rule whereby every man may judge himself whether he be of the world or of God.

And, first, it is clear from what has been said that no man has a title to the praise of God unless his heart is circumcised by humility; unless he is little, and base, and vile in his own eyes; unless he is deeply convinced of that inbred "corruption of his nature," "whereby he is very far gone from original righteousness," being prone to all evil, averse to all good, corrupt and abominable; having a "carnal mind which is enmity against God, and is not subject to the law of God, nor indeed can be," unless he continually feels in his inmost soul that without the Spirit of God resting upon him, he can neither think, nor desire, nor speak, nor act anything good, or well-pleasing in his sight. No man I say, has a title to the praise of God till he feels his want of God; nor indeed, till he seeketh that "honor which cometh of God only"; and neither desires nor pursues that which cometh of man, unless so far only as it tends to this.

2. Another truth, which naturally follows from what has been said, is that none shall obtain the honor that cometh of God, unless his heart be circumcised by faith, even a "faith of the operation of God"; unless, refusing to be any longer led by his senses, appetites, or passions, or even by that blind leader of the blind, so idolized by the world, natural reason, he lives and walks by faith; directs every step as "seeing him that is invisible"; "looks not at the things that are seen, which are temporal, but at the things that are not seen, which are eternal"; and governs all his desires, designs, and thoughts, all his actions and conversations, as one who is entered in within the veil, where Jesus sits at the right hand of God.

3. It were to be wished that they were better acquainted with this faith, who employ much of their time and pains in laying another foundation, in grounding religion on the eternal *fitness* of things, on the intrinsic *excellence* of virtue, and the *beauty* of actions flowing from it—on the *reasons* as they term them, of good and evil, and the *relations* of beings to each other. Either these accounts of the grounds of Christian duty coincide with the scriptural or not. If they do, why are well-meaning men perplexed, and drawn from the weightier matters of the law, by a cloud of terms whereby the easiest truths are explained into obscurity? If they are not, then it behooves them to consider who is the author of this new doctrine; whether he is likely to be an angel from heaven who preacheth another gospel than that of Christ Jesus—though, if he were, God, not we, hath pronounced his sentence: "Let him be accursed."

4. Our gospel, as it knows no other foundation of good works than faith, or of faith than Christ, so it clearly informs us we are not his disciples while we either deny him to be the author, or his Spirit to be the inspirer and perfecter, both of our faith and works. "If any man have not the Spirit of Christ, he is none of his." He alone can quicken those who are dead unto God, can breathe into them the breath of Christian life, and so prevent*, accompany, and follow them with his grace as to bring their good desires to good effect. And, as many as are thus led by the Spirit of God, they are the sons of God." This is God's short and plain account of true religion and virtue; and "other foundation can no man lay."

5. From what has been said, we may, thirdly, learn that none is truly "led by the Spirit" unless that "Spirit bear witness with his spirit, that he is a child of God"; unless he see the prize and the crown before him, and "rejoice in hope of the glory of God." So greatly have they erred who have taught that, in serving God, we ought not to have a view to our own happiness! Nay, but we are often and expressly taught of God to have "respect unto the recompense of reward," to balance toil with the "joy set before us," these "light afflictions" with that "exceeding weight of glory." Yea, we are "aliens to the covenant of promise," we are "without God in the world," until God, "of his abundant mercy, hath begotten us again unto a living hope of the inheritance incorruptible, undefiled, and that fadeth not away."

6. But if these things are so, it is high time for those persons to deal faithfully with their own souls—who are so far from finding in themselves this joyful assurance that they fulfill the terms, and shall obtain the promises, of that covenant, as to quarrel with the covenant itself, and blaspheme the terms of it, to complain they are too severe, and that no man ever did or shall live up to them! What is this but to reproach God, as if he were a hard master requiring of his servants more than he enables them to perform?—as if he had mocked the helpless works of his hands by binding them to impossibilities, by commanding them to overcome where neither their own strength nor his grace was sufficient for them?

7. These blasphemers might almost persuade those to imagine themselves guiltless, who, in the contrary extreme, hope to fulfill the commands of God without taking any pains at all. Vain hope! That a child of Adam should ever expect to see the kingdom of Christ and of God without striving, without *agonizing*, first "to enter in at the strait gate." That one who was "conceived and born in sin," and whose "inward parts are very wickedness," should once entertain a thought of being "purified as his Lord is pure" unless he tread in his steps, and "take up his cross daily"; unless he "cut off his right hand," and "pluck out the right eye, and cast it from him"; that he should ever dream of shaking off his old opinions, passions, tempers, of being "sanctified throughout in spirit, soul, and body," without a constant and continued course of general self-denial!

8. What less than this can we possibly infer from the above-cited words of St. Paul, who, living "in infirmities, in reproaches, in necessities, in persecutions, in distresses" for Christ's sake; who, being full of "signs, and wonders, and mighty deeds"; who, having been "caught up into the third heaven" yet reckoned, as a late author strongly expresses it, that all his virtues would be insecure, and even his salvation in danger, without this constant self-denial? "So run I," says he, "not as uncertainly; so fight I, not as one that beateth the air." By which he plainly teaches us that he who does not thus run, who does not thus deny himself daily, does run uncertainly, and fighteth to as little purpose as he that "beateth the air."

9. To as little purpose does he talk of "fighting the fight of faith," as vainly hope to attain the crown of incorruption (as we may, lastly, infer from the preceding observations), whose heart is not circumcised by love. Cutting off both the lust of the flesh, the lust of the eye, and the pride of life—engaging the whole man, body, soul, and spirit, in the ardent pursuit of that one object—is so essential to a child of God that, without it, whosoever liveth is counted dead before him. "Though I speak with the tongues of men and of angels, and have not love, I am as sounding brass, or a tinkling cymbal. Though I have the gift of prophecy, and understand all mysteries, and all knowledge; and though I have all faith, so as to remove mountains, and have not love, I am nothing." Nay, "though I give all my goods to feed the poor, and my body to be burned, and have not love, it profiteth me nothing."

10. Here, then, is the sum of the perfect law; this is the true circumcision of the heart. Let the spirit return to God that gave it, with the whole train of its affections. "Unto the place from whence all the rivers came, thither let them flow again." Other sacrifices from us he would not; but the living sacrifice of the heart he hath chosen. Let it be continually offered up to God through Christ, in flames of holy love. And let no creature be suffered to share with him: for he is a jealous God. His throne will he not divide with another: he will reign without a rival. Be no design, no desire admitted there, but what has him for its ultimate object. This is the way wherein those children of God once walked, who, being dead, still speak to us: "Desire not to live, but to praise his name; let all your thoughts, words, and works, tend to his glory. Set your heart firm on him, and on other things only as they are in and from him. Let your soul be filled with so entire a love of him that you may love nothing but for his sake." "Have a pure intention of heart, a steadfast regard to his glory in all your actions." "Fix your eye upon the blessed hope of your calling, and make all the things of the world minister unto it." For then, and not till then, is that "mind in us which was also in Christ Jesus"; when, in every motion of our heart, in every word of our tongue, in every work of our hands, we "pursue nothing but in relation to him, and in subordination to his pleasure"; when we, too, neither think, nor speak, nor act, to fulfill our "own will, but the will of him that sent us"; when, whether we eat, or drink, or whatever we do, we do all to the glory of God.

Lesson 10—A Catholic Spirit: Toward Christian Unity

Is thine heart right, as my heart is with thy heart?
It is. If it be, give me thine hand.

2 Kings 10:15; *KJV*

"If thine heart be right, as mine with thy heart," love all mankind, thine enemies,
the enemies of God, strangers, as a brother in Christ. . . . Though we cannot walk alike, . . .
cannot think alike, . . . may we not love alike?

John Wesley, *Catholic Spirit,* §Intro.[II],3,4

OUR STARTING POINT

Over the past twenty centuries, Christians have had disagreements on matters of faith that have split the visible Christian church. On what basis can Wesleyans seek Christian unity, for the sake of outreach and mission? Can we find a universal (catholic) spirit common to all who love God in Christ?

READING

Read daily the reflection and prayer about Christian unity as the Body of Christ. In addition:

Day 1   Scan the entire sermon *Catholic Spirit* (1750) and carefully read the Introduction. Scan Lesson 10.

Day 2   Read Part I, §§I.1-18. What is meant by "Is your heart right"?

Day 3   Read Part II, §§II.1-8. What is meant by "Give me your hand"?

Day 4   Read Part III, §§III.1-6. Is the catholic spirit "indifference" to doctrine or worship?

Day 5   Reread the entire sermon and consider the words of Charles Wesley's hymn, "Catholic Love" (provided on the fourth page of this lesson).

Day 6   List some beliefs on which you think Christian communities might agree to disagree but in such differences be able to maintain essential Christian unity. Reread the lesson and answer the questions at the end.

Day 7   Rest.

REFLECTION

I [Paul] . . .beg you to lead a life worthy of the calling to which you have been called, with all humility and gentleness, with patience, bearing with one another in love, making every effort to maintain the unity of the Spirit in the bond of peace. There is one body and one Spirit, just as you were called to the one hope of your calling, one Lord, one faith, one baptism, one God and Father of all, who is above all and through all and in all. But each of us was given grace according to the measure of Christ's gift. . . . The gifts he gave were . . . to equip the saints for the work of ministry, for building up the Body of Christ, until all of us come to the unity of the faith and of the knowledge of the Son of God, to maturity, to the measure of the full stature of Christ.

Eph. 4:1-7; 11-13; *NRSV*

PRAYER

God of all love,

Fill us with your transforming love, that we may share that love with all your children. Help us to understand and believe all your promises. Teach us to see your face in the hearts of others, even in those with whom we disagree. Confirm in us your righteousness, that we may be agents of righteousness to all your creation. Give us wisdom to discern your holy will for our lives. Give us your power to be agents of peace with justice and mercy. And help us to find ways to make the one Body of Christ more effective in ministry and more visible in unity. Amen.

Prayer concerns for this week:

Daily Reflections

Day 1   Scan the entire sermon *Catholic Spirit* and carefully read the introduction. Scan Lesson 10.

Meaning for me:

Day 2   Read Part I, §§I.1-18. What is meant by, "Is your heart right"?

Meaning for me:

Day 3   Read Part II, §§II.1-8. What is meant by, "Give me your hand"?

Meaning for me:

Day 4   Read Part III, §§III.1-6. Is the catholic spirit "indifference" to doctrine or worship?

Meaning for me:

Day 5   Reread the entire sermon and consider the words of Charles Wesley's hymn, "Catholic Love" (provided on the fourth page of this lesson).

Meaning for me:

Day 6   List some beliefs on which you think Christian communities might agree to disagree but in such differences be able to maintain essential Christian unity. Reread the lesson and answer the questions at the end.

Meaning for me:

The Nature of a Catholic Spirit

Common to Christians in all denominations, associations, and churches should be a universal spirit of love for God in Christ and love for others. Such a universal spirit is called a "catholic spirit." Note that the term "catholic" (as used in the Apostles' Creed) means "universal" and does not refer to the Roman Catholic Church.

The believer who has a catholic spirit "is steadily fixed in his religious principles in what he believes to be the truth as it is in Jesus…[yet] his heart is enlarged toward all mankind, those he knows and those he does not; he embraces with strong and cordial affection neighbors and strangers, friends and enemies" (§III.4). Having the attitude of a catholic spirit is part of living a sanctified life and growing in holiness towards the image of God.

Mere "opinions" must not divide us. ("Opinion" in this sermon is not one's personal view, but rather a reference to points of belief that distinguish one group of Christians from another.) Non-essential doctrines, for example, must not divide us. Patterns of worship must not divide us. The particular characteristics of specific congregations to which Christians belong must not divide us.

Wesley acknowledges that Christians differ in the way they think and the way they live out their Christian life. The danger noted by Wesley is that such differences can become "grand hindrances" to practicing the double commandment to love God and to love our neighbor.

Wesley is not promoting an indifference to *"all opinions"*(§III.6)—particularly *essential* doctrines—nor an indifference to *how* we practice our worship. Neither does Wesley promote indifference to being a member of a congregation.

Wesley was not a pluralist—there are some essential doctrines that are non-negotiable for the Christian. Having a catholic spirit does not mean having a lowest-common-denominator Christianity, in which beliefs are not important. Rather, the believer is "fixed as the sun in his judgment concerning the main branches of Christian doctrine." Examples of such "main branches" of essential doctrine include the Trinity, Christ's deity and humanity, and the resurrection. Indifference to essential beliefs about our faith results in being "driven to and fro, and tossed about with every wind of doctrine." Such is the "spawn of hell, not the offspring of heaven." (§III.1).

Yet, beyond these essential doctrines, Christians may also hold firmly to various non-essential beliefs and practices. Adhering to such various beliefs and practices should not preclude us from having Christian fellowship with others who differ from us.

Further, Wesley affirms that the Christian with a catholic spirit makes firm choices about the ways in which to worship God "in spirit and in truth." Specifically (§III.2): *[The person] of a truly catholic spirit, having weighed all things in the balance of the sanctuary, has no doubt, no scruple at all, concerning that particular*

NOTES, REFLECTIONS, AND QUESTIONS

If we cannot as yet think alike in all things, at least we may love alike. . . . let us resolve, first, not to hurt one another . . . secondly, . . . to speak nothing harsh or unkind of each other. . . . thirdly, . . . to harbor no unkindly thought, no unfriendly temper towards each other . . . fourthly, endeavor to help each other on in whatever we are agreed leads to the Kingdom. So far as we can, let us always rejoice to strengthen each other's hands in God.[1]

John Wesley, *A Letter to a Roman Catholic*, §§16-17.

Unity in Christ as Head of the Church

Regardless of differences, all Christian communities are unified by honoring Jesus Christ as their head. We recognize differences in understanding our faith, practicing worship, and how we express love of neighbor. We know that such differences can form different congregations and associations of congregations in faithful expression of love of God in Christ, worship, and love of others. Yet we need to celebrate the commonality of our love of God in Jesus Christ through the Holy Spirit and find the means to make the unity of the universal Body of Christ more visible in the world.

mode of worship wherein he joins. He is clearly convinced that this manner of worshipping God is both scriptural and rational.

Wesley thus encouraged allegiance to a particular congregation of believers. In that particular congregation, the believer participates in the means of grace as practiced by that community. The Christian with a catholic spirit "pours out his soul in public prayer," "joins in public praise and thanksgiving," and "rejoices to hear the word of reconciliation, the gospel of the grace of God." In that community each believer "watches over" the others in love, holding these others accountable to their professed beliefs and common practices—"admonishing, exhorting, comforting, reproving, and every way building up each other in the faith" (§III.3). (Accountability in small groups was an effective principle of discipleship introduced by Wesley.) "Methodists, then, should be ever firm in their convictions, acknowledging the right of private judgment, and yet ever be open to genuine Christian fellowship—not an easy task for any communion of faith."[2]

Wesley was convinced that the issues dividing different groups of Christians pertained primarily to non-essential opinions, and to "the different ways those opinions are expressed."[3] By contrast, Wesley sought unity of Christian believers on the basis of holy living, love for one another, and a commitment to basic Christian beliefs. A believer with catholic spirit (§III.5):

- *Values and praises God for "knowledge of the things of God, the true scriptural manner of worshipping [God], and . . . union with a [specific] congregation fearing God and working righteousness*
- *Loves . . . all, of whatever opinion or worship, or congregation, who believe in the Lord Jesus Christ; who love God and man; who, rejoicing to please and fearing to offend God, are careful to abstain from evil, and [are] zealous of good works.*

Christian Unity

Wesley notes that "a difference in opinions or modes of worship may prevent an entire external union" but he insists that such differences need not prevent "union in affection." Wesley calls us to be of one heart with other Christians and to unite "all the children of God." In such Christian fellowship, we can "forward one another in love and good works" (§4). Our unity is necessary for the furthering of the work of evangelism and mission. For example, hurricane victims need to be assisted; racism needs to be eliminated; and non-believers need to hear the gospel of Jesus Christ—and we can't do all of this alone!

Seeking unity of the one Body of Christ—the Church—is based on respect for one another's opinions, modes of worship, and the character of our congregations. We do not hide our differences but rather carefully articulate them in order to seek mutual understanding. Our common mission may be stated as such:

> *Sent as his disciples, the people of God have to witness to and participate in God's reconciliation, healing, and transformation of creation. The Church's relation to Christ entails that faith and community require discipleship. The integrity of the mission of the Church, of its very being as God's instrument, therefore is at stake in witness through proclamation*

NOTES, REFLECTIONS, AND QUESTIONS

Weary of all this wordy strife,
These notions, forms, and modes, and names,
To thee, the way, the Truth, the Life,
Whose love my simple heart inflames,
Divinely taught, at last I fly,
With thee and thine to live and die.

Forth from the midst of Babel brought,
Parties and sects I cast behind;
Enlarge my heart, and free my thought,
Where'er the latent truth I find
The latent truth with joy to own,
And bow to Jesus' name alone.

Join'd to the hidden church unknown
In this sure bond of perfectness
Obscurely safe, I dwell alone
And glory in th' uniting grace,
To me, to each believer given,
To all thy saints in earth and heaven.

Charles Wesley, "Catholic Love," *Methodist 1889 Hymnal* (unnumbered in Supplement)

To confess the unity of the church is to say that each of the parts are dependant upon the others for making up the one church of Christ. We are really one, but we really need with utmost urgency to take unity that is real and make it more visibly available. We must do that by healing those tears in the fabric, by taking the unity that is real and increasing its visibility.[5]

R. Kendall Soulen

and concrete actions with all people of goodwill for justice, peace, and integrity of creation.[4]

An Example: Contemporary and Traditional Worship

Wesley would have been disturbed by today's worship "wars" between those who value the use of contemporary musical instruments and songs and those who value a traditional style. Wesley was aware that the use of any type of musical instrument, such as an organ, was controversial in early Protestant churches, but he was willing to be innovative. It is safe to assume that Wesley would affirm the value of contemporary and traditional worship (as well as other forms)—all of which express the gospel uniquely in each culture.

Renewal of the Universal Church

Making the oneness of Christ's universal Church visible is an ecumenical task that requires continued renewal of those elements of faith that are shared by all: Holy Scripture, saving faith, holistic spirituality, accountable discipleship, formative worship, and missional vocation. These are central to the Wesleyan tradition and comprise, to a large extent, what Wesley meant by holiness and going on to perfection. Such renewal and holiness requires an active role of each believer in the universal Church. Such discipleship works for peace with justice and the integrity of creation—to recover and live the image that God has already provided for us.

RESPONDING FAITHFULLY

Why do you think there are so many different types of congregations and denominations?

_____

_____

_____

_____

_____

Do you need to repent and ask for forgiveness for things that may have caused division in your church?

_____

_____

_____

What opinions have you held that might have caused unnecessary division in the church?

How can you help heal and move beyond differences of non-essential beliefs in your church?

LEARNING MORE

The following may be of interest:
- William J. Abraham, *Wesley for Armchair Theologians*, pp. 149-152.
- Paul Chilcote, *Praying in the Wesley Spirit: 52 Prayers for Today*, pp. 120-122.
- World Council of Churches, *The Nature and Purpose of the Church*, Faith and Order Paper 181 (1998).

LOOKING AHEAD

The Danger of Riches—addressing the question, Why has Christianity done so little good in the world?

Teacher Helps provides follow-up questions that may be useful in class discussions.

END NOTES

[1] John Wesley, *Letter to a Roman Catholic*, §§16-17, found in Richard P. Heitzenrater, *The Elusive Mr Wesley*, 2nd Edition. Nashville: Abingdon Press, 1995, pp. 192-198.
[2] Kenneth J. Collins, *John Wesley: A Theological Journey*. Nashville: Abingdon Press, 2003, p. 163.
[3] Richard P. Heitzenrater, *Wesley and the People Call Methodists*. Nashville: Abingdon Press, 1995, p. 222.
[4] World Council of Churches, *The Nature and Purpose of the Church: A Stage on the Way to a Common Statement*, Faith and Order Paper 181, WCC Publications, Geneva, Switzerland, 1998, §47 (p. 22).
[5] Kendall Soulen, Lecture, March 30, 2006.

Reading for Lesson 10. Catholic Spirit (1750)

And when he was departed thence, he lighted on Jehonadab the son of Rechab coming to meet him,
and he saluted him, and said to him, Is thine heart right, as my heart is with thy heart?
And Jehonadab answered: It is. If it be, give me thine hand (2 Kings 10:15).

Introduction

I. Let us consider the question proposed by Jehu to Jehonadab, "Is thine heart right, as my heart is with thy heart?"

II. "If thine heart be right, as mine with thy heart," love all mankind, thine enemies, the enemies of God, strangers, as a brother in Christ.

III. We may learn from hence what a catholic spirit is.

1. It is allowed even by those who do not pay this great debt that love is due to all mankind, the royal law, "Thou shalt love thy neighbor as thyself," carrying its own evidence to all that hear it. And that, not according to the miserable construction put upon it by the zealots of old times, "Thou shalt love thy neighbor," thy relation, acquaintance, friend, "and hate thine enemy." Not so; "I say unto you," said our Lord, "Love your enemies, bless them that curse you, do good to them that hate you, and pray for them that despitefully use you and persecute you; that ye may be the children," may appear so to all mankind, "of your Father which is in heaven, who maketh his sun to rise on the evil and on the good, and sendeth rain on the just and on the unjust."

2. But it is sure, there is a peculiar love which we owe to those that love God. So David: "All my delight is upon the saints that are in the earth, and upon such as excel in virtue." And [from one] greater than he: "A new commandment I give unto you, that ye love one another as I have loved you, that ye also love one another. By this shall all men know that ye are my disciples, if ye have love one to another" (John 13:34-35). This is that love on which the Apostle John so frequently and strongly insists. "This," saith he, "is the message that ye heard from the beginning, that we should love one another" (1 Jn. 3:11). "Hereby perceive we the love of God, because he laid down his life for us. And we ought," if love should call us thereto, "to lay down our lives for the brethren" (v. 16). And again: "Beloved, let us love one another; for love is of God. He that loveth not, knoweth not God; for God is love" (4:7-8). "Not that we loved God, but that he loved us, and sent his Son to be the propitiation for our sins. Beloved, if God so loved us, we ought also to love one another" (vs. 10-11).

3. All men approve of this; but do all men practice it? Daily experience shows the contrary. Where are even the Christians who "love one another, as he hath given us commandment"? How many hindrances lie in the way! The two grand, general hindrances are, first, that they cannot all think alike; and, in consequence of this, secondly, they cannot all walk alike; but in several smaller points their practice must differ in proportion to the difference of their sentiments.

4. But although a difference in opinions or modes of worship may prevent an entire external union, yet need it prevent our union in affection? Though we cannot think alike, may we not love alike? May we not be of one heart, though we are not of one opinion? Without all doubt, we may. Herein all the children of God may unite, notwithstanding these smaller differences. These remaining as they are, they may forward one another in love and in good works.

5. Surely in this respect the example of Jehu himself, as mixed a character as he was, is well worthy [of] both the attention and imitation of every serious Christian. "And when he was departed thence, he lighted on Jehonadab the son of Rechab coming to meet him. And he saluted him, and said to him, Is thine heart right, as my heart is with thy heart? And Jehonadab answered, It is. If it be, give me thine hand." [2 Kings 10:15]

The text naturally divides itself into two parts. First, a question proposed by Jehu to Jehonadab: "Is thine heart right, as my heart is with thy heart?" Secondly, an offer made on Jehonadab's answering, "It is."—"If it be, give me thine hand."

I.

1. And, first, let us consider the question proposed by Jehu to Jehonadab, "Is thine heart right, as my heart is with thy heart?"

The very first thing we may observe in these words, is that here is no inquiry concerning Jehonadab's opinions. And yet it is certain, he held some which were very uncommon, indeed quite peculiar to himself; and some which had a close influence upon his practice; on which, likewise, he laid so great a stress as to entail them upon his children's children, to their latest posterity.

This is evident from the account given by Jeremiah, many years after his death: "I took Jaazaniah and his brethren, and all his sons, and the whole house of the Rechabites, . . . and set before them pots full of wine, and cups, and said unto them, Drink ye wine. But they said, We will drink no wine; for Jonadab," or Jehonadab, "the son of Rechab, our father" (it would be less ambiguous, if the words were placed thus: "Jehonadab *our father, the son of* Rechab," out of love and reverence to whom he probably desired his descendants might be called by his name) "commanded us, saying, ye shall drink no wine, neither ye nor your sons for ever. Neither shall ye build house[s], nor sow seed; nor plant vineyard[s], nor have any; but all your days ye shall dwell in tents . . . . And we have obeyed, and done according to all that Jonadab our father commanded us (Jer. 35:3-10).

2. And yet Jehu (although it seems to have been his manner, both in things secular and religious, to *drive furiously*) does not concern himself at all with any of these things, but lets Jehonadab abound in his own sense. And neither of them appears to have given the other the least disturbance touching the opinions which he maintained.

3. It is very possible that many good men now also may entertain peculiar opinions; and some of them may be as singular* herein as even Jehonadab was. And it is certain, so long as *we know* but *in part*, that all men will not see all things alike. It is an unavoidable consequence of the present weakness and shortness of human understanding, that several men will be of several minds, in religion as well as in common life. So it has been from the beginning of the world, and so it will be "till the restitution of all things."

4. [Further]: although every man necessarily believes that every particular opinion which he holds is true (for to believe any opinion is not true, is the same thing as not to hold it); yet can no man be assured that all his own opinions, taken together, are true. Nay, every thinking man is assured they are not, seeing *humanum est errare et nescire*: "To be ignorant of many things, and to mistake in some, is the necessary condition of humanity." This, therefore, [as] he is sensible, is his own case. He knows, in the general, that he himself is mistaken; although in what particulars he mistakes he does not, perhaps cannot, know.

5. I say "perhaps he cannot know"; for who can tell how far invincible ignorance may extend? Or (what comes to the same thing) invincible prejudice, which is often so fixed in tender minds, that it is afterwards impossible to tear up what has taken so deep a root. And who can say, unless he knew every circumstance attending it, how far any mistake is culpable? Seeing all guilt must suppose some concurrence of the will, of which he only can judge who searcheth the heart.

6. Every wise man, therefore, will allow others the same liberty of thinking which he desires they should allow him; and will no more insist on their embracing his opinions than he would have them to insist on his embracing theirs. He bears with those who differ from him, and only asks him with whom he desires to unite in love that single question, "Is thine heart right, as my heart is with thy heart?"

7. We may, secondly, observe that here is no inquiry made concerning Jehonadab's mode of worship, although it is highly probable there was, in this respect also, a very wide difference between them. For we may well believe Jehonadab, as well as all his posterity, worshipped God at Jerusalem! Whereas Jehu did not; he had more regard to state-policy than religion. And, therefore, although he slew the worshippers of Baal, and "destroyed Baal out of Israel," yet from the convenient sin of Jeroboam, the worship of the "golden calves," he "departed not" (2 Kings 10:29).

8. But even among men of an upright heart, men who desire to "have a conscience void of offence," it must needs be that, as long as there are various opinions, there will be various ways of worshipping God; seeing a variety of opinion[s] necessarily implies a variety of practice.

And as in all ages men have differed in nothing more than in their opinions concerning the Supreme Being, so in nothing have they more differed from each other, than in the manner of worshipping him. Had this been only in the heathen world, it would not have been at all surprising; for we know these "by" their "wisdom knew not God"; nor, therefore, could they know how to worship him. But is it not strange that even in the Christian world, although they all agree in the general, "God is a Spirit, and they that worship him must worship him in spirit and in truth"; yet the particular modes of worshipping God are almost as various as among the heathens?

9. And how shall we choose among so much variety? No man can choose for, or prescribe to, another. But everyone must follow the dictates of his own conscience, in simplicity and godly sincerity. He must be fully persuaded in his own mind and then act according to the best light he has. Nor has any creature power to constrain another to walk by his own rule. God has given no right to any of the children of men thus to lord it over the conscience of his brethren. But every man must judge for himself, as every man must give an account of himself to God.

10. Although, therefore, every follower of Christ is obliged, by the very nature of the Christian institution, to be a member of some particular congregation or other, some church, as it is usually termed (which implies a particular manner of worshipping God; for "two cannot walk together unless they be agreed"); yet none can

be obliged by any power on earth but that of his own conscience, to prefer this or that congregation to another, this or that particular manner of worship.

     I know it is commonly supposed that the place of our birth fixes the church to which we ought to belong; that one, for instance, who is born in England, ought to be a member of that which is styled* the Church of England, and consequently, to worship God in the particular manner which is prescribed by that church. I was once a zealous maintainer of this; but I find many reasons to abate of this zeal. I fear it is attended with such difficulties as no reasonable man can get over. Not the least of which is that if this rule had [taken] place, there could have been no Reformation from popery; seeing it entirely destroys the right of private judgment, on which that whole Reformation stands.

    11. I dare not, therefore, presume to impose my mode of worship on any other. I believe it is truly primitive* and apostolic. But my belief is no rule for another.

     I ask not, therefore, of him with whom I would unite in love, Are you of my church, of my congregation? Do you receive the same form of church government, and allow the same church officers, with me? Do you join in the same form of prayer wherein I worship God? I inquire not, "Do you receive the Supper of the Lord in the same posture and manner that I do? Nor whether, in the administration of baptism, you agree with me in admitting sureties for the baptized, in the manner of administering it; or the age of those to whom it should be administered. Nay, I ask not of you (as clear as I am in my own mind) whether you allow baptism and the Lord's Supper at all. Let all these things stand by: we will talk of them, if need be, at a more convenient season. My only question at present is this, "Is thine heart right, as my heart is with thy heart?"

    12. But what is properly implied in the question? I do not mean, What did Jehu imply therein, but what should a follower of Christ understand thereby, when he proposes it to any of his brethren?

    The first thing implied is this: Is thy heart right with God? Dost thou believe his being and his perfections? His eternity, immensity, wisdom, power; his justice, mercy, and truth? Dost thou believe that he now "upholdeth all things by the word of his power?" And that he governs even the most minute, even the most noxious, to his own glory, and the good of them that love him? Hast thou a divine evidence, a supernatural conviction, of the things of God? Dost thou "walk by faith not by sight"? "Looking not at temporal things, but things eternal"?

    13. Dost thou believe in the Lord Jesus Christ, "God over all, blessed for ever"? Is he "revealed in thy soul"? Dost thou know Jesus Christ and him crucified? Does he dwell in thee, and thou in him? Is he formed in thy heart by faith? Having absolutely disclaimed all thy own works, thy own righteousness, hast thou "submitted thyself unto the righteousness of God," "which is by faith in Christ Jesus"? Art thou "found in him, not having thy own righteousness, but the righteousness which is by faith"? And art thou, through him, "fighting the good fight of faith, and laying hold of eternal life"?

    14. Is thy faith *energoumene di' agapes*—filled with the energy of love? Dost thou love God (I do not say "above all things," for it is both an unscriptural and an ambiguous expression), but "with all thy heart, and with all thy mind, and with all thy soul, and with all thy strength"? Dost thou seek all thy happiness in him alone? And dost thou find what thou seekest? Does thy soul continually "magnify the Lord, and thy spirit rejoice in God thy Savior"? Having learned "in everything to give thanks," dost thou find it is a "joyful and a pleasant thing to be thankful"? Is God the center of thy soul, the sum of all thy desires? Art thou accordingly laying up thy treasure in heaven, and counting all things else dung and dross? Hath the love of God cast the love of the world out of thy soul? Then thou art "crucified to the world"; thou art dead to all below; and thy "life is hid with Christ in God."

    15. Art thou employed in doing, "not thy own will, but the will of him that sent thee"? Of him that sent thee down to sojourn here awhile, to spend a few days in a strange land, till, having finished the work he hath given thee to do, thou return to thy Father's house? Is it thy meat and drink "to do the will of thy Father which is in heaven"? Is thine eye single in all things? Always fixed on him? Always looking unto Jesus? Dost thou point at him in whatsoever thou doest? In all thy labor, thy business, thy conversation? Aiming only at the glory of God in all. "Whatsoever thou doest, either in word or deed, doing it all in the name of the Lord Jesus; giving thanks unto God, even the Father, through him"?

    16. Does the love of God constrain thee to serve him with fear, to "rejoice unto him with reverence"? Art thou more afraid of displeasing God than either of death or hell? Is nothing so terrible to thee as the thought of offending the eyes of his glory? Upon this ground, dost thou "hate all evil ways," every transgression of his holy and perfect law. And herein "exercise thyself to have a conscience void of offence toward God and toward man?"

    17. Is thy heart right toward thy neighbor? Dost thou love as thyself all mankind without exception?

    "If you love those only that love you, what thank have ye? Do you "love your enemies"? Is your soul full of good-will, of tender affection, toward them? Do you love even the enemies of God? The unthankful and unholy?

Do your bowels yearn over them? Could you "wish yourself" temporally "accursed" for their sake? And do you show this by "blessing them that curse you, and praying for those that despitefully use you and persecute you"?

18. Do you show your love by your works? While you have time as you have opportunity, do you in fact "do good to all men"—neighbors or strangers, friends or enemies, good or bad?

Do you do them all the good you can? Endeavoring to supply all their wants; assisting them both in body and soul, to the uttermost of your power? If thou art thus minded, may every Christian say—yea, if thou art but sincerely desirous of it, and following on till thou attain—then "thy heart is right, as my heart is with thy heart."

II.

1. "If it be, give me thine hand." I do not mean, "Be of my opinion." You need not; I do not expect or desire it. Neither do I mean, "I will be of your opinion." I cannot; it does not depend on my choice. I can no more think than I can see or hear as I will. Keep you your opinion, I mine; and that as steadily as ever.

You need not even endeavor to come over to me, or bring me over to you. I do not desire you to dispute those points, or to hear or speak one word concerning them. Let all opinions alone on one side and the other. Only "give me thine hand."

2. I do not mean, "Embrace my modes of worship," or, "I will embrace yours." This also is a thing which does not depend either on your choice or mine. We must both act as each is fully persuaded in his own mind. Hold you fast that which you believe is most acceptable to God, and I will do the same.

I believe the episcopal form of church government to be scriptural and apostolic. If you think the presbyterian or independent is better, think so still, and act accordingly. I believe infants ought to be baptized, and that this may be done either by dipping or sprinkling. If you are otherwise persuaded, be so still, and follow your own persuasion. It appears to me that forms of prayer are of excellent use, particularly in the great congregation. If you judge extemporary prayer to be of more use, act suitably to your own judgment. My sentiment is that I ought not to forbid water wherein persons may be baptized; and that I ought to eat bread and drink wine as a memorial of my dying Master. However, if you are not convinced of this, act according to the light you have. I have no desire to dispute with you one moment upon any of the preceding heads. Let all these smaller points stand aside. Let them never come into sight. "If thine heart is as my heart," if thou lovest God and all mankind, I ask no more: "Give me thine hand."

3. I mean, first, love me. And that not only as thou lovest all mankind; not only as thou lovest thine enemies, or the enemies of God, those that hate thee, that "despitefully use thee and persecute thee"; not only as a stranger, as one of whom thou knowest neither good nor evil. I am not satisfied with this. No; "If thine heart be right, as mine with thy heart," then love me with a very tender affection, as a friend that is closer than a brother; as a brother in Christ, a fellow citizen of the New Jerusalem, a fellow soldier engaged in the same warfare, under the same Captain of our salvation. Love me as a companion in the kingdom and patience of Jesus, and a joint heir of his glory.

4. Love me (but in a higher degree than thou dost the bulk of mankind) with the love that is *long-suffering and kind*; that is patient if I am ignorant or out of the way, bearing and not increasing my burden; and is tender, soft, and compassionate still; that *envieth not* if at any time it please God to prosper me in his work even more than thee. Love me with the love that *is not provoked*, either at my follies or infirmities or even at my acting (if it should sometimes so appear to thee) not according to the will of God. Love me so as to *think no evil* of me; to put away all jealousy and evil-surmising. Love me with the love that *covereth all things*; that never reveals either my faults or infirmities; that *believeth all things*, is always willing to think the best, to put the fairest construction on all my words and actions, that *hopeth all things*, either that the thing related was never done; or not done with such circumstances as are related, or, at least, that it was done with a good intention, or in sudden stress of temptation. And hope to the end that whatever is amiss will, by the grace of God, be corrected, and whatever is wanting, supplied, through the riches of his mercy in Christ Jesus.

5. I mean, secondly, commend me to God in all thy prayers; wrestle with him in my behalf, that he would speedily correct what he sees amiss and supply what is wanting in me.

In thy nearest access to the throne of grace, beg of him who is then very present with thee, that my heart may be more as thy heart, more right both toward God and toward man; that I may have a fuller conviction of things not seen, and a stronger view of the love of God in Christ Jesus; may more steadily walk by faith, not by sight, and more earnestly grasp eternal life. Pray that the love of God and of all mankind may be more largely poured into my heart; that I may be more fervent and active in doing the will of my Father which is in heaven, more zealous of good works, and more careful to abstain from all appearance of evil.

6. I mean, thirdly, provoke me to love and to good works. Second thy prayer, as thou hast opportunity, by speaking to me, in love, whatsoever thou believest to be for my soul's health. Quicken me in the work which God has given me to do, and instruct me how to do it more perfectly.

Yea, "smite me friendly and reprove me," whereinsoever I appear to thee to be doing rather my own will than the will of him that sent me. O speak and spare not, whatever thou believest may conduce, either to the amending my faults, the strengthening my weakness, the building me up in love, or the making me more fit, in any kind, for the Master's use.

7. I mean, lastly, love me not in word only, but in deed and in truth. So far as in conscience thou canst (retaining still thy own opinions and thy own manner of worshipping God), join with me in the work of God, and let us go on hand in hand. And thus far, it is certain, thou mayest go.

Speak honorably, wherever thou art, of the work of God, by whomsoever he works, and kindly of his messengers. And, if it be in thy power, not only sympathize with them when they are in any difficulty or distress, but give them a cheerful and effectual assistance, that they may glorify God on thy behalf.

8. Two things should be observed with regard to what has been spoken under this last head. The one, that whatsoever love, whatsoever offices of love, whatsoever spiritual or temporal assistance, I claim from him whose heart is right, as my heart is with his, the same I am ready, by the grace of God, according to my measure, to give him. The other, that I have not made this claim in behalf of myself only, but of all whose heart is right toward God and man, that we may all love one another as Christ hath loved us.

III.

1. One inference we may make from what has been said. We may learn from hence what is a catholic spirit.

There is scarce any expression which has been more grossly misunderstood and more dangerously misapplied, than this. But it will be easy for any who calmly consider the preceding observations to correct any such misapprehensions of it, and to prevent any such misapplication.

For, from hence we may learn, first, that a catholic spirit is not *speculative* latitudinarianism. It is not an indifference to all opinions. This is the spawn of hell, not the offspring of heaven. This unsettledness of thought, this being "driven to and fro, and tossed about with every wind of doctrine," is a great curse, not a blessing, an irreconcilable enemy, not a friend, to true catholicism. A man of a truly catholic spirit has not now his religion to seek. He is fixed as the sun in his judgment concerning the main branches of Christian doctrine. It is true, he is always ready to hear and weigh whatsoever can be offered against his principles. But as this does not show any wavering in his own mind, so neither does it occasion any.

He does not halt between two opinions, nor vainly endeavor to blend them into one. Observe this, you who know not what spirit ye are of, who call yourselves men of a catholic spirit only because you are of a muddy understanding; because your mind is all in a mist; because you have no settled, consistent principles, but are for jumbling all opinions together. Be convinced that you have quite missed your way: you know not where you are. You think you are got into the very spirit of Christ, when, in truth, you are nearer the spirit of Antichrist. Go first and learn the first elements of the gospel of Christ, and then shall you learn to be of a truly catholic spirit.

2. From what has been said, we may learn, secondly, that a catholic spirit is not any kind of *practical* latitudinarianism. It is not indifference as to public worship, or as to the outward manner of performing it. This, likewise, would not be a blessing but a curse. Far from being an help thereto, it would, so long as it remained, be an unspeakable hindrance to the worshipping of God in spirit and in truth. But the man of a truly catholic spirit, having weighed all things in the balance of the sanctuary, has no doubt, no scruple at all, concerning that particular mode of worship wherein he joins. He is clearly convinced that *this* manner of worshipping God is both scriptural and rational. He knows none in the world which is more scriptural, none which is more rational. Therefore, without rambling hither and thither, he cleaves close thereto, and praises God for the opportunity of so doing.

3. Hence we may, thirdly, learn that a catholic spirit is not indifference to all congregations. This is another sort of latitudinarianism, no less absurd and unscriptural than the former. But it is far from a man of a truly catholic spirit. He is fixed in his congregation as well as his principles. He is united to one, not only in spirit, but by all the outward ties of Christian fellowship. There he partakes of all the ordinances of God. There he receives the Supper of the Lord. There he pours out his soul in public prayer, and joins in public praise and thanksgiving. There he rejoices to hear the word of reconciliation, the gospel of the grace of God. With these his nearest, his best-beloved brethren, on solemn occasions, he seeks God by fasting. These particularly he watches over in love, as they do over his soul, admonishing, exhorting, comforting, reproving, and every way building up each other in the faith. These he regards as his own household; and therefore, according to the ability God has given him, naturally cares for them, and provides that they may have all the things that are needful for life and godliness.

4. But while he is steadily fixed in his religious principles in what he believes to be the truth as it is in Jesus; while he firmly adheres to that worship of God which he judges to be most acceptable in his sight; and while he is united by the tenderest and closest ties to one particular congregation—his heart is enlarged toward all mankind, those he knows and those he does not; he embraces with strong and cordial affection neighbors and strangers, friends and enemies. This is catholic or universal love. And he that has this is of a catholic spirit. For love alone gives the title to this character: catholic love is a catholic spirit.

5. If, then, we take this word in the strictest sense, a man of a catholic spirit is one who, in the manner above-mentioned, gives his hand to all whose hearts are right with his heart. One who knows how to value and praise God for all the advantages he enjoys, with regard to the knowledge of the things of God, the true scriptural manner of worshipping him; and, above all, his union with a congregation fearing God and working righteousness. One who, retaining these blessings with the strictest care, keeping them as the apple of his eye, at the same time loves—as friends, as brethren in the Lord, as members of Christ and children of God, as joint partakers now of the present kingdom of God, and fellow heirs of his eternal Kingdom—all, of whatever opinion or worship, or congregation, who believe in the Lord Jesus Christ; who love God and man; who, rejoicing to please and fearing to offend God, are careful to abstain from evil and zealous of good works. He is the man of a truly catholic spirit who bears all these continually upon his heart; who, having an unspeakable tenderness for their persons and longing for their welfare, does not cease to commend them to God in prayer, as well as to plead their cause before men; who speaks comfortably to them and labors, by all his words, to strengthen their hands in God. He assists them to the uttermost of his power in all things, spiritual and temporal. He is ready "to spend and be spent for them"; yea, to lay down his life for their sake.

6. Thou, O man of God, think on these things! If thou art already in this way, go on. If thou hast heretofore mistook the path, bless God who hath brought thee back! And now run the race which is set before thee, in the royal way of universal love. Take heed, lest thou be either wavering in thy judgment, or straitened in thy bowels. But keep an even pace, rooted in the faith once delivered to the saints and grounded in love, in true catholic love, till thou art swallowed up in love for ever and ever!

Lesson 11–The Dangers of Riches

They that will be rich fall into temptation and a snare, and into many foolish
and hurtful desires, which drown men in destruction and perdition.

1 Tim. 6:9

I ask, then, in the name of God, Who of you "desire to be rich?" . . . Who of you desires to have more
than the plain necessaries and conveniences of life? Stop! Consider! What are you doing?
Evil is before you! Will you rush upon the point of a sword? By the grace of God, turn and live!

Open your eyes! Look all around you! Are the richest men the happiest? Have those the largest share
of content[ment] who have the largest possessions? Is not the very reverse true? Is it not a common
observation, that the richest of men are, in general, the most discontented, the most miserable?

John Wesley, The Danger of Riches; §§II.2,10

OUR STARTING POINT

The consumer-driven culture in which many Christians live is a major obstacle to growth in holiness.
Christians constantly face the temptation to pursue the material things of this world, rather than continuing
to pursue holiness. Riches become a problem when they direct our time, energy, and attention away from God.

READING

Read daily the reflection and prayer about the need for Christians to be faithful to God and not to the tangible things of this world. *The Danger of Riches* (1781) deals with how Christians can faithfully live in the places they find themselves.

Day 1   Scan the sermon *The Danger of Riches.* Scan the lesson.
Day 2   Read the Introduction and Part I, §§I.1-I.8. Who are "they who will be rich"?
Day 3   Read Part I, §§I.9-I.19. How do those that desire riches fall into temptation?
Day 4   Read Part II, §§II.1-10. Gain all you can, save all you can, give all you can.
Day 5   Read Part II, §§II.11-20. Read about the grave spiritual danger that comes from desiring riches.
Day 6   Reread the lesson and answer the questions at the end.
Day 7   Rest.

REFLECTION

Jesus said to his disciples, "Truly I tell you, it is hard for the rich to enter the kingdom of heaven. Again, I tell you, it is easier for a camel to go through the eye of a needle than for the rich to enter the kingdom of God." When the disciples heard this, they were greatly astonished and asked, "Who then can be saved?" Jesus looked at them and said, "With human beings this is impossible, but with God all things are possible."

Matt. 19:23-26; TNIV

PRAYER

Pray daily before study:
Lord Jesus,

Thank you for making it possible for me to enter the kingdom of God! Help me to be loyal to you and your kingdom, not to the things of this world. All that I have and all that I am are yours. Help me to spend my life and my resources in ways that bring you honor and glory. Amen.

Prayer concerns for this week:

Daily Reflections

Day 1   Scan the sermon *The Danger of Riches*. Scan the lesson.

Meaning for me:

Day 2   Read the Introduction and Part I, §§I.1-I.8. Who are "they who will be rich"?

Meaning for me:

Day 3   Read Part I, §§I.9-I.19. How do those that desire riches fall into temptation?

Meaning for me:

Day 4   Read Part II, §§II.1-10. Gain all you can, save all you can, give all you can.

Meaning for me:

Day 5   Read Part II, §§II.11-20. Read about the grave spiritual danger that comes from desiring riches.

Meaning for me:

Day 6   Reread the lesson and answer the questions at the end.

Meaning for me:

Obstacles in the Way of Salvation

We have learned quite a bit about the Way of Salvation. In this lesson we will consider some potential obstacles to our growth in holiness, particularly the major obstacle that John Wesley saw— the danger of wealth and affluence.

Through the final decades of his ministry [Wesley] issued a series of warnings that the increasing wealth of the Methodists correlated directly with a decline in their spiritual growth and in the progress of the revival.[2]
Randy Maddox, *Responsible Grace.*

One of the most interesting results of the early Methodist revival was that it encouraged people to stop wasting their pay on frivolous things. For example, many men who had spent large amounts of their pay on liquor stopped drinking, began saving more money, and took it home to their families. Over time, the result was that people who had been poor began to accumulate some measure of wealth. The idea of "rich" Methodists, however, made Wesley very uncomfortable because affluence diverts our attention from a God-centered life. So, as the movement continued to mature, Wesley increasingly felt the need to address how Christians should live faithfully in relation to their material possessions.

As you read *The Danger of Riches*, you may feel that, at times, Wesley was being overly concerned about this issue. In the passage quoted from the sermon at the right, for example, his language is very pointed and strong. It is hard to read this sermon without feeling guilty and, perhaps, becoming slightly defensive. As you read this sermon, you may ask yourself, "Isn't this a ridiculous standard? Is it realistic? Isn't this a little fanatical?"

Who of you desires to have more than the plain necessaries and conveniences of life? Stop! Consider! What are you doing? Evil is before you! Will you rush upon the point of a sword? By the grace of God, turn and live!
John Wesley, *The Danger of Riches*, §II.2

Wesley did use strong language in order to highlight what is at stake for us as we wrestle with the things of this world that divide our loyalty to God. But so does Jesus![1] For instance, Jesus makes stark statements about wealth and possessions, such as: "No one can serve two masters. Either you will hate the one and love the other, or you will be devoted to the one and despise the other. You cannot serve both God and money." (Matt. 6:24; *TNIV*)

In another sermon about wealth and possessions, *Causes of the Inefficacy of Christianity*, Wesley sought to answer a haunting question: "Why has Christianity done so little good in the world?" Toward the end of his life, Wesley looked at the revival and wondered why Methodists were not making more spiritual progress. Even though scriptural Christianity was preached and Christian discipline was practiced, Wesley felt that the movement was failing in the goal of restoring souls in the image of God. Worldly influences seemed to have penetrated the lives of religious people more deeply than faith in Jesus Christ and a desire to follow him, no matter the cost. These influences and desires thus became obstacles to Methodism's ability to accomplish its goal of "spreading Scriptural holiness."

Therefore, as Wesley surveyed the Methodist movement, he became convinced that one of the main sources of the problem was how people dealt with their money. Wesley believed that this was the major obstacle that caused many Christians to stop growing in holiness and even to fall away from the grace they had already received. He believed that wealth was dangerous because it fed the desire of having more, of wanting to be rich. This desire

Have they not hurt you already, have they not wounded you in the tenderest part, by slackening, if not utterly destroying, your 'hunger and thirst after righteousness'? Have you now the same longing that you had once, for the whole image of God? . . . Have they not cooled (if not quenched) your love to God? . . . And if your love of God is in anywise decayed, so is also your love of neighbor . . . If you lose love, you lose all.
John Wesley, *The Danger of Riches*, §II.12

gradually divided the loyalties of Christians so that their zeal for growing in holiness would slowly be undermined and tamed. The ultimate result would be that Christians look and live just like the rest of the world. They gradually come to serve the world and its priorities, rather than serving Jesus Christ and having the priorities that come as the result of being one of his disciples.

Stewardship Is the Issue

Wesley's sermons dealing with wealth are based on the conviction that all that we have comes as a gift from God and that our primary loyalty should always be to Jesus Christ. The ultimate goal for Christians, in dealing with money and possessions, is to be good stewards of what God has entrusted to us. For Christians, this means that we use what God has entrusted to us in the same way the Lord Jesus would use it if he were in direct control of it, instead of us. As contemporary Wesleyan theologian Rebekah Miles has commented, "When Christians use their money properly to serve God and neighbor, they are acting as God's faithful stewards. But when Christians use money improperly, by hoarding it or using it for their own luxury, they are robbing God as well as the poor for whom excess wealth is intended."[3] This sentiment echoes many of the themes in Wesley's writing on wealth.

The Solution: Gain, Save, and (Most of All) Give All You Can

As Wesley considered the situation facing Methodism and as he searched the Scriptures, he found a solution that he believed would enable Christians to keep their focus on being followers of Christ, rather than on acquiring more "stuff." First, Wesley challenged Christians to "gain all that they can."[4] Christians should be productive members of society. They should earn as much money as they can through the work they do. The only restraint on this is that the money must come in ways that are not sinful or would lead others into sin. Recent scandals in the business world serve as a powerful reminder of the ethical temptations that Christians face in the workplace. Wesley reminds us that we ought to live as Christians at work as well as in the rest of our lives.

After they gain all that they can, Wesley challenged Christians as faithful stewards to save all that they can. Wesley encouraged Christians to think about what they did with their money and to be frugal. In his own life, Wesley was constantly trying to find ways to save more money and to spend less. As his income began to increase due to selling some of the books he had published, he committed to living on the same amount of money on which he had lived before his income had risen.

In Wesley's day, Methodists were quite successful at these two practices. They were hard workers who earned what they could and they lived frugally; eventually some were able to accumulate significant savings. However, Wesley feared that those who gained and saved all that they could, but ignored the final exhortation—to give all that they can—were in a very dangerous situation.

NOTES, REFLECTIONS, AND QUESTIONS

Throughout Wesley's many admonitions about riches, we see that he is not concerned that his hearers give simply because it is the right thing to do, because it is a command of Scripture, because it is an expression of their faith, or because the poor need their help. Wesley instructs them to give both because giving will be a means of grace, strengthening their love and, just as important, because failure to give is a means of diminishment, weakening their love and endangering their very souls.[5]

Rebekah Miles, "Why Wesley Feared for the Souls of the Rich," *The Wesleyan Tradition: A Paradigm for Renewal*, pp. 108-109

Your way lies plain before your face; if you have courage, walk in it. Having gained, in a right sense, all you can, and saved all you can; in spite of nature, and custom, and worldly prudence, give all you can.

John Wesley, The Danger of Riches, §II.8

Let us for each other care,
each the other's burdens bear;
to thy church the pattern give,
show how true believers live.

Charles Wesley, "Jesus, Lord, we look to thee," *Methodist 1889 Hymnal #509*

Open your eyes! Look all around you! Are the richest men the happiest? Have those the largest share of content who have the largest possessions? Is not the very reverse true? Is it not a common observation, that the richest of men are, in general, the most discontented, the most miserable?

John Wesley, *The Danger of Riches*, §II.10

The advice to give all that you can was by far the most important recommended practice, and it was by far the most often ignored advice. Christians in Wesley's day, and in our own day, have found it very difficult to part with all the money so carefully earned and saved, once it was theirs. Still, giving all that you can was the most important part of the formula, because only by giving all would the Christian avoid falling into the "temptation and snare" (Tim. 6:9) of riches and comfortable living.

As noted earlier in this lesson, Jesus warned his disciples in the Sermon on the Mount (Matt. 6:24) that it is impossible to serve two masters, God and Money, for we will soon love one and come to hate the other. Jesus saw this in his ministry when the rich young man walked away from him because he could not part with his wealth. Ultimately, Jesus' concern—and consequently Wesley's concern—was with our hearts and our loyalty. This message is certainly relevant for living in our consumer-driven culture! It is so easy to believe promises of happiness that would come from wealth and possessions; and, once we begin to believe such empty promises, it is a small step from enjoying our wealth to worshipping it, to the detriment of our faith and to the destruction of our souls.

NOTES, REFLECTIONS, AND QUESTIONS

Just then a man came up to Jesus and asked, "Teacher, what good thing must I do to get eternal life?"

Jesus answered, "If you want to be perfect, go sell your possessions and give to the poor, and you will have treasure in heaven. Then come, follow me." When the young man heard this, he went away sad, because he had great wealth.

Matt. 19:16,21-22; *TNIV*

Do you gain all you can, and save all you can? Then you must, in the nature of things, grow rich. Then if you have any desire to escape the damnation of hell, give all you can; otherwise I can have no more hope of your salvation, than of that of Judas Iscariot.[6]

John Wesley, *Causes of the Inefficacy of Christianity*, §17

RESPONDING FAITHFULLY

Read the Scripture passages that are referenced in this lesson. What other passages of Scripture can you think of that relate to wealth and possessions? Do these passages confirm or challenge Wesley's ideas?

_____

_____

What do you find to be the major obstacles to living in this world faithfully as a Christian? How are your money and possessions an obstacle to holy living?

_____

_____

Does this lesson have any implications for how Christians today think about going into debt in order to make purchases?

_____

_____

Do you gain, save, and give all that you can? What is one specific thing that you can do in order to pledge your allegiance to the kingdom of God, rather than the kingdom of wealth?

_____

_____

How can your church become a more faithful steward of the money with which God has blessed you?

_____

_____

_____

LEARNING MORE

Read other parts of Wesley's writing which deal with the danger of riches:
- *Causes of the Inefficacy of Christianity*
- *On God's Vineyard*
- *The Use of Money.*

Read parts of:
- Henry H. Knight III., *Eight Life-Enriching Practices of United Methodists*, Ch. 8.
- John O. Gooch, *John Wesley for the 21ˢᵗ Century: Set Apart for Social Witness*, Ch. 8.

LOOKING AHEAD

Christian Perfection—the goal of sanctification.

Teacher Helps provides follow-up questions that may be useful in class discussions.

END NOTES

[1] To read more about the attitudes of Jesus in the New Testament about wealth and possession, see Sondra Ely Wheeler, *Wealth as Peril and Obligation: The New Testament on Possessions.*
[2] Randy L. Maddox, *Responsible Grace*, op. cit., p. 245.
[3] Rebekah Miles, "Why Wesley Feared for the Souls of the Rich," Paul Wesley Chilcote, Editor, *The Wesleyan Tradition: A Paradigm for Renewal.* Nashville: Abingdon Press, 2002. p. 105.
[4] The following material Wesley first articulated in his famous sermon, *The Use of Money.*
[5] Miles, op. cit., pp. 108-109.
[6] John Wesley, "Causes of the Inefficacy of Christianity," July 2, 1789, §18. Found in Jackson, *Works*, Volume III, Sermon CXVI.

Reading for Lesson 11. The Danger of Riches (1781)

They that will be rich fall into temptation and a snare, and into many foolish and hurtful desires, which drown men in destruction and perdition (1 Tim. 6:9).

Introduction

1. How innumerable are the ill consequences which have followed from men's not knowing, or not considering, this great truth [1 Tim. 6:9]! And how few are there even in the Christian world that either know or duly consider it! Yea, how small is the number of those, even among real Christians, who understand and lay it to heart! Most of these too pass it very lightly over, scarce remembering there is such a text in the Bible. And many put such a construction upon it, as makes it of no manner of effect. "They that will be rich," say they, "that is, will be rich at all events, who will be rich right or wrong, that are resolved to carry their point, to compass this end, whatever means they use to attain it—they 'fall into temptation,' and into all the evils enumerated by the Apostle." But truly, if this were all the meaning of the text, it might as well have been out of the Bible.

2. This is so far from being the whole meaning of the text, that it is no part of its meaning. The Apostle does not here speak of gaining riches unjustly, but of quite another thing: his words are to be taken in their plain, obvious sense, without any restriction or qualification whatsoever. St. Paul does not say, "They that will be rich *by evil means*, by theft, robbery, oppression, or extortion; they that will be rich by fraud or dishonest art; but simply, "they that will be rich." These, allowing, supposing the means they use to be ever so innocent, "fall into temptation and a snare, and into many foolish and hurtful desires, which drown men in destruction and perdition."

3. But who believes that? Who receives it as the truth of God? Who is deeply convinced of it? Who preaches this? Great is the company of preachers at this day, regular and irregular. But who of them, all openly and explicitly, preaches this strange doctrine? It is the keen observation of a great man, "The pulpit is a fearful preacher's stronghold." But who even in his stronghold, has the courage to declare so unfashionable a truth? I do not remember that in threescore years I have heard one sermon preached upon this subject. And what author, within the same term, has declared it from the press? At least, in the English tongue? I do not know one. I have neither seen nor heard of any such author. I have seen two or three who just touch upon it;

but none that treats of it professedly. I have myself frequently touched upon it in preaching, and twice in what I have published to the world: once in explaining our Lord's Sermon on the Mount, and once in the discourse on the "mammon of unrighteousness." But I have never yet either published or preached any sermon expressly upon the subject. It is high time I should—that I should at length speak as strongly and explicitly as I can, in order to leave a full and clear testimony behind me, whenever it pleases God to call me hence.

4. O that God would give me to speak *right* and *forcible* words! And you to receive them in honest and humble hearts! Let it not be said, "They sit before thee as my people, and they hear thy words; but they will not do them. Thou art unto them as one that hath a pleasant voice, and can play well on an instrument; for they hear thy words, but they do them not! O that ye may "not be forgetful hearers, but doers of the word," that ye may be "blessed in your deed! In this hope I shall endeavor,

I. First, to explain the Apostle's words; and,

II. Secondly, to apply them.

But O! "Who is sufficient for these things? Who is able to stem the general torrent? To combat all the prejudices, not only of the vulgar, but of the learned and the religious world? Yet nothing is too hard for God! Still his grace is sufficient for us. In his name, then, and by his strength I will endeavor to explain the words of the Apostle.

I.

1. And, first, let us consider, what it is to "be rich." What does the Apostle mean by this expression?

The preceding verse fixes the meaning of this: "Having food and raiment" (literally *covering*, for the word includes *lodging* as well as *clothes*), "let us be therewith content." "But they that will be rich"; that is, who will have more than these; more than food and coverings. It plainly follows, whatever is more than these is, in the sense of the Apostle, *riches*; whatever is above the plain necessaries or at most conveniences, of life. Whoever has sufficient food to eat, and raiment to put on, with a place where to lay his head, and something over, is *rich*.

2. Let us consider, secondly, what is implied in that expression, "they that will be rich." And does not this imply, first, they that desire to be rich, to have more than *food* and *coverings*; they that seriously and deliberately desire more than food to eat, and raiment to put on, and a place where to lay their head—more than the plain necessaries and conveniences of life? All, at least, who allow themselves in this desire, who see no harm in it, desire to be rich.

3. And so do, secondly, all those that calmly, deliberately, and of set purpose *endeavor* after more than food and coverings; that aim at and endeavor after, not only so much worldly substance as will procure them the necessaries and conveniences of life, but more than this, whether to lay it up, or lay it out in superfluities. All these undeniably prove their "desire to be rich" *by their endeavors after it.*

4. Must we not, thirdly, rank among those that desire to be rich all that, in fact, "lay up treasures on earth"—a thing as expressly and clearly forbidden by our Lord as either adultery or murder? It is allowed (1) that we are to provide necessaries and conveniences for those of our own household; (2) that men in business are to lay up as much as is necessary for the carrying on of that business; (3) that we are to leave our children what will supply them with necessaries and conveniences after we have left the world; and (4) that we are to provide things honest in the sight of all men, so as to "owe no man anything"? But to lay up any more, when this is done, is what our Lord has flatly forbidden. When it is calmly and deliberately done, it is a clear proof of our desiring to be rich. And thus to lay up money is no more consistent with good conscience, than to throw it into the sea.

5. We must rank among them, fourthly, all who *possess* more of this world's goods than they use according to the will of the [divine] Donor: I should rather say, of the Proprietor, for he only *lends* them to us; or, to speak more strictly, entrusts them to us as stewards, reserving the *property* of them to himself. And, indeed, he cannot possibly do otherwise, seeing they are the work of his hands; he is, and must be, the Possessor of heaven and earth. This is his inalienable right; a right he cannot divest himself of. And, together with that portion of his goods which he hath lodged in our hands he has delivered to us a writing, specifying the purposes for which he has entrusted us with them. If therefore we keep more of them in our hands than is necessary for the preceding purposes, we certainly fall under the charge of "desiring to be rich." Over and above that, we are guilty of burying our Lord's talent in the earth, and on that account are liable to be pronounced wicked, because unprofitable, servants.

6. Under this imputation of "desiring to be rich," fall, fifthly, all "lovers of money." The word properly means, those that *delight in money*; those that take pleasure in it; those that seek their happiness therein, that brood over their gold and silver, bills or bonds. Such was the man described by the fine Roman painter, who broke out into that natural soliloquy:

. . . *Populus me sibilat, at mihi plaudo Ipse domi simul ac nummos contemplor in arca quoties.*

[The following is Francis's translation of these lines from Horace [Satires]:

"Let them his on, While, in my own opinion fully blest, I count my money, and enjoy my chest."—Edit.]

If there are any vices which are not natural to man, I should imagine this is one—as money of itself does not seem to gratify any natural desire or appetite of the human mind; and as, during an observation of sixty years, I do not remember one instance of a man given up to the love of money, till he had neglected to employ this precious talent according to the will of his Master. After this, sin was punished by sin—and this evil spirit was permitted to enter into him.

7. But beside this gross sort of covetousness, the love of money, there is a more refined species of covetousness, termed by the great Apostle, *pleonexia*—which literally means *a desire of having more*, more than we have already. And those also come under the denomination of "they that will be rich." It is true that this desire, under proper restrictions, is innocent; nay, commendable. But when it exceeds the bounds (and how difficult is it not to exceed them!), then it comes under the present censure.

8. But who is able to receive these hard sayings? Who can believe that they are the great truths of God? Not many wise, not many noble, not many famed for learning; none, indeed, who are not taught of God. And who are they whom God teaches? Let our Lord answer: "If any man be willing to do his will, he shall know of the doctrine whether it be of God." Those who are otherwise minded will be so far from receiving it, that they will not be able to understand it. Two as sensible men as most in England sat down together, some time since, to read over and consider that plain discourse on, "Lay not up for yourselves treasures upon earth." After much deep consideration, one of them broke out, "Positively, I cannot understand it. Pray, do *you* understand it, Mr. L.? Mr. L. honestly replied, "Indeed, not I. I cannot conceive what Mr. W.[1] means. I can make nothing at all of it." So utterly blind is our natural understanding touching the truth of God!

9. Having explained the former part of the text, "They that will be rich," and pointed out in the clearest manner I could, the persons spoken of; I will now endeavor, God being my helper, to explain what is spoken of them: "They fall into temptation and a snare, and into many foolish and hurtful desires, which drown men in destruction and perdition."

"They fall into temptation." This seems to mean much more than simply, "they are tempted." They *enter into the temptation*: they fall plump down into it. The waves of it compass them about and cover them all over. Of those who thus enter into temptation, very few escape out of it. And the few that do are sorely scorched by it, though not utterly consumed. If they escape at all, it is with the skin of their teeth, and with deep wounds that are not easily healed.

10. They fall, secondly, "into a snare," the snare of the devil, which he hath purposely set in their way. I believe the Greek word properly means a gin, a steel trap, which shows no appearance of danger. But as soon as any creature touches the spring, it suddenly closes, and either crushes its bones in pieces, or consigns it to inevitable ruin.

11. They fall, thirdly, "into many foolish and hurtful desires" (*anoetous*—silly, senseless, fantastic); as contrary to reason, to sound understanding, as they are to religion; *hurtful*, both to body and soul, tending to weaken, yea, destroy every gracious and heavenly temper; [and] destructive of that faith which is of the operation of God, of that hope which is full of immortality; of love to God and to our neighbor, and of every good word and work.

12. But what desires are these? This is a most important question, and deserves the deepest consideration.

In general, they may all be summed up in one, the desiring happiness out of [without] God. This includes, directly, or remotely, every foolish and hurtful desire. St. Paul expresses it by "loving the creature more than the Creator"; and by being "lovers of pleasure more than lovers of God." In particular, they are (to use the

---

[1] Ed: "W." presumably refers to John Wesley himself.

exact and beautiful enumeration of St. John) "the desire of the flesh, the desire of the eyes, and the pride of life"—all of which the desire of riches naturally tends both to beget and to increase.

13. "The desire of the flesh" is generally understood in far too narrow a meaning. It does not, as is commonly supposed, refer to one of the senses only, but takes in all the pleasures of sense, the gratification of any of the outward senses. It has reference to the *taste* in particular. How many thousands do we find at this day, in whom the ruling principle is the desire to enlarge the pleasure of *tasting*! Perhaps they do not gratify this desire in a gross manner, so as to incur the imputation of intemperance; much less so as to violate health or impair their understanding by gluttony or drunkenness. But they live in a genteel, regular sensuality; in an elegant epicurism, which does not hurt the body, but only destroys the soul, keeping it at a distance from all true religion.

14. Experience shows that the imagination is gratified chiefly by means of the eye. Therefore, "the desire of the eyes," in its natural sense, is the desiring and seeking happiness in gratifying the imagination. Now, the imagination is gratified either by grandeur, by beauty, or by novelty—chiefly by the last, for neither grand nor beautiful objects please any longer than they are new.

15. Seeking happiness in *learning*, of whatever kind, falls under "the desire of the eyes"; whether it be in history, languages, poetry, or any branch of natural or experimental philosophy. Yea, we must include the several kinds of learning, such as geometry, algebra, and metaphysics. For if our supreme delight be in any of these, we are herein gratifying "the desire of the eyes."

16. "The pride of life" (whatever else that very uncommon, expression *he alazoneia tou biou*, may mean) seems to imply chiefly, the *desire of honor*, of the esteem, admiration, and applause of men; as nothing more directly tends both to beget and cherish pride than the honor that cometh of men. And as *riches* attract much admiration, and occasion much applause, they proportionably minister food for pride, and so may also be referred to this head.

17. *Desire of ease* is another of these foolish and hurtful desires; desire of avoiding every cross, every degree of trouble, danger, difficulty; a desire of slumbering out of life, and going to heaven (as the vulgar say) upon a feather-bed. Everyone may observe how riches first beget, and then confirm and increase this desire, making men more and more soft and delicate; more unwilling, and indeed more unable, to "take up their cross daily"; to "endure hardship as good soldiers of Jesus Christ," and to "take the kingdom of heaven by violence."

18. Riches, either desired or possessed, naturally lead to some or other of these foolish and hurtful desires; and by affording the means of gratifying them all, naturally tend to increase them. And there is a near connection between unholy desires and every other unholy passion and temper. We easily pass from these to pride, anger, bitterness, envy, malice, revengefulness; to a head-strong, unadvisable, unreprovable spirit: indeed to every temper that is earthly, sensual, or devilish. All these the desire or possession of riches naturally tends to create, strengthen, and increase.

19. And by so doing, in the same proportion as they prevail, they "pierce men through with many sorrows"; sorrows from remorse, from a guilty conscience; sorrows flowing from all the evil tempers which they inspire or increase; sorrows inseparable from those desires themselves, as every unholy desire is an uneasy desire; and sorrows from the contrariety of those desires to each other, whence it is impossible to gratify them all. And, in the end, "they drown" the body in pain, disease, "destruction," and the soul in everlasting "perdition."

II.

1. I am, in the second place, to apply what has been said. And this is the principal point. For what avails the clearest knowledge, even of the most excellent things, even of the things of God, if it go no farther than speculation, if it be not reduced to practice? He that hath ears to hear, let him hear! And what he hears, let him instantly put in practice. O that God would give me the thing which I long for: that, before I go hence and am no more seen, I may see a people wholly devoted to God, crucified to the world, and the world crucified to them! A people truly given up to God, in body, soul, and substance! How cheerfully should I then say, "Now lettest thou thy servant depart in peace"!

2. I ask, then, in the name of God, who of *you* "desire to be rich"? Which of *you* (ask your own hearts in the sight of God) seriously and deliberately desire (and perhaps applaud yourselves for so doing, as no small instance of your *prudence*) to have more than food to eat, and raiment to put on, and a house to cover you? Who of you desires to have more than the plain necessaries and conveniences of life? Stop! Consider! What are you doing? Evil is before you! Will you rush upon the point of a sword? By the grace of God, turn and live!

3. By the same authority I ask, who of you are *endeavoring* to be rich? To procure for yourselves more than the plain necessaries and conveniences of life? Lay, each of you, your hand to your heart, and seriously inquire,

"Am I of that number? Am I laboring, not only for what I want, but for more than I want? May the Spirit of God say to everyone whom it concerns, "Thou art the man!"

4. I ask, thirdly, who of you are in fact "laying up for yourselves treasures upon earth"? Increasing in goods? Adding, as fast as you can, house to house, and field to field! As long as *thou* thus "dost well unto thyself, men will speak good of thee." They will call thee a wise, a prudent man! A man that *minds the main chance.* Such is, and always has been, the wisdom of the world. But God saith unto thee, "Thou fool! Art thou not 'treasuring up to thyself wrath against the day of wrath, and revelation of the righteous judgment of God'?"

5. Perhaps you will ask, "But do not you yourself advise, to gain all we can, and to save all we can? And is it possible to do this without both *desiring* and *endeavoring to be rich*? Nay, suppose our endeavors are successful, without actually laying up treasures upon earth? I answer, It is possible. You may gain all you can without hurting either your soul or body; you may save all you can, by carefully avoiding every needless expense; and yet never lay up treasures on earth, nor either desire or endeavor so to do.

6. Permit me to speak as freely of myself as I would of another man. I *gain all I can* (namely, by writing) without hurting either my soul or body. I *save all I can*, not willingly wasting anything, not a sheet of paper, not a cup of water. I do not lay out anything, not a shilling, unless as a sacrifice to God. Yet by *giving all I can*, I am effectually secured from "laying up treasures upon earth." Yea, and I am secured from either desiring or endeavoring it as long as I give all I can. And that I do this, I call all that know me, both friends and foes, to testify.

7. But some may say, "Whether you endeavor it or no, you are undeniably *rich*. You have more than the necessaries of life." I have. But the Apostle does not fix the charge, barely on *possessing* any quantity of goods, but on possessing more than we employ according to the will of the Donor.

Two-and-forty years ago, having a desire to furnish poor people with cheaper, shorter, and plainer books than any I had seen, I wrote many small tracts, generally a penny apiece; and afterwards several larger. Some of these had such a sale as I never thought of; and, by this means, I unawares became rich. But I never desired or endeavored after it. And now that it is come upon me unawares, I lay up no treasures upon earth: I lay up nothing at all. My desire and endeavor, in this respect is to "wind my bottom round the year." I cannot help leaving my books behind me whenever God calls me hence; but, in every other respect, my own hands will be my executors.

8. Herein, my brethren, let you that are rich, be even as I am. Do you that possess more than food and raiment ask: "What shall we do? Shall we throw into the sea what God hath given us?" God forbid that you should! It is an excellent talent; it may be employed much to the glory of God. Your way lies plain before your face; if you have courage, walk in it. Having *gained*, in a right sense, *all you can*, and *saved all you can*—in spite of nature, and custom, and worldly prudence—*give all you can*. I do not say, "Be a good Jew, giving a tenth of all you possess." I do not say, "Be a good Pharisee, giving a fifth of all your substance." I dare not advise you to give half of what you have; no, nor three quarters; but all! Lift up your hearts, and you will see clearly in what sense this is to be done.

> If you desire to be a "faithful and a wise steward," out of that portion of your Lord's goods which he has for the present lodged in your hands, but with the right of resumption whenever it pleaseth him: (1) provide things needful for yourself—food to eat, raiment to put on, whatever nature moderately requires for preserving you both in health and strength; and (2) provide these for your wife, your children, your servants, or any others who pertain to your household. If, when this is done, there be an overplus left, then do good to "them that are of the household of faith." If there be an overplus still, "as you have opportunity, do good unto all men." In so doing, you give all you can; nay, in a sound sense, all you have. For all that is laid out in this manner, is really given to God. You render unto God the things that are God's, not only by what you give to the poor, but also by that which you expend in providing things needful for yourself and your household. [The Use of Money, §III.3]

9. O ye Methodists, hear the word of the Lord! I have a message from God to all men, but to *you* above all. For above forty years I have been a servant to you and to your fathers. And I have not been as a reed shaken with the wind: I have not varied in my testimony. I have testified to you the very same thing from the first day even until now. But "who hath believed our report?" I fear, not many rich. I fear there is need to apply to some of *you* those terrible words of the Apostle: "Go to now, ye rich men! Weep and howl for the miseries which shall come upon you. Your gold and silver is cankered, and the rust of them shall witness against you, and shall eat your flesh, as it were fire." Certainly it will, unless ye both save all you can and give

all you can. But who of you hath considered this since you first heard the will of the Lord concerning it? Who is now determined to consider and practice it? By the grace of God begin today!

10. O ye lovers of money, hear the word of the Lord! Suppose ye that money, though multiplied as the sand of the sea, can give happiness? Then you are "given up to a strong delusion, to believe a lie"—a palpable lie, confuted daily by a thousand experiments. Open your eyes! Look all around you! Are the richest men the happiest? Have those the largest share of content[ment] who have the largest possessions? Is not the very reverse true? Is it not a common observation, that the richest of men are, in general, the most discontented, the most miserable? Had not the far greater part of them more content when they had less money? Look into your breasts. If you are increased in goods, are you proportionably increased in happiness? You have more substance, but have you more content? You know the contrary. You know that, in seeking happiness from riches, you are only striving to drink out of empty cups. And let them be painted and gilded ever so finely, they are empty still.

11. O ye that *desire* or *endeavor to be rich*, hear ye the word of the Lord! Why should ye be stricken any more? Will not even experience teach you wisdom? Will ye leap into a pit with your eyes open? Why should you any more "fall into temptation"? It cannot be but temptation will beset you, as long as you are in the body. But though it should beset you on every side, why will you *enter into* it? There is no necessity for this: it is your own voluntary act and deed. Why should you any more plunge yourselves *into a snare*, into the trap Satan has laid for you, that is ready to break your bones in pieces. to crush your soul to death? After fair warning, why should you sink any more into "foolish and hurtful desires"? Desires as foolish, as inconsistent with reason as they are with religion itself—desires that have done you more hurt already than all the treasures upon earth can countervail.

12. Have they not hurt you already, have they not wounded you in the tenderest part, by slackening, if not utterly destroying, your "hunger and thirst after righteousness? Have you now the same longing that you had once, for the whole image of God? Have you the same vehement desire, as you formerly had, of "going on unto perfection?" Have they not hurt you by weakening your *faith*? Have you now faith's "abiding impression, realizing things to come"? Do you endure, in all temptations, from pleasure or pain, "seeing him that is invisible?" Have you every day, and every hour, an uninterrupted sense of his presence? Have they not hurt you with regard to your *hope*? Have you now a hope full of immortality? Are you still big with earnest expectation of all the great and precious promises? Do you now "taste the powers of the world to come"? Do you "sit in heavenly places with Christ Jesus"?

13. Have they not so hurt you, as to stab your religion to the heart? Have they not cooled (if not quenched) your *love to God*? This is easily determined. Have you the same delight in God which you once had? Can you now say,

I nothing want beneath, above; Happy, happy in thy love!

I fear not. And if your love of God is in any wise decayed, so is also your love of your neighbor. You are then hurt in the very life and spirit of your religion! If you lose love, you lose all.

14. Are not you hurt with regard to your *humility*? If you are increased in goods, it cannot well be otherwise. Many will think you a better, because you are a richer, man; and how can you help thinking so yourself? Especially considering the commendations which some will give you in simplicity, and many with a design to serve themselves of you.

If you are hurt in your humility it will appear by this token: you are not so teachable as you were, not so advisable; you are not so easy to be convinced, not so easy to be persuaded. You have a much better opinion of your own judgment and are more attached to your own will. Formerly one might guide you with a thread; now one cannot turn you with a cart-rope. You were glad to be admonished or reproved, but that time is past. And you now account a man your enemy because he tells you the truth. O let each of you calmly consider this, and see if it be not your own picture!

15. Are you not equally hurt with regard to your *meekness*? You had once learned an excellent lesson of him that was meek as well as lowly in heart. When you were reviled, you reviled not again. You did not return railing for railing, but contrariwise, blessing. Your love was *not provoked*, but enabled you on all occasions to overcome evil with good. Is this your case now? I am afraid not. I fear you cannot "bear all things." Alas, it may rather be said, you can bear nothing: no injury, nor even affront! How quickly are you ruffled! How readily does that occur: "What! To use *me* so! What insolence is this! How did he dare to do it! I am not now what I was once. Let him know I am now able to defend myself." You mean, to revenge yourself. And it is much if you are not willing, as well as able; if you do not take your fellow servant by the throat.

16. And are you not hurt in your *patience* too? Does your love now "endure all things"? Do you still "in patience possess your soul," as when you first believed? O what a change is here! You have again learnt to be frequently out of humor. You are often fretful; you feel, nay, and give way to peevishness. You find abundance of things go so cross that you cannot tell how to bear them!

> Many years ago, I was sitting with a gentleman in London, who feared God greatly and generally gave away, year by year, nine-tenths of his yearly income. A servant came in and threw some coals on the fire. A puff of smoke came out. The baronet threw himself back in his chair and cried out, "O Mr. Wesley, these are the crosses I meet with daily!" Would he not have been less impatient, if he had had fifty, instead of five thousand, pounds a year?

17. But to return. Are not you who have been successful in your endeavors to increase in substance, insensibly sunk into softness of mind, if not of body too? You no longer rejoice to "endure hardship, as good soldiers of Jesus Christ." You no longer "rush into the kingdom of heaven, and take it as by storm." You do not cheerfully and gladly "deny yourselves, and take up your cross daily." You cannot deny yourself the poor pleasure of a little sleep, or of a soft bed, in order to hear the word that is able to save your souls! Indeed, you "cannot go out so early in the morning; besides it is dark, nay, cold; perhaps rainy, too. Cold, darkness, rain, all these together—I can never think of it." You did not say so when you were a poor man. You then regarded none of these things. It is the change of circumstances which has occasioned this melancholy change in your body and mind. You are but the shadow of what you were! What have riches done for you?

> "But it cannot be expected I should do as I have done, for I am now grown old." Am not I grown old as well as you? Am not I in my seventy-eighth year? Yet, by the grace of God, I do not slack my pace yet. Neither would *you*, if you were a poor man still.

18. You are so deeply hurt that you have well-nigh lost your zeal for works of mercy, as well as of piety. You once pushed on, through cold or rain, or whatever cross lay in your way, to see the poor, the sick, the distressed. You went about doing good, and found out those who were not able to find you. You cheerfully crept down into their cellars, and climbed up into their garrets:

To supply all their wants,
And spend and be spent in assisting his saints.

You found out every scene of human misery, and assisted according to your power:

Each form of woe your generous pity moved;
Your Savior's face you saw, and, seeing, loved.

Do you now tread in the same steps? What hinders? Do you fear spoiling your silken coat? Or is there another lion in the way? Are you afraid of catching vermin? And are you not afraid lest the roaring lion should catch *you*? Are you not afraid of him that hath said, "Inasmuch as ye have not done it unto the least of these, ye have not done it unto me"? What will follow? "Depart, ye cursed, into everlasting fire prepared for the devil and his angels!"

19. In time past how mindful were you of that word: "Thou shalt not hate thy brother in thy heart: Thou shalt in any wise reprove thy brother, and not suffer sin upon him!" You *did* reprove, directly or indirectly, all those that sinned in your sight. And happy consequences quickly followed. How good was a word spoken in season! It was often as an arrow from the hand of a giant. Many a heart was pierced. Many of the stout-hearted, who scorned to hear a sermon,

Fell down before his cross subdued,
And felt his arrows dipped in blood.

But which of you now has that compassion for the ignorant, and for them that are out of the way? They may wander on for *you*, and plunge into the lake of fire, without let or hindrance. Gold hath steeled your hearts. You have something else to do.

Unhelp'd, unpitied let the wretches fall.

20. Thus have I given you, O ye gainers, lovers, possessors of riches, one more (it may be the last) warning. O that it may not be in vain! May God write it upon all your hearts! Though "it is easier for a camel to go through the eye of a needle, than for a rich man to enter into the kingdom of heaven," yet the things impossible with men are possible with God. Lord, speak! And even the rich men that hear these words shall enter thy kingdom—shall "take the kingdom of heaven by violence," shall "sell all for the pearl of great price"— shall be "crucified to the world, and count all things dung, that they may win Christ!"

Lesson 12–Christian Perfection

For it is by grace you have been saved, through faith.

Eph. 2:8; NIV

Look for [Christian perfection] then every day, every hour, every moment! Why not this hour, this moment? Certainly you may look for it now, if you believe it is by faith. And by this token you may surely know whether you seek it by faith or by works. If by works, you want something to be done first, **before** you are sanctified. You think, I must first be or do thus or thus. Then you are seeking it by works unto this day. If you seek it by faith, you may expect it **as you are**; and if as you are, then expect it **now**. It is of importance to observe that there is an inseparable connection between these three points, expect it **by** faith, expect it **as you are**, and expect it **now**!

John Wesley, *The Scripture Way of Salvation*; §III.18 (emphasis in the original)

Pure and spotless let us be . . . perfectly restored in thee.

Charles Wesley, "Love Divine, All Loves Excelling" (1747)

OUR STARTING POINT

Sanctification is the process of growing in holiness. For Wesley, sanctification—like justification—is received by grace through faith. The goal and the logical result of the process of sanctification is being perfected in love—loving God and neighbor completely.

READING

Read daily the reflection and prayer about every Christian's calling to "go on to perfection." *The Scripture Way of Salvation* (1765) discusses salvation as involving both justification and sanctification. It also points to the possibility of full salvation, which for Wesley means being perfected in love.

Day 1   Read the Introduction and scan the rest of the sermon. Faith and salvation sum up the essence of Christian faith. Scan Lesson 12.

Day 2   Read Part I, §§I.1-9. Salvation is a present reality, not simply something that will happen in the future.

Day 3   Read Part II, §§I.1-4. We are justified and sanctified by faith.

Day 4   Read Part III, §§III.1-6. Faith is the sole condition for both our justification and sanctification.

Day 5   Read Part III, §§III.7-13. Read about the importance of repentance and works of piety and mercy for salvation.

Day 6   Read Part III, §§III.14-18. Sanctification is by faith and leads to entire sanctification, perfection in love. This is also by faith. Reread the lesson and answer the questions at the end.

Day 7   Rest.

REFLECTION

It is God's will that you should be sanctified . . . For God did not call us to be impure, but to live a holy life.

1 Thess. 4:3,7; *TNIV*

PRAYER

Lord Jesus, when I think about the possibility of perfection, there are so many things that come to mind. As I reflect on who I am and what I've done, the possibility of perfection seems unattainable. I know without a doubt that I cannot make myself perfect. But as I read the Scriptures, I see that it is your will that I love God and neighbor completely, that I not only receive forgiveness, but that I actually live a holy life. So, help me not to despair over how far away I am currently from perfection. Rather, help me to see that this is part of your will for my life and that when I am weak you are strong. Help me to have faith that if my being made perfect in love is your will, then you are certainly able to do this in and for me. Fill me with your presence and the desire simply to do your will and to follow you all the days of my life. Amen.

Prayer concerns for this week:

Daily Reflections

Day 1   Read the Introduction and scan the rest of the sermon. Faith and salvation sum up the essence of Christian faith. Scan Lesson 12.

Meaning for me:

Day 2   Read Part I, §§I.1-9. Salvation is a present reality, not simply something that will happen in the future.

Meaning for me:

Day 3   Read Part II, §§II.1-4. We are justified and sanctified by faith.

Meaning for me:

Day 4   Read Part III, §§III.1-6. Faith is the sole condition for both our justification and sanctification.

Meaning for me:

Day 5   Read Part III, §§III.7-13. Read about the importance of repentance and works of piety and mercy for salvation.

Meaning for me:

Day 6   Read Part III, §§III.14-18. Sanctification is by faith and leads to entire sanctification, perfection in love. This is also by faith. Reread the lesson and answer the questions at the end.

Meaning for me:

Summarizing the Way of Salvation

By this point in our series we have read sermons dealing with the Wesleyan understanding of prevenient, justifying, and sanctifying grace. As we discuss the sermon, *The Scripture Way of Salvation*, we will notice how Wesley brings together all of these ideas into one coherent Way of Salvation. And we will add to our understanding of the Way of Salvation by looking more closely at Wesley's understanding of Christian perfection, or entire sanctification.

In *The Scripture Way of Salvation*, Wesley argued that the end, or purpose, of Christianity is "salvation; the means to attain it, faith" (§Intro.1). He then briefly discussed prevenient grace and established that both justification and sanctification are received by grace through faith, not by our attainment.

Once Wesley established that salvation is the purpose of Christianity and that faith is the means to it, he looked carefully at the extent to which Christians can expect to be saved in this life. Wesley argued that salvation "is not something at a distance—it is a present thing; a blessing which, through the free mercy of God, ye are now in possession of" (§I.1). This present salvation has the goal of being perfected in love—being saved "to the uttermost."[1] Entire sanctification, or Christian perfection, can be described most succinctly as a Christian's growth in holiness by God's grace until he or she reaches the goal of being perfected in love.

The Grand Depositum of the Wesleyan Revival

Wesley's doctrine of Christian perfection was and remains controversial, in part because it carried the doctrine of sanctification to its natural conclusion. If sanctification is the process of growing in holiness by God's grace, where does this growth lead? What is the goal, or the result in our lives toward which sanctification is moving? Wesley described the goal as entire sanctification or Christian perfection. Wesley stated that this is not just an elusive goal, but something that God actually wants Christians to reach.

Wesley argued that entire sanctification is the logical outcome of the process of sanctification, and that it is entirely in accord with the witness of Scripture. Wesley believed so strongly in this doctrine that he declared Christian perfection to be "the grand *depositum* which God has lodged with the people called Methodists; and for the sake of propagating this chiefly he appeared to have raised us up."[5] Further, "he believed that Methodism would remain vital only so long as it proclaimed" the message of entire sanctification.[6]

What Christian Perfection Is and Is Not

In another sermon, *Christian Perfection*,[7] Wesley discusses what Christian perfection is and is not. Christians are not perfect in knowledge in this life; full revelation will come when Christ returns.

NOTES, REFLECTIONS, AND QUESTIONS

This sermon [The Scripture Way of Salvation] is one of Wesley's most frequently read discourses and one of the most useful... Wesley recommended this sermon as a clear exposition of the teaching of the Bible about the way of salvation.[2]

Kenneth Kinghorn, *John Wesley on Christian Practice*

To Wesley's thinking, Christian growth was normative for every member of the congregation, not just a zealous elite.[3]

D. Michael Henderson, *John Wesley's Class Meeting: A Model for Making Disciples*

Be perfect, therefore, as your heavenly Father is perfect.

Matt. 5:48; *TNIV*

The doctrine of entire sanctification was the most controversial of Wesley's doctrines, and with good reason, for it carries the doctrine of sanctification to its logical conclusion, to the complete renewal of the human creature, insofar as that renewal is possible under the conditions of finitude.[4]

Theodore Runyon, *The New Creation*

Therefore, with minds that are alert and fully sober, set your hope on the grace to be brought to you when Jesus Christ is revealed at his coming. As obedient children, do not conform to the evil desires you had when you lived in ignorance. But just as he who called you is holy, so be holy in all you do; for it is written: "Be holy, because I am holy."

1 Peter 1:13-16; *TNIV*

Christians who have been perfected in love are also not free from mistakes. Similarly, freedom from infirmities is not implied by Christian perfection. Wesley clarifies that by infirmities he means "all inward or outward imperfections which are not of a moral nature."[8] Finally, Wesley argues that Christian perfection does not include freedom from temptations.

In other words, when we talk about Christian perfection, or entire sanctification, we are not talking about absolute perfection of performance or behavior. Rather, we are referring to a perfection of motive or intent within the believer. Robin Maas has nicely summarized what we mean by being perfected in love: "it means *loving to full capacity*."[9]

The Wesleyan doctrine of Christian perfection means that the Christian has one motive: love for God and neighbor. According to Wesley's sermon, *On Perfection*, entire sanctification is the fulfillment of the greatest commandment (Matt. 22:37-39) to love the Lord with all your heart, soul, and mind and to love your neighbor as yourself. It is also having the same mind that was in Christ Jesus (Phil. 2:5).

Christian perfection involves the embodiment of the fruits of the spirit that Paul speaks of in Gal. 5:22-23. And perfection brings us nearer to the goal of restoring the image of God, which is the overall aim of the Way of Salvation. Perfection is where the root of original sin is finally extinguished. Steve Harper has summarized a contemporary understanding of Christian perfection as having singleness of intention, power over sin, radical dependence on Christ, equipment for ministry, and an experience in which to grow.[10]

Christian perfection is a dynamic experience of growth, not a fixed state or condition. When we are asked, "Do you expect to be perfected in love?" and we answer affirmatively, we are making a claim about Christ's work and God's power, not our ability.

How We Are Made Perfect in Love

Now that we have an idea of what was and was not contained in the idea of Christian perfection, we can look more closely at *how* we are made perfect by God's grace. For Wesley, "faith is the condition, and the only condition, of sanctification, exactly as it is of justification" (§III.3). Wesley describes the faith by which we are made perfect as having four main characteristics. Christians are made perfect by having faith (1) that God has promised in the Scriptures to do this, (2) that what God has promised God is able to perform, (3) that God is able and willing to do it now, and, finally, (4) that God actually does it (§§III.14-17).

While Wesley emphasizes the importance of faith for Christian perfection, he also lifts up the importance of repentance (§§III.2,5,6) and good works for entire sanctification. Works of piety (such as prayer, searching the Scriptures, partaking of the Lord's Supper, and fasting) and works of mercy (such as feeding the hungry, clothing the naked, entertaining the stranger, and visiting those who are in prison or sick) are necessary in order for the

"Teacher, which is the greatest commandment in the Law?" Jesus replied, "'Love the Lord your God with all your heart and with all your soul and with all your mind.' This is the first and greatest commandment. And the second is like it: 'Love your neighbor as yourself.'"

Matt. 22:36-39; *TNIV*

May the God of peace himself *sanctify you entirely*; and may your spirit and soul and body be kept sound and blameless at the coming of our Lord Jesus Christ. The one who calls you is faithful, and he will do this.

1 Thess. 5:23-24; *NRSV*

Come, Almighty to deliver,
let us all thy life receive;
Suddenly return and never,
nevermore thy temples leave.
Thee we would be always blessing,
serve thee as thy hosts above,
Pray and praise thee without ceasing,
glory in thy perfect love.

Finish, then, thy new creation;
pure and spotless let us be.
Let us see thy great salvation
perfectly restored in thee;
Changed from glory into glory,
till in heaven we take our place,
Till we cast our crowns before thee,
lost in wonder, love, and praise.

Charles Wesley, "Love Divine, All Loves Excelling" (1747)—*UM Hymnal* #384; *AME Hymnal* #455; *CME Hymnal* #44; *Afr. Amer. Heritage Hymnal* #440; *Free Methodist Ch. & The Wesleyan Ch. Hymnal* #335; *Ch. of Nazarene Hymnal* #507

children of God to work out their salvation (§§III.9,10). It is important for us to understand that we are *made* perfect by grace; we do not perfect ourselves. Nevertheless, we are not passive in the process of our growth in holiness. God wills that we participate in the process of the renewal of our souls in the image of our creator.

The Scriptural Foundation of Christian Perfection

Finally, it is crucial to emphasize the scriptural foundations for Wesley's doctrine of entire sanctification. Wesley did not invent or create anything new—he simply preached and taught what he found in Scripture. Jesus would not have said "be perfect as your heavenly Father is perfect" if this were impossible. Several passages that provide Biblical support for the possibility of being made perfect in love include Matt. 5:48; 2 Cor. 13:9; 1 Thess. 3:13; 4:3; Heb. 12:14; 1 Peter 1:14-16; and 1 Jn. 4:12,17. If we believe that God wants to fill us with a single intention—to love God and neighbor—then Christian perfection does nothing more than affirm that the work which God *wants* to do in us, God is *able* to do in us. As Theodore Runyon has said, "If God's aim is a new creation, can ours be any less?"[11]

NOTES, REFLECTIONS, AND QUESTIONS

Wesley was convinced that the Christian life did not have to remain a life of continual struggle. He believed that both Scripture and Christian tradition attested that God's loving grace can transform our lives to the point where our own love for God and others becomes a "natural response.... To deny this possibility would be to deny the sufficiency of God's empowering grace—to make the power of sin greater than that of grace.[12]

Randy Maddox, *Responsible Grace*, p. 188

Examination of Preachers (1766)

From the very beginnings of the Wesleyan movement, candidates for full-time preaching have been asked essentially the same series of questions. The first four are as follows[13]:

1. Have you faith in Christ?

2. Are you going on to perfection?

3. Do you expect to be perfected in love in this life?

4. Are you groaning after it?

RESPONDING FAITHFULLY

What are the possibilities and the limitations of Christian perfection?

Read the Scripture passages that are referenced in this lesson (above). How strong do you think the scriptural case is for Wesley's understanding of perfection?

How would your life be different from this day forward if you took seriously Wesley's advice of expecting to be made perfect in love by faith, as you are?

_____

_____

_____

_____

_____

Think of someone you know (or have known) who seems to be "going on to perfection." What characteristics do you see manifest in his or her life?

_____

_____

_____

_____

_____

How would your congregation be different if the members believed and sought to live into Wesley's understanding of entire sanctification or Christian perfection?

_____

_____

_____

_____

_____

_____

LEARNING MORE

Read other parts of Wesley's writing which deal with his explanation of Christian perfection:
* *Christian Perfection*
* *On Perfection*
* *A Plain Account of Christian Perfection.*

Read parts of:
* Randy L. Maddox, *Responsible Grace: John Wesley's Practical Theology*
* Harald Lindström, *Wesley and Sanctification.*

LOOKING AHEAD

God's New Creation—The Culmination of the Way of Salvation.

Teacher Helps provides follow-up questions that may be useful in class discussions.

END NOTES

[1] William B. Fitzgerald summarized the Way of Salvation in this way: "All need to be saved; all can be saved; all can know themselves to be saved; and all can be saved to the uttermost." John A Vickers, *A Dictionary of Methodism in Britain and Ireland*, p. 127.

[2] Kenneth Cain Kinghorn, Editor, *The Standard Sermons in Modern English*. Volume 2, *John Wesley on Christian Practice*, Nashville: Abingdon Press, 2002, p. 187.

[3] D. Michael Henderson, *John Wesley's Class Meeting: A Model for Making Disciples*. Nappanee, Indiana: Evangel Publishing House, 1997, p. 45.

[4] Runyon, op. cit., p. 91.

[5] John Wesley, "Letter to Robert Carr Brackenbury, September 15, 1790," Jackson, *Works*, vol.13 (*Letters*), p. 9.

[6] Steve Harper, *The Way to Heaven: The Gospel According to John Wesley*. Grand Rapids, Zondervan, 1983, p. 88.

[7] Some excerpts from this sermon are provided in Teacher Helps.

[8] John Wesley, *Christian Perfection*, §I.7.

[9] Robin Maas, *Crucified Love*. Nashville: Abingdon Press, 1989, p. 30.

[10] Steve Harper, op. cit., pp. 84-87.

[11] Theodore Runyon, *The New Creation*: John Wesley's Theology Today. Nashville: Abingdon Press, 1998, p. 233.

[12] Randy Maddox, *Responsible Grace*, op. cit., p. 188.

[13] John Wesley, *Minutes of the Methodist Conferences*, London: Mason, 1862, Vol. 1 (1744-1798), p. 54; quoted in Richard P. Heitzenrater, *Wesley and the People Called Methodists*. Nashville: Abingdon Press, 1994, p. 235. Compare *The Book of Discipline of The United Methodist Church 2004*, §336: Have you faith in Christ? Are you going on the perfection? Do you expect to be made perfect in love in this life? Are you earnestly striving after it?

Reading for Lesson 12. The Scripture Way of Salvation (1765)

Ye are saved through faith (Eph. 2:8).

Introduction

1. Nothing can be more intricate, complex, and hard to be understood than religion, as it has been often described. And this is not only true concerning the religion of the heathens, even many of the wisest of them, but concerning the religion of those also who were, in some sense, Christians; yea, and men of great name in the Christian world, men who seemed to be pillars thereof. Yet how easy to be understood, how plain and simple a thing, is the genuine religion of Jesus Christ; provided only that we take it in its native form, just as it is described in the oracles of God! It is exactly suited, by the wise Creator and Governor of the world, to the weak understanding and narrow capacity of man in his present state. How observable is this, both with regard to the end it proposes, and the means to attain that end! The end is, in one word, salvation; the means to attain it, faith.

2. It is easily discerned that these two little words—I mean faith and salvation—include the substance of all the Bible, the marrow, as it were, of the whole Scripture. So much the more should we take all possible care to avoid all mistake concerning them, and to form a true and accurate judgment concerning both the one and the other.

3. Let us then seriously inquire,

I. What is Salvation?

II. What is that faith whereby we are saved? and,

III. How we are saved by it.

I.

1. And, first, let us inquire, What is *salvation*? The salvation which is here spoken of is not what is frequently understood by that word, the going to heaven, eternal happiness. It is not the soul's going to paradise, termed by our Lord, "Abraham's bosom." It is not a blessing which lies on the other side death, or, as we usually speak, in the other world. The very words of the text itself put this beyond all question: "Ye *are* saved." It is not something at a distance: it is a present thing; a blessing which, through the free mercy of God, ye are now in possession of. Nay, the words may be rendered, and that with equal propriety, "Ye *have been* saved." So that the salvation which is here spoken of might be extended to the entire work of God, from the first dawning of grace in the soul, till it is consummated in glory.

2. If we take this in its utmost extent, it will include all that is wrought in the soul by what is frequently termed "natural conscience," but more properly, "preventing grace"; all the drawings of the Father, the desires after God, which, if we yield to them, increase more and more; all that light wherewith the Son of God "enlighteneth everyone that cometh into the world"; *showing* every man "to do justly, to love mercy, and to walk humbly with his God"—all the *convictions* which his Spirit, from time to time, works in every child of man—although it is true, the generality of men stifle them as soon as possible, and after a while forget, or at least deny, that ever they had them at all.

3. But we are at present concerned only with that salvation which the Apostle is directly speaking of. And this consists of two general parts, justification and sanctification.

Justification is another word for pardon. It is the forgiveness of all our sins, and, what is necessarily implied therein, our acceptance with God. The price whereby this hath been procured for us (commonly termed "the meritorious cause of our justification"), is the blood and righteousness of Christ; or, to express it a little more clearly, all that Christ hath done and suffered for us till he "poured out his soul for the transgressors." The immediate effects of justification are: the peace of God, a "peace that passeth all understanding"; and a "rejoicing in hope of the glory of God," "with joy unspeakable and full of glory."

4. And at the same time that we are justified, yea, in that very moment, *sanctification* begins. In that instant we are born again, born from above, born of the Spirit. There is a *real* as well as a *relative* change. We are inwardly renewed by the power of God. We feel "the love of God shed abroad in our heart by the Holy Ghost which is given unto us": producing love to all mankind, and more especially to the children of God; expelling the love of the world, the love of pleasure, of ease, of honor, of money, together with pride, anger, self-will, and every other evil temper—in a word, changing the earthly, sensual, devilish mind into "the mind which was in Christ Jesus."

5. How naturally do those who experience such a change imagine that all sin is gone; that it is utterly rooted out of their heart, and has no more any place therein! How easily do they draw that inference, "I *feel* no sin; therefore, I *have* none. It does not *stir*; therefore, it does not *exist*. It has no *motion*; therefore, it has no *being*!"

6. But it is seldom long before they are undeceived, finding sin was only suspended, not destroyed. Temptations return, and sin revives, showing it was but stunned before, not dead. They now feel two principles in themselves, plainly contrary to each other, "the flesh lusting against the Spirit"; nature opposing the grace of God. They cannot deny that—although they still feel power to believe in Christ and to love God; and although his "Spirit" still "witnesses with their spirits that they are the children of God"—yet they feel in themselves sometimes pride or self-will, sometimes anger or unbelief. They find one or more of these frequently *stirring* in their heart, though not *conquering*; yea, perhaps "thrusting sore at them that they may fall"; but the Lord is their help.

7. How exactly did Macarius, fourteen hundred years ago, describe the present experience of the children of God?—"The unskillful," or inexperienced, "when grace operates, presently imagine they have no more sin. Whereas they that have discretion cannot deny that even we who have the grace of God may be molested again. For we have often had instances of some among the brethren, who have experienced such grace as to affirm that they had no sin in them; and yet, after all, when they thought themselves entirely freed from it, the corruption that lurked within was stirred up anew, and they were well-nigh burned up."

8. From the time of our being born again, the gradual work of sanctification takes place. We are enabled "by the Spirit" to "mortify the deeds of the body," of our evil nature; and as we are more and more dead to sin, we are more and more alive to God. We go on from grace to grace, while we are careful to "abstain from all appearance of evil," and are "zealous of good works," as we have opportunity, doing good to all men; while we walk in all his ordinances blameless, therein worshipping him in spirit and in truth; while we take up our cross, and deny ourselves every pleasure that does not lead us to God.

9. It is thus that we wait for entire sanctification; for a full salvation from all our sins—from pride, self-will, anger, unbelief; or, as the Apostle expresses it, "go on to perfection." But what is perfection? The word has various senses: here it means perfect love. It is love excluding sin; love filling the heart, taking up the whole capacity of the soul. It is love "rejoicing evermore, praying without ceasing, in everything giving thanks."

II.

But what is faith through which we are saved? This is the second point to be considered.

1. Faith, in general, is defined by the Apostle, *elegchos ou blepomenon*—an *evidence*, a divine *evidence and conviction* (the word means both) *of things not seen*—not visible, not perceivable either by sight, or by any other of the external senses. It implies both a supernatural *evidence* of God, and of the things of God; a kind of spiritual *light* exhibited to the soul; and a supernatural *sight* or perception thereof. Accordingly, the Scripture speaks of God's giving sometimes light, sometimes a power of discerning it. So St. Paul: "God, who commanded light to shine out of darkness, hath shined in our hearts, to give us the light of the knowledge of the glory of God in the face of Jesus Christ." And elsewhere the same Apostle speaks of "the eyes of" our "understanding being opened." By this two-fold operation of the Holy Spirit, having the eyes of our soul both *opened* and *enlightened*, we see the things which the natural "eye hath not seen, neither the ear heard." We have

a prospect of the invisible things of God; we see the *spiritual world*, which is all round about us, and yet no more discerned by our natural faculties than if it had no being. And we see the *eternal world*, piercing through the veil which hangs between time and eternity. Clouds and darkness then rest upon it no more, but we already see the glory which shall be revealed.

2. Taking the word in a more particular sense, faith is a divine *evidence* and *conviction*, not only that "God was in Christ, reconciling the world unto himself," but also that Christ loved *me*, and gave himself for *me*. It is by this faith (whether we term it the *essence*, or rather a *property* thereof) that we *receive Christ*; that we receive him in all his offices, as our Prophet, Priest, and King. It is by this that he is "made of God unto us wisdom, and righteousness, and sanctification, and redemption."

3. "But is this the *faith of assurance*, or *faith of adherence*?" The Scripture mentions no such distinction. The Apostle says, "There is one faith, and one hope of our calling"; one Christian, saving faith; "as there is one Lord," in whom we believe, and "one God and Father of us all." And it is certain, this faith necessarily implies an *assurance* (which is here only another word for *evidence*, it being hard to tell the difference between them) that Christ loved *me*, and gave himself for *me*. For "he that believeth" with the true living faith "hath the witness in himself." "The Spirit witnesseth with his spirit that he is a child of God." "Because he is a son, God hath sent forth the Spirit of his Son into his heart, crying, Abba, Father"; giving him an assurance that he is so, and a childlike confidence in him. But let it be observed that, in the very nature of the thing, the assurance goes before the confidence. For a man cannot have a childlike confidence in God till he knows he is a child of God. Therefore, confidence, trust, reliance, adherence, or whatever else it be called, is not the first, as some have supposed, but the second, branch or act of faith.

4. It is by this faith we are saved, justified, and sanctified, taking that word in its highest sense. But how are we justified and sanctified by faith? This is our third head of inquiry. And this being the main point in question, and a point of no ordinary importance, it will not be improper to give it a more distinct and particular consideration.

III.

1. And, first, how are we justified by faith? In what sense is this to be understood? I answer, faith is the condition, and the only condition, of justification. It is the *condition*: none is justified but he that believes; without faith no man is justified. And it is the *only condition*: this alone is sufficient for justification. Everyone that believes is justified, whatever else he has or has not. In other words: no man is justified till he believes; every man when he believes is justified.

2. "But does not God command us to repent also? Yea, and to 'bring forth fruits meet for repentance'—to cease, for instance, from doing evil, and learn to do well? And is not both the one and the other of the utmost necessity, insomuch that if we willingly neglect either, we cannot reasonably expect to be justified at all? But if this be so, how can it be said that faith is the only condition of justification?" God does undoubtedly command us both to repent, and to bring forth fruits meet for repentance; which, if we willingly neglect, we cannot reasonably expect to be justified at all. Therefore, both repentance and fruits meet for repentance are, in some sense, necessary to justification. But they are not necessary in the *same sense* with faith, nor in the *same degree*. Not in the *same degree*; for those fruits are only necessary *conditionally*, if there be time and opportunity for them. Otherwise a man may be justified without them, as was the *thief* upon the cross (if we may call him so; for a late writer has discovered that he was no thief, but a very honest and respectable person!), but he cannot be justified without faith; this is impossible. Likewise, let a man have ever so much repentance, or ever so many of the fruits meet for repentance, yet all this does not at all avail: he is not justified till he believes. But the moment he believes, with or without those fruits, yea, with more or less repentance, he is justified—not in the *same sense*, for repentance and its fruits are only *remotely* necessary, necessary in order to [have] faith; whereas faith is *immediately* and *directly* necessary to justification. It remains that faith is the only condition, which is *immediately* and *proximately* necessary to justification.

3. "But do you believe we are sanctified by faith? We know you believe that we are justified by faith; but do not you believe, and accordingly teach, that we are sanctified by our works?" So it has been roundly and vehemently affirmed for these five-and-twenty years. But I have constantly declared just the contrary, and that in all manner of ways. I have continually testified in private and in public that we are sanctified as well as justified by faith. And, indeed, the one of these great truths does exceedingly illustrate the other. Exactly as we are justified by faith, so are we sanctified by faith. Faith is the condition, and the only condition, of

sanctification, exactly as it is of justification. It is the *condition*: none is sanctified but he that believes; without faith no man is sanctified. And it is the *only condition*: this alone is sufficient for sanctification. Everyone that believes is sanctified, whatever else he has or has not. In other words, no man is sanctified till he believes; every man when he believes is sanctified.

4. "But is there not a repentance consequent upon, as well as a repentance previous to, justification? And is it not incumbent on all that are justified to be 'zealous of good works'? Yea, are not these so necessary, that if a man willingly neglect them, he cannot reasonably expect that he shall ever be sanctified in the full sense; that is, perfected in love? Nay, can he grow at all in grace, in the loving knowledge of our Lord Jesus Christ? Yea, can he retain the grace which God has already given him? Can he continue in the faith which he has received, or in the favor of God? Do not you yourself allow all this, and continually assert it? But, if this be so, how can it be said that faith is the only condition of sanctification?"

5. I do allow all this, and continually maintain it as the truth of God. I allow there is a repentance consequent upon, as well as a repentance previous to, justification. It is incumbent on all that are justified to be zealous of good works. And these are so necessary, that if a man willingly neglect them, he cannot reasonably expect that he shall ever be sanctified. He cannot grow in grace, in the image of God, the mind which was in Christ Jesus; nay, he cannot retain the grace he has received; he cannot continue in faith, or in the favor of God. What is the inference we must draw herefrom? Why, that both repentance, rightly understood, and the practice of all good works—works of piety, as well as works of mercy (now properly so called, since they spring from faith), are, in some sense, necessary to sanctification.

6. I say "repentance rightly understood"; for this must not be confounded with the former repentance. The repentance consequent upon justification is widely different from that which is antecedent to it. This implies no guilt, no sense of condemnation, no consciousness of the wrath of God. It does not suppose any doubt of the favor of God, or any "fear that hath torment." It is properly a conviction, wrought by the Holy Ghost, of the *sin* which still *remains* in our heart, of the *phronema sarkos, the carnal mind*, which "does still *remain*" (as our Church speaks) "even in them that are regenerate"; although it does no longer *reign*: it has not now dominion over them. It is a conviction of our proneness to evil, of a heart bent to backsliding, of the still continuing tendency of the flesh to lust against the Spirit. Sometimes, unless we continually watch and pray, it lusteth to pride, sometimes to anger, sometimes to love of the world—love of ease, love of honor, or love of pleasure—more than of God. It is a conviction of the tendency of our heart to self-will, to atheism, or idolatry; and above all, to unbelief; whereby, in a thousand ways, and under a thousand pretenses, we are ever departing, more or less, from the living God.

7. With this conviction of the sin remaining in our hearts, there is joined a clear conviction of the sin remaining in our lives; still *cleaving* to all our words and actions. In the best of these we now discern a mixture of evil, either in the spirit, the matter, or the manner of them—something that could not endure the righteous judgment of God, were he extreme to mark what is done amiss.

Where we least suspected it, we find a taint of pride or self-will, of unbelief or idolatry; so that we are now more ashamed of our best duties than formerly of our worst sins. And hence we cannot but feel that these are so far from having anything meritorious in them, yea, so far from being able to stand in sight of the divine justice, that for those also we should be guilty before God, were it not for the blood of the covenant.

8. Experience shows that—together with this conviction of sin *remaining* in our hearts and *cleaving* to all our words and actions, as well as the guilt which on account thereof we should incur were we not continually sprinkled with the atoning blood—one thing more is implied in this repentance; namely, a conviction of our helplessness, of our utter inability to think one good thought, or to form one good desire; and much more to speak one word aright, or to perform one good action, but through his free, almighty grace, first preventing us, and then accompanying us every moment.

9. "But what good works are those, the practice of which you affirm to be necessary to sanctification?" First, all works of piety, such as public prayer, family prayer, and praying in our closet; receiving the Supper of the Lord; searching the Scriptures, by hearing, reading, meditating; and using such a measure of fasting or abstinence as our bodily health allows.

10. Secondly, all works of mercy, whether they relate to the bodies or souls of men—such as feeding the hungry, clothing the naked, entertaining the stranger, visiting those that are in prison, or sick, or variously afflicted; such as the endeavoring to instruct the ignorant, to awaken the stupid sinner, to quicken the lukewarm, to confirm the wavering, to comfort the feeble-minded, to succor the tempted, or contribute in any

manner to the saving of souls from death. This is the repentance, and these the "fruits meet for repentance," which are necessary to full sanctification. This is the way wherein God hath appointed his children to wait for complete salvation.

11. Hence may appear the extreme mischievousness of that seemingly innocent opinion that there is no sin in a believer, that all sin is destroyed, root and branch, the moment a man is justified. By totally preventing that repentance, it quite blocks up the way to sanctification. There is no place for repentance in him who believes there is no sin either in his life or heart. Consequently, there is no place for his being perfected in love, to which that repentance is indispensably necessary.

12. Hence it may likewise appear that there is no possible danger in *thus* expecting full salvation. For suppose we were mistaken, suppose no such blessing ever was or can be attained, yet we lose nothing. Nay, that very expectation quickens us in using all the talents which God has given us; yea, in improving them all, so that when our Lord cometh, he will receive his own with increase.

13. But to return; though it be allowed that both this repentance and its fruits are necessary to full salvation; yet they are not necessary either in the *same sense* with faith, or in the *same degree*. Not in the *same degree*; for these fruits are only necessary *conditionally*, if there be time and opportunity for them. Otherwise a man may be sanctified without them. But he cannot be sanctified without faith. Likewise, let a man have ever so much of this repentance, or ever so many good works, yet all this does not at all avail: he is not sanctified till he believes. But the moment he believes, with or without those fruits, yea, with more or less of this repentance, he is sanctified. Not in the *same sense*, for this repentance and these fruits are only *remotely* necessary— necessary in order to [have] the continuance of his faith, as well as the increase of it; whereas faith is *immediately* and *directly* necessary to sanctification. It remains that faith is the only condition which is *immediately* and *proximately* necessary to sanctification.

14. "But what is that faith whereby we are sanctified—saved from sin, and perfected in love?" It is a divine evidence and conviction, first, that God hath promised it in the Holy Scripture. Till we are thoroughly satisfied of this, there is no moving one step farther. And one would imagine there needed not one word more to satisfy a reasonable man of this, than the ancient promise, "Then will I circumcise thy heart, and the heart of thy seed, to love the Lord thy God with all thy heart, and with all thy soul." How clearly does this express the being perfected in love!—how strongly imply the being saved from all sin! For as long as love takes up the whole heart, what room is there for sin therein?

15. It is a divine evidence and conviction, secondly, that what God hath promised he is able to perform. Admitting, therefore, that "with men it is impossible" to "bring a clean thing out of an unclean," to purify the heart from all sin, and to fill it with all holiness; yet this creates no difficulty in the case, seeing "with God all things are possible." And surely no one ever imagined it was possible to any power less than that of the Almighty! But if God speaks, it shall be done. God saith, "Let there be light; and there" is "light"!

16. It is, thirdly, a divine evidence and conviction that he is able and willing to do it now. And why not? Is not a moment to him the same as a thousand years? He cannot want more time to accomplish whatever is his will. And he cannot want or stay for any more *worthiness* or *fitness* in the persons he is pleased to honor. We may therefore boldly say, at any point of time, "Now is the day of salvation!" "Today, if ye will hear his voice, harden not your hearts!" "Behold, all things are now ready! Come unto the marriage!"

17. To this confidence that God is both able and willing to sanctify us *now*, there needs to be added one thing more—a divine evidence and conviction that *he doeth it*. In that hour it is done. God says to the inmost soul, "According to thy faith be it unto thee"! Then the soul is pure from every spot of sin; it is clean "from all unrighteousness." The believer then experiences the deep meaning of those solemn words, "If we walk in the light as he is in the light, we have fellowship one with another, and the blood of Jesus Christ his Son cleanseth us from all sin."

18. "But does God work this great work in the soul *gradually* or *instantaneously*?" Perhaps it may be gradually wrought in some. I mean in this sense—they do not advert to the particular moment wherein sin ceases to be. But it is infinitely desirable, were it the will of God, that it should be done instantaneously; that the Lord should destroy sin "by the breath of his mouth," in a moment, in the twinkling of an eye. And so he generally does, a plain fact of which there is evidence enough to satisfy any unprejudiced person. *Thou* therefore look for it every moment! Look for it in the way above described; in all those *good works* whereunto thou art "created anew in Christ Jesus." There is then no danger: you can be no worse, if you are no better, for that expectation. For were you to be disappointed of your hope, still you lose nothing. But you shall not be disappointed of your hope: it will come, and will not tarry. Look for it then every day, every hour, every moment!

Why not this hour, this moment? Certainly you may look for it *now*, if you believe it is by faith. And by this token you may surely know whether you seek it by faith or by works. If by works, you want something to be done *first, before* you are sanctified. You think, "I must first *be* or *do* thus or thus." Then you are seeking it by works unto this day. If you seek it by faith, you may expect it *as you are*; and, if as you are, then expect it *now*. It is of importance to observe that there is an inseparable connection between these three points—expect it *by faith*; expect it *as you are*; and expect it *now*! To deny one of them is to deny them all; to allow one is to allow them all. Do *you* believe we are sanctified by faith? Be true then to your principle and look for this blessing just as you are, neither better nor worse; as a poor sinner that has still nothing to pay, nothing to plead, but "Christ *died*." And if you look for it as you are, then expect it *now*. Stay for nothing. Why should you? Christ is ready. And he is all you want. He is waiting for you. He is at the door! Let your inmost soul cry out,

Come in, come in, thou heavenly Guest!
    Nor hence again remove;
But sup with me, and let the feast
    Be everlasting love.

Lesson 13—God's New Creation: The Culmination of the Way of Salvation

Behold, I make all things new (Rev. 21:5; *KJV*).

The earth shall be full of the knowledge of the Lord, as the waters cover the sea (Isa. 11:9; *KJV*). [In God's new creation, there will be] . . . a deep, an intimate, an uninterrupted union with God; a constant communion with the Father and his Son Jesus Christ, through the Spirit; a continual enjoyment of the Three-One God, and of all the creatures in him!

John Wesley, *The New Creation*, §18

The loving knowledge of God, producing uniform, uninterrupted holiness and happiness, shall cover the earth, shall fill every soul of man.

John Wesley, *The General Spread of the Gospel*, §8

OUR STARTING POINT

We sometimes try to imagine what life would be like in a "new heaven" and a "new earth." Surely it must transcend our current experience. What is this "kingdom of God" about which Jesus preached? What does the reign of God in Christ really mean?

The new creation refers to God's work restoring the entire world, and it also refers to our personal lives. As we grow in holiness, and eventually go to be with Jesus Christ, we will be glorified—then creation will be made completely new!

READING

Read daily the reflection and prayer about the new heaven and the new earth. Unlike the other lessons—which were based on the text of only one sermon—this lesson includes selections from two of Wesley's sermons.

Day 1   Scan *The New Creation* and *The General Spread of the Gospel*. Scan Lesson 13.
Day 2   Read *The New Creation*, §§1-5,7,18. Read about a new heaven and a new earth.
Day 3   Read *The General Spread of the Gospel*, §§1,7-10. God's work in the souls of people.
Day 4   Read *The General Spread of the Gospel*, §§13-16. God has begun a revival.
Day 5   Read *The General Spread of the Gospel*, §§20-22,25-27. God's promise to bring about the kingdom of God.
Day 6   Read about Christ's commission to us to spread the gospel: Matt. 28:16-20 and Acts 1:1-11. Reread the lesson and answer the questions at the end.
Day 7   Rest.

REFLECTION

Then I saw a new heaven and a new earth; for the first heaven and the first earth had passed away, and the sea was no more. And I saw the holy city, the new Jerusalem, coming down out of heaven from God, prepared as a bride adorned for her husband. [A voice from the throne proclaims] "God himself will be with them; he will wipe every tear from their eyes. Death will be no more; mourning and crying and pain will be no more, for the first things have passed away. . . . See, I am making all things new. . . . It is done! I am the Alpha and the Omega, the beginning and the end. To the thirsty I will give water as a gift from the spring of the water of life. Those who conquer will inherit these things, and I will be their God and they will be my children."

Rev. 21:1-6a; *NRSV*

PRAYER

O Great Ruler of heaven and earth, I thirst for eternal life perfected in you. Give me the grace to taste eternal life now and to see your kingdom come. Open my heart, and teach me about the promises you have made to your people throughout the ages, so that I will be motivated to participate in making your reign real in my own time and place. Amen.

Prayer concerns for this week:

Daily Reflections

Day 1   Scan the sermons *The New Creation* and *The General Spread of the Gospel*. Scan Lesson 13.

Meaning for me:

Day 2   Read *The New Creation*, §§1-5,7,18. Read about a new heaven and a new earth.

Meaning for me:

Day 3   Read *The General Spread of the Gospel*, §§1,7-10. God's work in the souls of people.

Meaning for me:

Day 4   Read *The General Spread of the Gospel*, §§13-16. God has begun a revival.

Meaning for me:

Day 5   Read *The General Spread of the Gospel*, §§20-22,25-27. God's promises to bring about the Kingdom of God.

Meaning for me:

Day 6   Read about Christ's commission to us to spread the gospel: Matt. 28:16-20 and Acts 1:1-11. Reread the lesson and answer the questions at the end.

Meaning for me:

Kingdom of God

Wesley believed the Kingdom of God can come to exist here on earth and be tasted in the midst of our daily lives. This Kingdom comes when God's will is done on earth as it is in heaven, which we affirm in the Lord's Prayer. God's reign begins to take place inwardly in individuals whose lives are directed in godliness and holiness, in which the image of God for each person is gradually restored to what God has intended. God's reign is reflected outwardly in the acts of mercy undertaken by such individuals, in love of neighbor as well as love of God. Thus, both the inward dimension and the outward dimension of God's love are intensified as the in-breaking of the Kingdom of God takes place.

Both individuals and congregations of individuals become agents in the work of bringing to realization the dominion of God. In both individuals and congregations, the Holy Spirit is the source of strength and power for this transformation of the earth.

Glorification. God is working to establish the reign of God in our individual lives and throughout the whole of creation. But what is the ultimate goal of God's redemptive work? For individual Christians, the culminating aspect of Wesley's Way of Salvation will be our complete deliverance from the presence of sin, when believers fully recover the holiness that God intended for us from the time of our creation. God will provide this ultimate freedom from sin to all who are sincerely growing in grace.

Wesley asserted that, most often, this "triumph" of grace will be given to us at the moment of death. Death is not something to be feared for the Christian, but rather should be welcomed because of God's gracious promise of eternal life. Wesley wrote in the Preface to his Sermons: "I am a spirit coming from God and returning to God; just hovering over the great gulf, till a few moments hence I am no more seen—I drop into an unchangeable eternity! I want to know one thing, the way to heaven."[1] Leaving this life is simply a transition to eternal life with God in glory—our glorification with God. As Charles Wesley wrote: "Till in heaven we take our place; till we cast our crowns before him, lost in wonder, love, and praise."[2]

Resurrection. One of the main things Christians believe about death and the end times is that Jesus Christ has been raised from the dead. We believe that the life in Christ was so abundant, so overflowing, that death could not contain it. On the third day, Jesus' life burst forth from the tomb and revealed God's ultimate victory over the forces of sin, evil, and ultimately even death itself.

The resurrection of Jesus Christ from the dead is the source of our ultimate hope. When we face our own death, or the death of a loved one, or any of our human limitations, we can rejoice that God is in control, because we have already seen that when God is in control the result is resurrection and new life.

Judgment. Implicit in Christ's resurrection is an element of judgment. Paul writes that "the end will come, when he [Jesus] hands over the kingdom to God the Father... For he must reign until he has put all his enemies under his feet. The last enemy to

NOTES, REFLECTIONS, AND QUESTIONS

For this also we pray in those words, "Thy kingdom come." We pray for the coming of his everlasting kingdom, the kingdom of glory in heaven, which is the continuation and perfection of the kingdom of grace on earth. Consequently this, as well as the preceding petition, is offered up for the whole intelligent creation, who are all interested in this grand event, the final renovation of all things, by God's putting an end to misery and sin, to infirmity and death, taking all things into his own hands, and setting up the kingdom which endureth throughout all ages.

John Wesley, *Upon Our Lord's Sermon on the Mount: Discourse Six*, §III.8

Come, thou long expected Jesus,
born to set thy people free;
from our fears and sins release us,
let us find our rest in thee.

Israel's strength and consolation,
hope of all the earth thou art;
dear desire of every nation,
joy of every longing heart.

By thine own eternal spirit
rule in all our hearts alone;
by thine all sufficient merit,
raise us to thy glorious throne.

Charles Wesley, "Come, Thou Long Expected Jesus" (1744)—*UM Hymnal* #196; *AME Church Hymnal* #103; *CME Hymnal* #625; *Nazarene Hymnal* #181

[A person] knows there can be no happiness on earth but in the enjoyment of God and in the foretaste of those "rivers of pleasure which flow at his right hand for evermore."

John Wesley, *Journal*, October 14, 1738

But Christ has been raised from the dead... For the trumpet will sound, the dead will be raised imperishable... then the saying that is written will come true: "Death has been swallowed up in victory. Where, O death, is your victory? Where, O death, is your sting?"

1 Cor. 15:20, 52, 54-55; *TNIV*

be destroyed is death" (1 Cor. 15:24-26). God's ultimate affirmation of his good creation includes a word of judgment to the forces of sin, evil, and death—all of which will be destroyed.

New Creation

Cosmic Redemption of God's Grace Reaching All of Creation. In Rev. 21:5, the Triune God speaks, "Behold, I make all things new."[3] The work of bringing about a new creation is thus a process—a process begun already on earth. Wesley understood this process to be a renewal of *all* creation, not just human lives. God's restoration of all of creation is a process that begins in our own lives, and in all forms of God's creation.

Rev. 21:1 proclaims a new heaven and a new earth—a new creation (see also 1 Cor. 5:17). The new creation is a new state of being. God's promises are all fulfilled. There is no longer any sin, misery, infirmity, or death. God reestablishes "universal holiness and happiness" (*The General Spread of the Gospel*, §27). The new creation is not an escape from the earth, but a vision of God coming down to earth in order to transform it—and us.

Eschatology. Eschatology is a theological term concerning the "end times" or "last things." Eschatology is about the study of end times—"the fulfillment of God's plan for human history."[4] Eschatology has two dimensions, one in the future and another achieved or realized in our present day on this earth. Realized eschatology is concerned about our lives here and now. It dwells on how God's purposes are made real in the final events of individual lives in the present age and the way those purposes affect present reality.[5] Wesley affirmed aspects of both these dimensions of eschatology. Following Jesus' preaching, Wesley said the Kingdom of God was both already present and not yet fully realized.

For Wesley, "the essence of heaven" is "the opportunity to see God, to know God, and to love God."[6] It is not surprising that Wesley believed that this essence of grace could be tasted in the present world but also be provided in overflowing bounty in the world to come.

Mission: Going into the World. From the beginning of God's relationship with Israel, God has blessed people and nations for the purpose of sharing that blessing.[7] We are blessed in order to be a blessing to others. We have been called into relationship with Jesus Christ. With that relationship comes both the privilege of knowing him, and the responsibility to move out in mission to the world.[8]

If we are under the lordship of Jesus Christ, there is no other option than to be sharing the gospel wherever we are. Our job, and indeed the church's job, is to point all of creation to Jesus Christ. If the purpose of the church is to bring all creation together in communion under the lordship of Jesus Christ, then the church must bring mission to the very center of its reason for existence. The church is to be a foretaste of the world to come.[9]

NOTES, REFLECTIONS, AND QUESTIONS

Ye servants of God, your Master proclaim,
and publish abroad his wonderful name;
the name all-victorious of Jesus extol,
his kingdom is glorious and rules over all.

God ruleth on high, almighty to save,
and still he is nigh, his presence we have;
the great congregation his triumph shall sing,
ascribing salvation to Jesus, our King.

Charles Wesley, "Ye servants of God" (1744)—
UM Hymnal #181; Free Methodist Ch. & The Wesleyan Ch. Hymnal #80; Ch. of Nazarene Hymnal #153

He [The Risen Christ] said to them: "It is not for you to know the times or dates the Father has set by his own authority. But you will receive power when the Holy Spirit comes on you; and you will be my witnesses in Jerusalem, and in all Judea and Samaria, and to the ends of the earth."

Acts 1: 7-8; NIV

Then [the Risen] Jesus came to them and said, "All authority in heaven and on earth has been given to me. Therefore go and make disciples of all nations, baptizing them in the name of the Father and of the Son and of the Holy Spirit, and teaching them to obey everything I have commanded you. And surely I am with you always, to the very end of the age."

Matt. 28:18-20; NIV

Wesley stated it well (*The General Spread of the Gospel*, §27):

[God] is already renewing the face of the earth. And we have strong reason to hope that the work he hath begun, he will carry on unto the day of the Lord Jesus; that he will never intermit this blessed work of his Spirit, until he has fulfilled all his promises, until he hath put a period to sin, and misery, and infirmity, and death; and re-established universal holiness and happiness, and caused all the inhabitants of the earth to sing together, "Hallelujah, the Lord God omnipotent reigneth! Blessing, and glory, and wisdom, and honor, and power, and might, be unto our God forever and ever!" (Rev. 7:12)

NOTES, REFLECTIONS, AND QUESTIONS

I am confident of this, that the one who began a good work among you will bring it to completion by the day of Christ Jesus.

Phil. 1:6; *NRSV*

RESPONDING FAITHFULLY

Have you become a new creation in Christ Jesus? In what specific ways can that personal transformation make a difference for the Kingdom of God?

Wesley believed the Kingdom of God is in the present, as well as in the future. Describe your experience of the Kingdom of God in the present time.

How can you be a part of spreading scriptural holiness? How can your faith community be active in this task?

We are called to share our blessings with others. Name one thing you can do today to witness to the love of Jesus Christ in the world.

LEARNING MORE

The following works of John Wesley may be of interest:
- *Explanatory Notes on the New Testament* (for Rev. 21:1-7)
- *The General Deliverance*
- *In What Sense Are We To Leave the World.*

Read parts of:
- Theodore Runyon, *The New Creation: John Wesley's Theology Today*
- Randy L. Maddox, "The Triumph of Responsible Grace" (Ch. 9), *Responsible Grace: John Wesley's Practical Theology* (pp. 230-256)
- Craig C. Hill, *In God's Time: The Bible and the Future.*

Additional readings on the new creation from the Gospels:
- Matt. 5-7 or Luke 11-13
- Matt. 13; Mark 4,10; or Luke 18
- Mark 13 or Luke 21.

Additional readings from the Epistles of Paul:
- Rom. 14:17
- 1 Cor. 6:9-10
- Gal. 5:16-25.

Teacher Helps provides follow-up questions that may be useful in class discussions.

END NOTES

[1] *The Works of John Wesley*, Bicentennial Edition, 1:105.
[2] Charles Wesley, "Love Divine, All Loves Excelling" (1747).
[3] Compare the NRSV, "See, I am making all things new."
[4] Craig C. Hill, *In God's Time: The Bible and the Future*, p. 3. See also Larry J. Kreitzer, "Eschatology," *Dictionary of Paul and His Letters*, pp. 253-269.
[5] Maddox, op. cit., p. 235.
[6] Maddox, *Ibid*, p. 252.
[7] See Genesis 12:3.
[8] Lesslie Newbigin, *The Open Secret: An Introduction to the Theology of Mission.* Grand Rapids, Michigan, William B. Eerdman's Publishing Company, 1995, p. 73.
[9] See, for example, Newbigin, *Ibid.*

First Reading for Lesson 13. Selections from The New Creation (1785)

Behold, I make all things new (Rev. 21:5.)

1. What a strange scene is here opened to our view! How remote from all our natural apprehensions! Not a glimpse of what is here revealed was ever seen in the heathen world. Not only the modern, barbarous, uncivilized heathens have not the least conception of it, but it was equally unknown to the refined, polished heathens of ancient Greece and Rome. And it is almost as little thought of or understood by the generality of Christians: I mean, not barely those that are nominally such, that have the form of godliness without the power, but even those that, in a measure, fear God and study to work righteousness.

2. It must be allowed that after all the researches we can make, still our knowledge of the great truth which is delivered to us in these words is exceedingly short and imperfect. As this is a point of mere revelation, beyond the reach of all our natural faculties, we cannot penetrate far into it, nor form any adequate conception of it. But it may be an encouragement to those who have in any degree tasted of the powers of the world to come to go as far as we can go, interpreting Scripture by Scripture, according to the analogy of faith.

3. The Apostle, caught up in the visions of God, tells us in the first verse of the chapter, "I saw a new heaven and a new earth," and adds (Rev. 21:5), "He that sat upon the throne said" (I believe the only words which he is said to utter throughout the whole book), "Behold, I make all things new."

4. Very many commentators entertain a strange opinion that this relates only to the present state of things, and gravely tell us that the words are to be referred to the flourishing state of the church, which commenced after the heathen persecutions. Nay, some of them have discovered that all which the Apostle speaks concerning the "new heaven and the new earth" was fulfilled when Constantine the Great poured in riches and honors upon the Christians. What a miserable way is this of making void the whole counsel of God, with regard to all that grand chain of events, in reference to his church, yea, and to all mankind, from the time that John was in Patmos unto the end of the world! Nay, the line of this prophecy reaches farther still. It does not end with the present world, but shows us the things that will come to pass when this world is no more.

5. For, thus saith the Creator and Governor of the universe: "Behold, I make all things new"—all which are included in that expression of the Apostle, "A new heaven and a new earth." . . .

7. . . . This is the introduction to a far nobler state of things, such as it has not yet entered into the heart of men to conceive—the universal restoration which is to succeed the universal destruction. For "we look," says the Apostle, "for new heavens and a new earth, wherein dwelleth righteousness" (2 Pet. 3:7ff). . . .

18. But the most glorious of all will be the change which then will take place on the poor, sinful, miserable children of men. These had fallen in many respects, as from a greater height, so into a lower depth, than any other part of the creation. But they shall "hear a great voice out of heaven, saying, "Behold, the tabernacle of God is with men, and he will dwell with them, and they shall be his people, and God himself shall be their God" (Rev. 21:3-4). Hence will arise an unmixed state of holiness and happiness far superior to that which Adam enjoyed in paradise. In how beautiful and affecting a manner is this described by the Apostle: "God shall wipe away all tears from their eyes; and there shall be no more death, neither sorrow, nor crying, neither shall there be any more pain: for the former things are done away"! As there will be no more death, and no more pain or sickness preparatory thereto; as there will be no more grieving for, or parting with, friends; so there will be no more sorrow or crying. Nay, but there will be a greater deliverance than all this; for there will be no more sin. And, to crown all, there will be a deep, an intimate, an uninterrupted union with God; a constant communion with the Father and his Son Jesus Christ, through the Spirit; a continual enjoyment of the Three-One God, and of all the creatures in him!

Second Reading for Lesson 13. Selections from The General Spread of the Gospel (1783)

The earth shall be full of the knowledge of the Lord, as the waters cover the sea (Isa. 11:9).

1. In what a condition is the world at present! How does darkness, intellectual darkness, ignorance, with vice and misery attendant upon it, cover the face of the earth! From the accurate inquiry made with indefatigable pains by our ingenious countryman, Mr. Brerewood (who traveled himself over a great part of the known world, in order to form the more exact judgment), supposing the world to be divided into thirty parts, nineteen of them are professed heathens, altogether as ignorant of Christ, as if he had never come into the world. Six of the remaining parts are professed Mahometans [Muslims], so that only five in thirty are so much as nominally Christians! . . .

7. The Western Churches seem to have the pre-eminence over all these in many respects. They have abundantly more knowledge. They have more scriptural and more rational modes of worship. Yet two-thirds of them are still involved in the corruptions of the Church of Rome; and most of these are entirely unacquainted with either the theory or practice of religion. And as to those who are called Protestants, or Reformed, what acquaintance with it have they? Put Papists and Protestants, French and English together, the bulk of one and of the other nation; and what manner of Christians are they? Are they "holy as he that hath called them is holy"? Are they filled with "righteousness, and peace, and joy in the Holy Ghost"? Is there "that mind in them which was also in Christ Jesus"? And do they "walk as Christ also walked"? Nay, they are as far from it as hell is from heaven!

8. Such is the present state of mankind in all parts of the world! But how astonishing is this, if there is a God in heaven and if his eyes are over all the earth! Can he despise the work of his own hand? Surely this is one of the greatest mysteries under heaven! How is it possible to reconcile this with either the wisdom or goodness of God? And what can give ease to a thoughtful mind under so melancholy a prospect? What but the consideration that things will not always be so, that another scene will soon be opened? God will be jealous of his honor. He will arise and maintain his own cause. He will judge the prince of this world and spoil him of his usurped dominion. He will give his Son "the heathen for his inheritance and the uttermost parts of the earth for his possession." "The earth shall be filled with knowledge of the Lord, as the waters cover the sea." The loving knowledge of God, producing uniform, uninterrupted holiness and happiness, shall cover the earth, shall fill every soul of man.

9. "Impossible!" will some men say, "Yea, the greatest of all impossibilities, that we should see a Christian world—yea, a Christian nation, or city! How can these things be?" On one supposition, indeed, not only all impossibility, but all difficulty vanishes away. Only suppose the Almighty to act irresistibly, and the thing is

done; yea, with just the same ease as when "God said, Let there be light; and there was light." But then, man would be man no longer—his inmost nature would be changed. He would no longer be a moral agent, any more than the sun or the wind; as he would no longer be endued with liberty—a power of choosing or self-determination. Consequently, he would no longer be capable of virtue or vice, of reward or punishment.

10. But setting aside this clumsy way of cutting the knot which we are not able to untie, how can all men be made holy and happy, while they continue men? While they still enjoy both the understanding, the affections, and the liberty which are essential to a moral agent? There seems to be a plain, simple way of removing this difficulty, without entangling ourselves in any subtle, metaphysical disquisitions. As God is One, so the work of God is uniform in all ages. May we not then conceive how he will work on the souls of men in times to come, by considering how he does work now, and how he has wrought in times past? . . .

13. Let us observe what God has done already. Between fifty and sixty years ago, God raised up a few young men, in the University of Oxford, to testify those grand truths, which were then little attended to: that without holiness no man shall see the Lord; that this holiness is the work of God, who worketh in us both to will and to do; that he doeth it of his own good pleasure, merely for the merits of Christ; that this holiness is the mind that was in Christ, enabling us to walk as he also walked; that no man can be thus sanctified till he is justified; and that we are justified by faith alone. These great truths they declared on all occasions, in private and in public, having no design but to promote the glory of God, and no desire but to save souls from death.

14. From Oxford, where it first appeared, the little leaven spread wider and wider. More and more saw the truth as it is in Jesus, and received it in the love thereof. More and more found "redemption through the blood of Jesus, even the forgiveness of sins." They were born again of his Spirit, and filled with righteousness, and peace, and joy in the Holy Ghost. It afterwards spread to every part of the land, and a little one became a thousand. It then spread into North Britain and Ireland; and, a few years after, into New York, Pennsylvania, and many other provinces in America, even as high as Newfoundland and Nova Scotia. So that, although at first this "grain of mustard seed" was "the least of all the seeds"; yet, in a few years, it grew into a "large tree, and put forth great branches."

15. Generally, when these truths—justification by faith in particular—were declared in any large town, after a few days or weeks there came suddenly on the great congregation (not in a corner, [but] at London, Bristol, Newcastle-upon-Tyne, in particular) a violent and impetuous power, which,

> Like mighty wind or torrent fierce,
> Did then opposers all o'er-run.

And this frequently continued, with shorter or longer intervals, for several weeks or months. But it gradually subsided, and then the work of God was carried on by gentle degrees; while that Spirit, in watering the seed that had been sown, in confirming and strengthening them that had believed,

> Deign'd his influence to infuse,
> Secret, refreshing as the silent dews.

And this difference in his usual manner of working was observable not only in Great Britain and Ireland, but in every part of America, from south to north, wherever the word of God came with power.

16. Is it not then highly probable that God will carry on his work in the same manner as he has begun? That he will carry it on, I cannot doubt; however Luther may affirm, that a revival of religion never lasts above a generation—that is, thirty years; (whereas the present revival has already continued above fifty)—or however prophets of evil may say, "All will be at an end when the first instruments are removed." There will then, very probably, be a great shaking; but I cannot induce myself to think that God has wrought so glorious a work, to let it sink and die away in a few years. No; I trust this is only the beginning of a far greater work, the dawn of "the latter-day glory."

17. And is it not probable, I say, that he will carry it on in the same manner as he has begun? At the first breaking out of this work in this or that place, there may be a shower, a torrent of grace; and so at some other particular seasons, which "the Father has reserved in his own power:" . . .

20. Then shall be fully accomplished to the house of Israel, the spiritual Israel, of whatever people or nation, that gracious promise: "I will put my laws in their minds, and write them in their hearts, and I will be to them a God, and they shall be to me a people. And they shall not teach every man his neighbor, and every man his brother, saying, 'Know the Lord'; for they shall all know me, from the least to the greatest. For I will be merciful to their unrighteousness, and their sins and their iniquities will I remember no more." Then shall

"the times of" universal "refreshment come from the presence of the Lord." The grand Pentecost shall "fully come," and "devout men in every nation under heaven," however distant in place from each other, shall "all be filled with the Holy Ghost"; and they will "continue steadfast in the apostles' doctrine, and in the fellowship, and in the breaking of bread, and in prayers." They will "eat their meat," and do all that they have to do, "with gladness and singleness of heart." "Great grace will be upon them all"; and they will be "all of one heart and of one soul."

The natural, necessary consequence of this will be the same as it was in the beginning of the Christian Church: "None of them will say, that [any] of the things which he possesses is his own; but they will have all things common. Neither will there be any among them that want; for as many as are possessed of lands or houses will sell them; and distribution will be made to every man, according as he has need." All their desires, meantime, and passions, and tempers will be cast in one mould, while all are doing the will of God on earth as it is done in heaven. All their "conversation will be seasoned with salt" and will "minister grace to the hearers"; seeing it will not be so much they that speak, "as the Spirit of their Father that speaketh in them." And there will be no "root of bitterness springing up," either to defile or trouble them. There will be no Ananias or Sapphira, to bring back the cursed love of money among them. There will be no partiality, no "widows neglected in the daily ministration." Consequently, there will be no temptation to any murmuring thought or unkind word of one against another, while

They all are of one heart and soul,
And only love informs the whole.

21. The grand stumbling-block being thus happily removed out of the way, namely, the lives of the Christians, the Mahometans will look upon them with other eyes and begin to give attention to their words. And as their words will be clothed with divine energy, attended with the demonstration of the Spirit and of power, those of them that fear God will soon take knowledge of the Spirit whereby the Christians speak. They will "receive with meekness the engrafted word," and will bring forth fruit with patience. From them the leaven will soon spread to those who till then, had no fear of God before their eyes. Observing the Christian dogs, as they used to term them, to have changed their nature—to be sober, temperate, just, benevolent—and that, in spite of all provocations to the contrary; from admiring their lives, they will surely be led to consider and embrace their doctrine. And then the Savior of sinners will say, "The hour is come; I will glorify my Father: I will seek and save the sheep that were wandering on the dark mountains. Now will I avenge myself of my enemy and pluck the prey out of the lion's teeth. I will resume my own, for ages lost: I will claim the purchase of my blood." So he will go forth in the greatness of his strength, and all his enemies shall flee before him. All the prophets of lies shall vanish away, and all the nations that had followed them shall acknowledge the great Prophet of the Lord, "mighty in word and deed"; and "shall honor the Son, even as they honor the Father."

22. And then, the grand stumbling-block being removed from the heathen nations also. . . . The holy lives of the Christians will be an argument they will not know how to resist. Seeing the Christians steadily and uniformly practice what is agreeable to the law written in their own hearts, their prejudices will quickly die away, and they will gladly receive "the truth as it is in Jesus." . . .

25. . . . For this is the promise: "For the Lord thy God will gather thee from all nations, whither the Lord thy God hath scattered thee. And the Lord thy God will bring thee into the land which thy fathers possessed, and thou shalt possess it. And the Lord thy God will circumcise thy heart, and the heart of thy seed, to love the Lord thy God with all thy heart, and with all thy soul" (Deut. 30:3ff). Again: "I will gather them out of all countries, whither I have driven them. And I will bring them again to this place, and I will cause them to dwell safely. And I will give them one heart, and one way, that they may fear me forever. I will put my fear into their hearts, that they shall not depart from me. And I will plant them in this land assuredly, with my whole heart and with my whole soul" (Jer. 32:37ff). Yet again: "I will take you from among the heathen, and gather you out of all countries, and will bring you into your own land. Then will I sprinkle clean water upon you, and ye shall be clean; from all your filthiness and from all your idols will I cleanse you. And ye shall dwell in the land that I gave to your fathers; and ye shall be my people, and I will be your God" (Ezek. 36:24ff).

26. At that time will be accomplished all those glorious promises made to the Christian Church, which will not then be confined to this or that nation, but will include all the inhabitants of the earth. "They shall not hurt nor destroy in all my holy mountain" (Isa. 11:9). "Violence shall no more be heard in thy land, wasting nor destruction within thy borders; but thou shalt call thy walls, 'Salvation,' and thy gates 'Praise.'"

Thou shalt be encompassed on every side with salvation, and all that go through thy gates shall praise God. "The sun shall be no more thy light by day; neither for brightness shall the moon give light unto thee; but the Lord shall be unto thee an everlasting light, and thy God thy glory." The light of the sun and moon shall be swallowed up in the light of his countenance shining upon thee. "Thy people also shall be all righteous, the work of my hands, that I may be glorified." "As the earth bringeth forth her bud, and the garden causeth the things that are sown in it to spring forth; so the Lord God will cause righteousness and praise to spring forth before all the nations" (Isa. 60:18ff; 61:11).

27. This I apprehend to be the answer, yea, the only full and satisfactory answer that can be given, to the objection against the wisdom and goodness of God, taken from the present state of the world. It will not always be thus. These things are only permitted for a season by the great Governor of the world, that he may draw immense, eternal good out of this temporary evil. This is the very key which the Apostle himself gives us in the words above recited: "God hath concluded them all in unbelief, that he might have mercy upon all!" In view of this glorious event, how well may we cry out, "O the depth of the riches both of the wisdom and knowledge of God!—although for a season "his judgments were unsearchable and his ways past finding out" (Rom. 11:32-33). It is enough that we are assured of this one point, that all these transient evils will issue well, will have a happy conclusion; and that "mercy first and last will reign." All unprejudiced persons may see with their eyes, that he is already renewing the face of the earth. And we have strong reason to hope that the work he hath begun he will carry on unto the day of the Lord Jesus; that he will never intermit this blessed work of his Spirit until he has fulfilled all his promises,—until he hath put a period to sin, and misery, and infirmity, and death; and re-established universal holiness and happiness, and caused all the inhabitants of the earth to sing together, "Hallelujah, the Lord God omnipotent reigneth!" "Blessing, and glory, and wisdom, and honor, and power, and might, be unto our God forever and ever!" (Rev. 7:12)

The Wesleyan Covenant

I am no longer my own, but thine.
Put me to what thou wilt, rank me with whom thou wilt.
Put me to doing, put me to suffering.
Let me be employed by thee or laid aside for thee,
Exalted for thee or brought low for thee.
Let me be full, let me be empty.
Let me have all things, let me have nothing.
I freely and heartily yield all things
To thy pleasure and disposal.
And now, O glorious and blessed God,
Father, Son, and Holy Spirit,
Thou art mine, and I am thine. So be it.
And the covenant which I have made on earth,
Let it be ratified in heaven. Amen.

Appendix A: Teacher Helps

Getting Started

Reading and Writing Assignment for the Participants. Each week (except for Lesson One), participants will read a Wesley sermon that corresponds to the theme of the lesson. It is suggested that the sermon should be read in one sitting on day one, then read again in pieces over the course of the week. (However, participants may choose any method of reading that works best for them.) Page one of each lesson supplies a six-day reading assignment for those who want to spread the reading out. The first page also presents a theological reflection and a prayer, which are to be used daily. Participants are encouraged to take notes or write down questions from the readings using the space furnished on the second page of the lesson, as well as on the right-hand side of the pages that follow. Life application questions ("Responding Faithfully") are located on the last page of each lesson. Recommended readings on Wesley's theology from other theologians are also given on the last page.

What Happens in the Class. A typical session will run approximately one and a half hours of actual in-class study time, depending on the amount of time allowed for class discussion and input, and not accounting for time spent sharing personal concerns or prayer, if desired. (The lesson can be adapted to more or less time.) Participants are expected to come prepared, having read the weekly reading assignments and having answered the questions. Based on a one and a half hour session for a group of 8 to 12 people, a sample class schedule is shown as follows. This sample schedule is only suggestive. Facilitators are encouraged to plan their own schedules to fit the needs of different sizes or types of groups.

Suggested Lesson Plan

- **Opening Prayer and Hymn Singing (10 minutes).** Both the prayer and a recommended Charles Wesley hymn are found in each lesson. If the music to the hymn is unknown to you or less familiar, the group may choose to read the words aloud as a choral reading. (Choral readings are explained below.)
- **Introduction (10 minutes).** The facilitator will introduce the main theme and the historical background of the assigned sermon text.
- **Small Group Discussion (25 minutes).** The facilitator may wish to divide a larger group into smaller groups of three or four. Each smaller group will be assigned a portion of the sermon to review in detail. Each group will share insights and questions with one another and designate someone to summarize the insights for the larger group as a whole.
- **Entire Group Discussion (40 minutes).** The entire group will reassemble, and each small group will share a summary of its discussion. This will be a time for general questions and answers. The facilitator will lead the discussion, weave in the Scriptures and hymns, and monitor the time. At least twenty minutes of discussion time should be used for discussing the questions listed under "Responding Faithfully," which is the life application portion for individual participants and their church communities.
- **Closing Prayer and Hymn Singing (5 minutes).**

Note for Obtaining Wesley's Sermons

Wesley's sermons may be found in the CD-ROM entitled: *The Works of John Wesley, The Bicentennial Edition,* Edited by Richard P. Heitzenrater, Abingdon Press. Sermons in the public domain are available from several websites, as noted in Appendix B (below):

http://gbgm-umc.org/UMhistory/Wesley/sermons/
http://wesley.nnu.edu/john_wesley/sermons/intro.htm

Choral Readings

A choral reading—speaking the hymn out loud in unison—is an alternative to singing a hymn. It is similar to reading poetry. An effective choral reading will have variety within the reading. For example, one person might read verse one out loud, and then everyone would read the chorus together out loud, then the men might read verse two, everyone read the chorus and the women would read verse three together. The idea is to have a rhythm of voices speaking the poetry so that the words reverberate deep into the souls of those who speak them. Sometimes a choral reading offers an effective way to hear and appropriate these profound words that were written by Charles Wesley.

Teacher Helps for Each Lesson

A.1 TEACHER HELPS FOR LESSON 1 (INTRODUCING THE WESLEYS)

The first lesson provides a brief biographical sketch of the lives of Charles and John Wesley, the two main characters of the Wesleyan movement. This sketch gives glimpses into their lives that will enable participants to understand how their spiritual journeys' relate to the Way of Salvation. The lesson is intended to provide participants the vocabulary and context for entering into a study of Wesleyan theology. Ideally, copies of this book would be distributed in advance so that participants will have the opportunity to read this lesson before the first meeting. If that is possible, then the class discussion could begin with the first question in the "Responding Faithfully" section, "What did you know about John and Charles Wesley before you began this lesson?" This lesson provides an opportunity for those in the class to discuss what they already knew about the Wesleys, and what information they have learned that is new. Were any misconceptions corrected by this lesson?

On the other hand, if the book cannot be distributed prior to the first group session, this lesson can be read through as a group. In this case, most of the class time will be used simply going through the lesson and discussing it. The above questions would then be explored as time permits.

A.2 TEACHER HELPS FOR LESSON 2 (CREATED IN THE IMAGE OF GOD)

Lesson 2 concentrates on the "one thing that is needful," which is the restoration of human beings to the perfect image of God. We often look for family resemblance in our own children. We might even try to see which parent's features are most prominent in our offspring. Ultimately, it is the perfect resemblance of our Creator which needs to be the most prominent feature in each of us.

The lesson reminds us that God created humanity in God's perfect image, but that image has been destroyed. At the heart of this issue is Wesley's concern for how humanity can be brought back into a right relationship with God.

Additional Questions for Discussion

1. What is the "one end of [our] existence"—our purpose in life? (See *One Thing Needful,* Intro., §2.)
2. The concept of being renewed in the image of God may be an entirely new idea for the class. This concept is central to the Wesleyan Way of Salvation. What do you think our churches would look like if we all understood this as the essential priority for Christians?

A.3 TEACHER HELPS FOR LESSON 3 (THE EFFECTS OF SIN)

Lesson 3 begins with a discussion of the nature of sin and the nature of evil. In general, sin is treated as anything that separates the believer from God; that causes a human to lose the image of God that God intends for each; or that inhibits the believer in coming to know God's will. Evil is a force that leads to sin or that leads away from what is good for creation.

Original sin is an infection of our original image as humans. Sin is a disease of the will, and sin has diseased our natural relationship with God and our neighbor. All people are in the condition of sin (Romans 3:23). Known sins simply complicate and illustrate the condition of sin. Thus, the curse of original sin becomes a description of our situation more than a prescription of our future life.

The fourth question under "Responding Faithfully" (regarding the "idols" that we set up in our lives) may be rather personal for class participants and so you may wish to discuss the answer to that question one-on-one, rather than with the entire group.

Additional Questions for Discussion
1. How would you describe the sinful nature of human beings at birth?
2. How do you react to describing our sinful nature as an inherited separation from God and our sinful acts as breaching our obligations to God and others?
3. In §II.8 Wesley speaks of pride. How does pride separate you from God?

Additional Study Material:

Why is there sin in the world? Because man was created in the image of God: Because he is not mere matter, a clod of earth, a lump of clay, without sense or understanding; but a spirit *like his Creator, a being endued not only with sense and understanding, but also with a will exerting itself in various affections. To crown all the rest, he was endued with* liberty; *a power of directing his own affections and actions; a capacity of determining himself, or of choosing good or evil. Indeed, had not man been endued with this, all the rest would have been of no use: Had he not been a free as well as an* intelligent *being, his understanding would have been as incapable of holiness, or any kind of virtue, as a tree or a block of marble. And having this power, a* power of choosing good or evil, *he chose the latter: He chose evil. Thus "sin entered into the world," and pain of every kind, preparatory to death.*

John Wesley, On the Fall of Man, §1

Every fresh alarming token more confirms the faithful word;
Nature (for its Lord hath spoken) must be suddenly restored:
From this national confusion, from this ruined earth and skies,
See the times of restitution, see the new creation rise!

Charles Wesley, "Righteous God! Whose Vengeful Phials," Methodist 1889 Hymnal #60

Important Note. These early lessons in the study may be difficult, either in terms of the reading or from a more spiritual perspective. For example, there may be some in the class who are feeling uncomfortable, convicted of sin, or perhaps even somewhat offended. It is important to remember the Scripture: "There is no one righteous, not even one; there is no one who understands, no one who seeks God. All have turned away, they have together become worthless; there is no one who does good, not even one" (Rom. 3:11-12; *NIV*). And again: "If we say that we have no sin, we deceive ourselves" (1 Jn. 1:8). Do not be discouraged, however, for we also read that: "if we confess our sins, he who is faithful and just will forgive our sins and cleanse us from all unrighteousness" (1 Jn. 1:9; *NRSV*).

A.4 Teacher Helps for Lesson 4 (Prevenient Grace: God's Loving Initiative)

Lesson 4 provides a brief introduction to the nature of God's grace, which will be amplified in subsequent chapters. Specifically, all humans need divine grace and without it there is no hope to overcome one's sin. Prevenient grace begins the process of the restoration of the image of God, by preparing one for justification and sanctification. This universal grace is given before we understand or acknowledge our need for it. The primary function of prevenient grace is to awaken us to the condition of our sin and to bring us to a point of conviction.

Additional Question for Discussion
1. In what ways does your church community reflect or not reflect a truly Wesleyan approach to its ministry, in which God's universal grace is offered, and people are provided with opportunities—during worship and at other times—to be "awakened" and "convinced" of their need for God?

Additional Study Material

The following Scriptures provide more examples of God's free, universal grace through the work of Jesus Christ:
*   I now realize how God does not show favoritism but accepts those from every nation who fear him and do what is right (Acts 10:34-35; *TNIV*).
*   God shows no partiality (Rom. 2:11; *NRSV*).
*   For there is one God and one mediator between God and human beings, Christ Jesus, himself human,

who gave himself as a ransom for all people (1 Tim. 2:5-6; *TNIV*).

- Jesus, who . . . suffered death, so that by the grace of God he might taste death for everyone Heb. 2:9; *TNIV*).

There is no man, unless he has quenched the Spirit, that is wholly void of the grace of God . . . Everyone has some measure of that light, some faint glimmering ray, which sooner or later, more or less, enlightens every man that cometh into the world. And everyone . . . feels more or less uneasy when he acts contrary to the light of his own conscience. So that no man sins because he has not grace, but because he does not use the grace which he hath.

John Wesley, On Working Out Our Own Salvation, §III.4

Father, whose everlasting love thy only Son for sinners gave,
Whose grace to all did freely move, and sent him down a world to save.

Help us thy mercy to extol, Immense, unfathom'd, unconfined;
To praise the Lamb who died for all, the general Savior of mankind.

Thy undistinguished regard was cast on Adam's fallen race;
For all thou hast in Christ prepared sufficient, sovereign, saving grace.

Jesus hath said, we all shall hope, preventing grace for all is free:
"And I, if I be lifted up, I will draw all men unto Me."

What soul those drawings never knew? with whom hath not thy Spirit strove?
We all must own that God is true, we all may feel that God is love.

O all ye ends of earth, behold the bleeding, all-atoning Lamb!
Look unto him for sinners sold, look and be saved through Jesu's name.

Behold the Lamb of God, who takes the sins of all the world away!
His pity no exception makes; but all that will receive him, may.

A world he suffer'd to redeem; for all he hath th' atonement made:
For those that will not come to him the ransom of his life was paid.

Charles Wesley, "Father, Whose Everlasting Love," *1877 Methodist Hymnal* (#39, pp.53-54).

A.5 TEACHER HELPS FOR LESSON 5 (THE ALMOST CHRISTIAN AND THE ALTOGETHER CHRISTIAN)

Lesson 5 focuses on the difference in Wesley's pastoral theology between an "Almost Christian" and a real or "Altogether Christian." This lesson highlights Wesley's own experience before he was a "real Christian" and it distinguishes between the two.

The Almost Christian is an impressively religious person who has the form but not the power of faith. John Wesley couldn't earn his salvation, though he tried with all of his might and by almost every means for thirteen years. How can we move from being an "almost" Christian to an "altogether" Christian—receiving justifying grace and the experience of the new birth? This will happen in God's time, but we can place ourselves in a position to receive it by: 1) using the means of grace (prayer, Scripture reading, attending worship, serving others, etc.); 2) having a posture of humility before God; 3) having an attitude of openness and expectancy for what we know that God will do, because of God's promises; and 4) actively inviting Christ into our lives.

Additional Questions for Discussion

1. A man said to Jesus, "Yes Lord I believe, help me overcome my unbelief" (Mark 9:24). Have you ever felt like that man? Does it encourage you that this man could ask those words directly to Jesus? Does that help "give us permission" to do the same?
2. As a community, do we act out the form of "living a life of faith in love" or do we model tolerance? (One way of understanding tolerance are those situations in which we do not hold each other accountable for Christian action.)
   Important Note: There may be some in the class who have not taken the opportunity to receive God's

grace in Jesus Christ. If there are those who have never invited Christ into their lives, time can be taken in class for individuals to ask Jesus Christ to be the Lord of their lives. Individuals may pray their own prayer of repentance and acceptance of God's grace, or the group may pray this prayer together:

> *Dear Jesus, I know that you created me to be in relationship with you. Forgive me for the times when I did not see you or recognize you in my life. I want to start to build our relationship. I know you came into this world for my sins, so that I may have life eternal with you. Please come into my heart and help me to grow into your perfect image. Amen.*

A.6 TEACHER HELPS FOR LESSON 6 (JUSTIFICATION: THE FORGIVENESS OF SINS)

In Lesson 6 we see the impact in Wesley's own life of his discovery of the importance of the doctrine of Justification. Wesley's understanding of justification shifted during his early ministry. In his early faith journey, he thought that sanctification would bring forth justification. After his trip to America and his subsequent discipleship with the Moravians, he understood that justification, or being forgiven by God, was a free gift of God given by grace through faith alone. This lesson emphasizes the meaning of justification and how it is experienced in the life of a believer. It points out that the doctrine of Justification is grounded in God's mercy and love.

Justification is the turning point of our lives, the time when we become aware of God's grace. Justification ("what God does for us in Jesus Christ") is (1) pardon, forgiveness of sin, "canceled sin", and (2) adoption (considered by God to be in a new relationship, a restoration of a right relationship with God). Grace aligns the person with God. There is no salvation earned by humans; no one deserves God's grace. A person is saved by grace (justifying grace) and the instrument of the grace is faith (Eph. 2:8-9). Faith is not just intellectual assent, but "a sure trust and confidence," an exercise of the will—but even this is a gift (Eph. 2:9). Faith is a gift, but it is not inevitable. A gift is not a gift until it is received, an accepting of our prior acceptance by God. Our acceptance is a grace-empowered acceptance. Faith is the human response to grace, that is to Jesus. See "And Can It Be That I Should Gain" [*United Methodist Hymnal*, #363; *African Methodist Episcopal Church Hymnal*, #459; *Free Methodist Church and The Wesleyan Church Hymnal*, #273; and *The Nazarene Hymnal*, #225]; and "Let Us Plead for Faith Alone" (especially v. 1) [*United Methodist Hymnal*, #385].

Additional Study Material

> *God does undoubtedly command us both to repent, and to bring forth fruits meet for repentance; which if we willingly neglect, we cannot reasonably expect to be justified at all; therefore both repentance, and fruits meet for repentance, are, in some sense, necessary to justification. But they are not necessary in the same sense with faith, nor in the same degree. Not in the same degree; for those fruits are only necessary conditionally; if there be time and opportunity for them. . . . Not in the same sense; for repentance and its fruits are only remotely necessary; necessary in order to [have] faith; whereas faith is immediately necessary to justification. It remains, that faith is the only condition, which is immediately and proximately necessary to justification.*

John Wesley, The Scripture Way of Salvation, §III.2

> *Faith alone is that evidence, that conviction, that demonstration of things invisible, whereby the eyes of our understanding being opened, and divine light poured in upon them, we "see the wondrous things of God's law"; the excellence and purity of it; the height, and depth, and length, and breadth thereof, and of every commandment contained therein. It is by faith that, beholding "the light of the glory of God in the face of Jesus Christ," we perceive, as in a glass, all that is in ourselves, yea, the inmost motions of our souls. And by this alone can that blessed love of God be "shed abroad in our hearts," which enables us so to love one another as Christ loved us.*

John Wesley, The Scripture Way of Salvation, §III.2

Near the end of his life, Wesley wrote of two dimensions of faith: the first, "a divine conviction of God and of the things of God"; and the second "a divine conviction of the invisible and eternal world" (*On Faith*, §1). That final sermon concludes with these poetic words from Charles Wesley ["Author of Faith, Eternal Word (1889 *Methodist Hymnal*, #95, v5)]:

The things unknown to feeble sense,
Unseen by reason's glimmering ray,

With strong, commanding evidence,
Their heavenly origin display.

Faith lends its realizing light:
The clouds disperse, the shadows fly;

The Invisible appears in sight,
And GOD is seen by mortal eye!

John Wesley, On Faith, §18

A.7   TEACHER HELPS FOR LESSON 7 (SPIRITUAL REBIRTH)

Lesson 7 describes the real change in the life of the believer—known to Wesley as the New Birth—that occurs simultaneously with the relative change of spiritual condition before God that is known as justification. The new birth is accompanied by an experience of assurance, in which God's spirit testifies to our spirit that we are children of God. This experience also marks the beginning of sanctification. Wesley believed that the new birth was essential for salvation and was to be distinguished from one's baptism.

Additional Question for Discussion

1. How would you describe the nature of your fellowship with God?

Additional Study Material

And as, in the natural birth, a man is born at once, and then grows larger and stronger by degrees; so in the spiritual birth, a man is born at once, and then gradually increases in spiritual stature and strength. The new birth, therefore, is the first point of sanctification, which may increase more and more unto the perfect day.

John Wesley, On God's Vineyard, §I.7

For additional material related to Lesson 7, see also the Teacher Helps for Lesson 5, "The Almost Christian and the Altogether Christian."

A.8   TEACHER HELPS FOR LESSON 8 (CHANNELS OF GOD'S GRACE)

Lesson 8 focuses on Wesley's admonition not to wait quietly for God's grace to be active in our lives, but to use the means of grace as a channel to God. The means of grace are to be used while we are waiting for God to act in justification and in sanctification. This lesson concentrates not so much on how to use each of the means of grace, but rather on how the means of grace work in our lives. (Should participants seek more information on how to use each means of grace, you may wish to consult Henry H. Knight, III, *Eight Life-Enriching Practices of United Methodists;* and Steve Harper, *Devotional Life in the Wesleyan Tradition.*) This lesson distinguishes between the instituted and prudential means of grace and the reasons we should use them. It focuses on the role of habitual use of the means of grace in the renewal of the image of God in the believer.

How do we grow in our grace-filled life? By using the means of grace—specific channels through which God conveys grace to people, the normal and ordinary ways that God uses to provide divine grace. In contrast to the Moravians, who wanted just to wait for God to come to them, Wesley said that faith is mediated through the agency of the Holy Spirit and the Spirit uses means of grace. These means are not ends in themselves, but they are the form of Christian discipleship, practices of habit and virtue formation (see Heb. 5:14). These spiritual disciplines (a disciplined spirituality) are structures that are provided to assist us to get home to God. The sacrament of communion, for instance, can be a "converting ordinance" for people. They are practices that we use in order to become more mature in Christ. Interestingly, the same means of grace that bring us to grace (prior to our justification) also keep us in Christ (as we are being sanctified). See *United Methodist Hymnal* #410 (v. 3); and #616 "Come, Sinners, to the Gospel Feast."

Additional Question for Discussion

1. In what ways can your congregation develop structures for accountable discipleship?

Additional Study Material

> Almighty God of truth and love,
> to me thy power impart;
> the mountain from my soul remove,
> the hardness from my heart.
>
> O may the least omission pain
> my reawakened soul,
> and drive me to that blood again,
> which makes the wounded whole.

Charles Wesley, "I Want a Principle Within" (v. 4; 1749)—*UM Hymnal #410; Free Methodist Ch. & The Wesleyan Ch. Hymnal #344*

A.9 TEACHER HELPS FOR LESSON 9 (SANCTIFICATION: GROWING IN HOLINESS)

Lesson 9 discusses Wesley's sermon *The Circumcision of the Heart* and his understanding of sanctification as a process of growth in holiness. Justification is related to, yet distinct from, sanctification. Wesley's understanding of sanctification as a process is discussed in light of his belief in the possibility of Christian perfection, or perfection in love. The qualities of the heart that has been circumcised (humility, faith, hope, and love) are discussed and attention is drawn to the way in which these qualities are listed sequentially as part of the process of growing in holiness.

There is a tension in Wesley as to whether Christian perfection is received instantaneously or is the result of a gradual process. He believed that entire sanctification could occur in a moment, though he recognized that the gradual process is more common. (See John Wesley, *The Scripture Way of Salvation*, §III.18, and this lesson in *The Circumcision of the Heart.*) The goal of sanctification is so intimately associated with the *process of becoming* sanctified that he often seems to talk about both justification and sanctification at the same time. Sometimes he uses the same terminology for both. Most commonly, however, he described justification as a point in time and sanctification as an ongoing process.

Additional Study Material

> *[In] the gradual work of sanctification . . . , we are enabled "by the Spirit" to "mortify the deeds of the body," of our evil nature; and as we are more and more dead to sin, we are more and more alive to God. We go on from grace to grace, while we are careful to "abstain from all appearance of evil," and are "zealous of good works," as we have opportunity, doing good to all men; while we walk in all his ordinances blameless, therein worshipping him in spirit and in truth; while we take up our cross, and deny ourselves every pleasure that does not lead us to God.*

John Wesley, *The Scripture Way of Salvation*, §I.8

> *It is thus that we wait for entire sanctification; for a full salvation from all our sins—from pride, self-will, anger, unbelief; or, as the Apostle expresses it, "go on to perfection." But what is perfection? The word has various senses: here it means perfect love. It is love excluding sin; love filling the heart, taking up the whole capacity of the soul. It is love "rejoicing evermore, praying without ceasing, in everything giving thanks."*

John Wesley, *The Scripture Way of Salvation*, §I.9

> *Convince them that the whole work of sanctification is not, as they imagined, wrought at once; that when they first believe they are but as new-born babes, who are gradually to grow up, and may expect many storms before they come to the full stature of Christ. Above all, let them be instructed, when the storm is upon them, not to reason with the devil, but to pray; to pour out their souls before God, and show him of their trouble.*

John Wesley, *The Wilderness State*, §III.14

. . . by sanctification we are saved from the power and root of sin, and restored to the image of God . . . [Sanctification] begins the moment we are justified, in the holy, humble, gentle, patient love of God and man. It gradually increases from that moment, as "a grain of mustard-seed, which, at first, is the least of all seeds," but afterwards puts forth large branches, and becomes a great tree; till, in another instant, the heart is cleansed, from all sin, and filled with pure love to God and man. But even that love increases more and more, till we "grow up in all things into him that is our Head"; till we attain "the measure of the stature of the fullness of Christ."

John Wesley, *On Working Out Our Own Salvation*, §III.1

A.10 Teacher Helps for Lesson 10 (A Catholic Spirit: Toward Christian Unity)

Lesson 10 discusses Wesley's sermon, *Catholic Spirit*, in light of his understanding of sanctification as a process of growth in holiness. Reference is made to the Apostle's Creed and to the reasoning behind "one holy, catholic, and apostolic church" (the unity of comprising the one body of Christ). The lesson discusses qualifications identified by Wesley for having a "common heart" and being willing to welcome and be welcomed into community.

Having the attitude of a catholic spirit is part of living a sanctified life. Mere "opinions" must not divide us. However, Wesley is not promoting a "speculative latitudinarianism," which is an indifference to essential doctrines. The believer is "fixed as the sun in his judgment concerning the main branches of Christian doctrine," such as the Trinity, Christ's deity, or the resurrection. Further, Wesley did not promote an indifference to how we practice our worship, which is called "practical latitudinarianism"—tongue twisters!

Additional Question for Discussion

1. Do you agree with Wesley that differences in non-essential beliefs, styles of worship, or the particular congregation to which one belongs should not preclude Christian fellowship?

Additional Study Material

Why is the church one church? The ultimate reality is in Jesus Christ, but, because Jesus Christ relates himself to all the different parts of the family, each part is rooted in him. If there is only one Jesus Christ, and if Jesus Christ is in communion with all the branches of the church, then Jesus Christ is already connecting those branches with each other. The church is disconnected because of sin; that is why the reconciling movement is so important, in which we acknowledge that we are broken and confess that we need to come together. We admit that we have fallen short of the glory of God's church and that all sides did things that gave to the ultimate splitting of the church. Part of healing is to acknowledge that Christians past and present not only contributed to division, but contributed unnecessarily.[13]

R. Kendall Soulen

Being the creature of God's own Word and Spirit, the Church is one, holy, catholic, and apostolic. These essential attributes of the Church are not its own qualities but are fully rooted in its dependence upon God through his Word and Spirit.

*It is **one** because the God who binds it to himself by Word and Spirit is the one creator and redeemer making the Church a foretaste and instrument for the redemption of all created reality.*

*It is **holy** because God is the holy one who in Jesus Christ has overcome all unholiness, sanctifying the Church by his word of forgiveness in the Holy Spirit and making it his own, the body of Christ.*

*It is **catholic** because God is the fullness of life who through Word and Spirit makes the Church the place and instrument of his saving, life-giving, fulfilling presence wherever it is, thereby offering the fullness of the revealed Word, all the means of salvation to people of every nation, race, class, sex, and culture.*

*It is **apostolic** because the Word of God that creates and sustains the Church is the Gospel primarily and normatively borne witness to by the apostles, making the communion of the faithful a community that lives in, and is responsible for, the succession of the apostolic truth throughout the ages.*

World Council of Churches, *The Nature and Purpose of the Church* [WCC 1998], §12 (pp. 9-10)

A.11 TEACHER HELPS FOR LESSON 11 (THE DANGER OF RICHES)

Lesson 11 introduces participants to Wesley's sermon *The Danger of Riches* and his perspective on wealth and possessions as they relate to Christian living. Wesley's definition of riches is highlighted as well as his exhortation to his followers to "gain all they can," "save all they can," and, most importantly, "give all they can." After completing this study participants will be able to understand Wesley's perspective on wealth and possessions as one that is concerned primarily with Wesley's overall concern of being renewed in the image of God. For Wesley, wealth and affluence have the potential to distract the disciple from what is most important, growing in holiness and loving God and neighbor. Being wealthy in itself is not a sin, but there is a question of loyalties: Do we idolize our accumulated material possessions or is our loyalty to Jesus Christ?

Additional Question for Discussion

1. It has been said that people can discover their true place of loyalty by analyzing two things: How they spend their time and how they spend their money (look at your checkbook, for example). In analyzing those two items, where would your loyalties lie?

A.12 TEACHER HELPS FOR LESSON 12 (CHRISTIAN PERFECTION)

Lesson 12 introduces participants to Wesley's sermon *The Scripture Way of Salvation*. After completing this lesson, participants will be able to see Wesley's Way of Salvation as a coherent process that leads to the goal of entire sanctification and glorification. Attention is given to the primary role that faith plays in both justification and sanctification. This lesson also focuses on the distinction between sanctification as a process of growth in holiness and Christian perfection as the goal to which sanctification leads. This lesson continues to discuss the issues that were raised in Lesson 9 dealing with sanctification and Christian perfection, providing a more detailed explanation of Wesley's understanding of Christian perfection.

Christian perfection is to have one motive: love for God and neighbor, the love by which we were loved by Christ. It occurs only via Christ's atonement; we are sanctified by grace just as we were justified by grace (Heb. 7:25; 12:2). (See *United Methodist Hymnal* #479, v. 4.) It is possible only by God (see Matt. 19:21, 25-26). This occurs only by depending on and abiding in Christ (John 15:4-5), not on our work. Christian perfection is not sinlessness, but rather, being made perfect in love, restored in a relationship in which we are motivated by love for God and others. It is a fulfillment of the virtues, a restoration of the image of God, and being made in the likeness of Christ. Perfect love is not a perfect life, according to God's standards of righteousness. We may still make mistakes and will still sin, but not knowingly sin. It is a perfection of motive (intent) rather than a perfection of performance (behavior), not achieved but received. Christian perfection is concerned with known acts, not the condition of sin. The penchant for sin remains, but does not reign.

Because this doctrine has often generated controversy, there is a particular need in this lesson to provide biblical support. Some relevant verses include: Heb. 12:14; 1 Jn. 4:12,17; Matt. 5:48; 1 Peter 1:14-16; 2 Cor. 13:9; 1 Thess. 3:13; 4:3. Class participants may wish to look up these verses and discuss their meaning.

Note that this sermon, "The Scripture Way of Salvation," is a useful summary of the entire Way of Salvation. William B. Fitzgerald summarized the Way of Salvation in this way (commonly called "The Four Alls of Methodism"): "All need to be saved" (from sin; see Lesson 3 on Original Sin); "all can be saved" (from sin; i.e., salvation by grace through faith; see Lesson 6 on Justification); "all can know themselves to be saved" (i.e., assurance; see Lesson 7); and "all can be saved to the uttermost" (i.e., Christian Perfection; see Lesson 12) [Vickers 2000, pp. 123, 127].

A.13 Teacher Helps for Lesson 13 (God's New Creation: The Culmination of the way of Salvation)

Lesson 13 focuses on the nature of the Kingdom of God, which is partly already present, partly coming to be present, and to a great extent still in the future. A discussion of what is meant by "glorification" is provided. Visions for a new heaven and a new earth are summarized, with reference to the Book of Revelation. The relation of the new creation to the Christian life is affirmed (e.g., justification, sanctification, church, and mission).

Additional Study Material

The new creation is God's ultimate purpose. Our life is an anticipation of heaven. (See "Love Divine, All Loves Excelling" *UMH* 384, v. 4.) We will continue to grow in grace until we are glorified with Christ. The scope of salvation is beyond you and me; it involves the redemption and healing of every aspect of the universe—which has social and ecological implications. The first sermon ("The New Creation") includes a lot of Wesley's specific speculations about the future of the created order. We do not need to agree with Wesley in the details of his speculation in order to agree with his spiritual trajectory—that God is renewing all things in order to bring us to our intended fulfillment in eternal fellowship with the Trinity.

Concluding Comments

Summary. You have completed some challenging, yet exciting and inspiring material. We have examined the basic elements of Wesley's Way of Salvation, starting with being created in the image of God and the separation of humans from God as described in Genesis 1-3. In all of our lives, beginning at birth, God's prevenient grace is present, leading to a conviction of sin, repentance, faith, and justification under the justifying dimension of grace. The change that results in our lives was described as new birth, and the high standards of the transformed life as becoming a "real" Christian. Channels of grace were identified. Sanctification and its goal of Christian perfection in love of God and neighbor were characterized, along with the need for unity of Christian communities that comprise the Body of Christ. We concluded with the present and future aspects of the Kingdom of God to which the good news of Jesus Christ was directed. In each discussion, we examined Scriptures and the ways in which both John and Charles Wesley proclaimed them. All these we celebrate in Christ's love for us and with us.

The Love Feast. The conclusion of this study could be an appropriate time for you to have a Love Feast together with your study group. Wesley was introduced to the Love Feast by the Moravians, and he often used the Love Feast format to fellowship with other believers. A Love Feast is reminiscent of the meals that Jesus shared with his inner circle of disciples, and it expresses community and fellowship with one another. You may use the Love Feast as described in *The United Methodist Book of Worship*[14] or you may design your own. A Love Feast is not communion. This "feast" may or may not include a meal of simple foods and beverages, but always includes prayer, testimony and praise to God. Often Scriptures are read and hymns are sung. Usually people are seated in a circle so that they can be in close fellowship with each other. A Love Feast can provide a fitting way to end this study of Wesley's Way of Salvation.

Appendix B: Resources

B.1 RESOURCES ON DISCIPLESHIP

DISCIPLE BIBLE STUDY   Abingdon Press (Cokesbury)
Jesus in the Gospels   Abingdon Press (Cokesbury)
Christian Believer   Abingdon Press (Cokesbury)

Accountable Discipleship

David Lowes Watson, *Covenant Discipleship: Christian Formation Through Mutual Accountability*. Nashville: Discipleship Resources, 1991.

Gayle Turner Watson, *Guide for Covenant Discipleship Groups*. Nashville: Discipleship Resources, 2000.

Steven W. Manskar, *Accountable Discipleship: Living in God's Household*. Nashville: Discipleship Resources, 2000.

Thomas R. Hawkins, *Cultivating Christian Community*. Nashville: Discipleship Resources, 2001.

Barb Nardi Kurtz, *The Heart's Journey: Christian Spiritual Formation in the Life of a Small Group*. Nashville: Discipleship Resources, 2001.

Shirley L. Ramsey and Edie Genung Harris, *Sprouts: Covenant Discipleship with Children*, Revised Edition. Nashville: Discipleship Resources, 2002.

David C. Sutherland, *Together in Love: Covenant Discipleship with Youth*. Nashville: Discipleship Resources, 1999.

Class Meetings

David Lowes Watson, *The Early Methodist Class Meeting*. Nashville: Discipleship Resources, 1985.

D. Michael Henderson, *John Wesley's Class Meeting: A Model for Making Disciples*. Nappanee, Indiana: Evangel Publishing House, 1997.

Devotions

Paul Wesley Chilcote, *Praying in the Wesley Spirit: 52 Prayers for Today*. Nashville: Upper Room Books, 2002.
Gregory S. Clapper, *As If the Heart Mattered: A Wesleyan Spirituality*. Nashville: Upper Room Books, 1997.
David Arthur deSilva, *Praying with John Wesley*. Nashville: Discipleship Resources, 2001.
Steve Harper, *Devotional Life in the Wesleyan Tradition*. Nashville: Upper Room Books, 1983.
Steve Harper, *Devotional Life in the Wesleyan Tradition*: A Workbook. Nashville: Upper Room Books, 1996.
Steve Harper, *Prayer and Devotional Life of United Methodists*. Nashville: Abingdon Press, 1999.

Life of John Wesley

Charles Sauer, *Pocket Story of John Wesley*, Revised Edition. Nashville: Discipleship Resources, 1988, 2002.
Charles Yrigoyen, Jr., *John Wesley: Holiness of Heart and Life*. Nashville: Abingdon Press, 1996 (with a study guide by Ruth A. Daugherty).

B.2 BOOKS

[Abraham 2005]   William J. Abraham, *Wesley for Armchair Theologians*. Louisville: Westminster John Knox Press, 2005.

[AMEH 1984]   *African Methodist Episcopal Church Hymnal*, African Methodist Episcopal Church, 1984.

[Armentrout n.d.]   Don S. Armentrout and Robert Boak Slocum, Editors, *An Episcopal Dictionary of the Church: A User Friendly Reference for Episcopalians*. New York: Church Publishing Incorporated (no date).

[Chadwick 1991]   Henry Chadwick (translator), Saint Augustine of Hippo, *Confessions*. Oxford: Oxford University Press, 1991.

[Beasley-Topliffe 1997]   Keith Beasley-Topliffe, Editor, *A Longing for Holiness: Selected Writings of John Wesley*. Nashville: Upper Room Books, 1997.

[Berger 1995]   Teresa Berger (translated by Timothy E. Kimbrough), *Theology in Hymns?: A Study of the Relationship of Doxology and Theology According to "A Collection of Hymns for the Use of the People Called Methodists (1780)."* Nashville: Kingswood Books, Abingdon Press, 1989 (translated in 1995).

[Burtner 1954]	Robert W. Burtner and Robert E. Chiles, Editors, *John Wesley's Theology: A Collection from His Works*. Nashville: Abingdon Press, 1954.
[CampbellT 1997]	Ted A. Campbell, et al., *Wesley and the Quadrilateral: Renewing the Conversation*. Nashville: Abingdon Press, 1997.
[CampbellT 1999]	Ted A. Campbell, *Methodist Doctrine: The Essentials*. Nashville: Abingdon Press, 1999.
[Carder 1996]	Kenneth L. Carder, *Living Our Beliefs: The United Methodist Way*. Nashville: Discipleship Resources, 1996.
[Chambers 1933]	Oswald Chambers, *My Utmost for His Highest: Selections for Every Day*. London: Simpkin, Marshall, 1933.
[Chilcote 1986]	Paul Wesley Chilcote, Editor, *Wesley Speaks on Christian Vocation*. Nashville: Discipleship Resources, 1986.
[Chilcote 1993]	Paul Wesley Chilcote, *She Offered Them Christ: The Legacy of Women Preachers in Early Methodism*. Nashville: Abingdon Press, 1993.
[Chilcote 2001]	Paul Wesley Chilcote, *Praying in the Wesley Spirit: 52 Prayers for Today*. Nashville: Upper Room Books, 2002.
[Chilcote 2002]	Paul Wesley Chilcote, Editor, *The Wesleyan Tradition: A Paradigm for Renewal*. Nashville: Abingdon Press, 2002.
[Chilcote 2004]	Paul Wesley Chilcote, *Recapturing the Wesleys' Vision: An Introduction to the Faith of John and Charles Wesley*. Downers Grove, Illinois: InterVarsity Press, 2004.
[CMEBOR n.d.]	*Christian Methodist Episcopal Church Book of Ritual (New and Revised)*, Christian Methodist Episcopal Church, General Board of Publications, Nashville, not dated.
[CMEH 1987]	*The Hymnal of the Christian Methodist Episcopal Church*. Nashville: Christian Methodist Episcopal Church, General Board of Publications, 1987.
[CollinsKJ 1989]	Kenneth J. Collins, *Wesley on Salvation: A Study in the Standard Sermons*. Grand Rapids Michigan. Francis Asbury Press, Zondervan Publishing House, 1989.
[CollinsKJ 1997]	Kenneth J. Collins, *The Scripture Way of Salvation: The Heart of John Wesley's Theology*. Nashville: Abingdon Press, 1997.
[CollinsKJ 1999]	Kenneth J. Collins, *A Real Christian: The Life of John Wesley*. Nashville: Abingdon Press, 1999.
[CollinsKJ 2001]	Kenneth J. Collins and John H. Tyson, Editors, *Conversion in the Wesleyan Tradition*, Nashville: Abingdon Press, 2001.
[CollinsKJ 2003]	Kenneth J. Collins, *John Wesley: A Theological Journey*. Nashville: Abingdon Press, 2003.
[Fieser 2006]	James Fieser, "David Hume (1711-1776) Writings on Religion," *The Internet Dictionary of Philosophy*, 2006
[Gilmore 1995]	Marshall Gilmore, Editor, *A Larger Catechism: For Members of the Christian Methodist Episcopal Church*. Nashville: Christian Methodist Episcopal Church, General Board of Publications, 1995.
[González 2005]	Justo L. González, *Essential Theological Terms*, Westminster John Knox Press, Louisville, KY, 2005.
[Gooch 2006]	John O. Gooch, *John Wesley for the 21st Century: Set Apart for Social Witness*. Nashville: Discipleship Resources, 2006.
[GP2 2000]	*Global Praise 2: Songs for Worship and Witness*, S.T. Kimbrough, Jr. (general editor) and Carlton R. Young (musical editor). New York: The General Board on Global Ministries, The United Methodist Church, GBGMusic, 2000.
[GP3 2004]	*Global Praise 3: More Songs for Worship and Witness*, S.T. Kimbrough, Jr. (general editor) and Carlton R. Young (musical editor). New York: The General Board on Global Ministries, The United Methodist Church, GBGMusic, 2004.
[Green 1977]	Keith Green, *Your Love Broke Through: The Worship Songs of Keith Green*, Volume 1 (The Ministry Years 1977-1979), Recording, Sparrow Records, February 1, 2002 (cd006521). http://www.sing365.com/music/lyric.nsf/Your-Love-Broke-Through-lyrics-Keith-Green/6A8B3E64DF5BF64948256AA2002C7E41
[Harper 2003]	Steve Harper, *The Way to Heaven: The Gospel According to John Wesley* [formerly titled, *John Wesley's Message for Today*]. Grand Rapids, Michigan: Zondervan Publishing House, 1983, 2003.
[Harvey 1964]	Van A. Harvey, *A Handbook of Theological Terms*. New York: Collier Books, Macmillan Publishing Company, 1964.

[Heitzenrater 1995]   Richard P. Heitzenrater, *Wesley and the People Called Methodists*. Nashville: Abingdon Press, 1995.

[Heitzenrater 2003]   Richard P. Heitzenrater, *The Elusive Mr. Wesley*, Second Revised Edition. Nashville: Abingdon Press, 1995.

[Henderson 1997]   D. Michael Henderson, *John Wesley's Class Meeting: A Model for Making Disciples*. Nappanee, Indiana: Evangel Publishing House, 1997.

[Hill 2002]   Craig C. Hill, *In God's Time—The Bible and the Future*. Grand Rapids, Michigan: William B. Eerdmans Publishing Company, 2002.

[Hoyt 1989]   Hoyt L. Hickman, *Worship Resources of the United Methodist Hymnal*. Nashville: Abingdon Press, 1989.

[Jones 1948]   E. Stanley Jones, *Gandhi: Portrayal of a Friend*. Nashville: Abingdon Press, 1948.

[Kimbrough 1992]   S.T. Kimbrough, Jr., *Charles Wesley: Poet and Theologian*. Nashville: Kingswood Books, Abingdon Press, 1992.

[Kinghorn 1992]   Kenneth Cain Kinghorn, *Gospel of Grace: The Way of Salvation in the Wesleyan Tradition*. Nashville: Abingdon Press, 1992.

[Kinghorn 2002]   Kenneth Cain Kinghorn, Editor, *The Standard Sermons in Modern English*. Nashville: Abingdon Press, 2002.
Volume 1, *John Wesley on Christian Belief*
Volume 2, *John Wesley on Christian Practices*
Volume 3, *John Wesley on the Sermon on the Mount* (Sermons 34-53).

[Knight 1992]   Henry H. Knight III, *The Presence of God in the Christian Life: John Wesley and the Means of Grace*. Metuchen, NJ: The Scarecrow Press, Inc., 1992.

[Knight 2001]   Henry H. Knight III, *Eight Life-Enriching Practices of United Methodists*. Nashville: Abingdon Press, 2001.

[Kreitzer 1993]   Larry J. Kreitzer, "Eschatology," *Dictionary of Paul and His Letters*. Downer's Grove, Illinois: InterVarsity Press, 1993, pp. 253-269.

[Langford 1991]   Thomas A. Langford, *Doctrine and Theology in The United Methodist Church*. Nashville: Kingswood Books, Abingdon Press, 1991.

[Lawson 1987]   John Lawson, *The Wesley Hymns As a Guide to Scriptural Teaching*. Grand Rapids, Michigan: Francis Asbury Press, Zondervan Publishing House, 1987.

[Lindstrom 1946]   Harald Lindstrom, *Wesley and Sanctification: A Study in the Doctrine of Salvation*. Wilmore, Kentucky: Francis Asbury Publishing Company, Incorporated, 1946 (re-published in 1981 with a foreword by Timothy L. Smith.

[Lodahl 2003]   Michael Lodahl, God of Nature and of Grace: Reading the World in a Wesleyan Way, Nashville: Kingswood Books, 2003.

[Logan 2005]   James C. Logan, *How Great a Flame: Contemporary Lessons from the Wesleyan Revival*. Nashville: Discipleship Resources, 2005.

[Maas 1989]   Robin Maas, *Crucified Love: The Practice of Christian Perfection*. Nashville: Abingdon Press, 1989.

[Maddox 1994]   Randy L. Maddox, *Responsible Grace: John Wesley's Practical Theology*. Nashville: Kingswood Books, Abingdon Press, 1994.

[Maddox 1998]   Randy L. Maddox, Editor, *Rethinking Wesley's Theology for Contemporary Methodism*. Nashville: Kingswood Books, Abingdon Press, 1998.

[Magoon 1857]   E.L. Magoon, *Sermons of the Rev. C.H. Spurgen of London with an Introduction and Sketch of His Life*. New York: Sheldon, Blakeman, and Company, 1857.

[Manskar 2004]   Steven W. Manskar, Diana L. Hynson, and Marjorie Hewitt Suchocki, *A Perfect Love, Understanding John Wesley's "A Plain Account of Christian Perfection,"* Expanded Edition. Nashville: Discipleship Resources, 2004.

[Marquardt 1992]   Manfred Marquardt, *John Wesley's Social Ethics: Praxis and Principles*, translated by John E. Steely and W. Stephen Gunter. Nashville: Abingdon Press, 1992.

[McClain 1990]   William B. McClain, *Black People in the Methodist Church: Wither Thou Goest*. Revised Edition. Nashville: Abingdon Press, 1984, 1990.

[McClain 1990]   William B. McClain, *Come Sunday: The Liturgy of Zion*. Nashville: Abingdon Press, 1990.

[Mercer 2000]   Jerry L. Mercer, *Living Deeply Our New Life in Christ: A Wesleyan Spirituality for Today*. Nashville: Discipleship Resources, 2000.

[Migliore 1991]   Daniel L. Migliore, *Faith Seeking Understanding: An introduction to Christian Theology*, Grand Rapids, Michigan: William B. Eerdmans Publishing Company, 1991.

[Miles 2002]   Rebekah Miles, "Why Wesley Feared for the Souls of the Rich," in Paul Wesley Chilcote, Editor, *The Wesleyan Tradition: A Paradigm for Renewal*. Nashville: Abingdon Press, 2002.

[Newman 2004]   John Henry Newman, "Difficulties of Latitudinarianism," *The Newman Reader: Works of John Henry Newman*, The National Institute for Newman Studies, 2004.

[Newbigin 1995]   Lesslie Newbigin, *The Open Secret: An Introduction to the Theology of Mission*. Grand Rapids, Michigan: William B. Eerdman's Publishing Company, 1995.

[Outler 1964]   Albert C. Outler, Editor, *John Wesley: A Representative Collection of His Writings*. New York: Oxford University Press, 1964. [Includes: John Wesley, "A Letter to a Roman Catholic" (July 18, 1749), pp. 493-499]

[Outler 1966]   Albert C. Outler, *That the World May Believe: A Study of Christian Unity*. New York: Joint Commission on Education and cultivation, Board of Missions of the Methodist Church, 1966.

[Outler 1991a]   Albert C. Outler and Richard P. Heitzenrater, Editors, *John Wesley's Sermons: An Anthology*. Nashville: Abingdon Press, 1991.

[Outler 1991b]   Albert C. Outler, *John Wesley's Sermons: An Introduction*. Nashville : Abingdon Press, 1991.

[Outler 1996]   Albert C. Outler, *Evangelism and Theology in the Wesleyan Spirit*. Nashville: Discipleship Resources, 1996.

[Rack 2002]   Henry D. Rack, *Reasonable Enthusiast: John Wesley and the Rise of Methodism*. Revised Edition. Nashville: Abingdon Press, 1992, 2002.

[Ruark 1987]   James E. Ruark, Editor, *Wesley's Notes on the Bible (John Wesley)*. An abridged edition of John Wesley's *Explanatory Notes Upon the Old and New Testaments*. Grand Rapids, Michigan: Francis Asbury Press, Zondervan Publishing House, 1987.

[Runyon 1998]   Theodore Runyon, *The New Creation: John Wesley's Theology Today*. Nashville: Abingdon Press, 1998.

[Sanchez 1992]   Diana Sanchez, Volume Editor, *The Hymns of the United Methodist Hymnal: Introduction to the Hymns, Canticles, and Acts of Worship*. Nashville: Abingdon Press, 1992.

[Schmidt 1999]   Jean Miller Schmidt, *Grace Sufficient: A History of Women in American Methodism, 1760-1939*. Nashville: Abingdon Press, 1999.

[Snyder 1980]   Howard A. Snyder, *The Radical Wesley and Patterns for Church Renewal*. Downers Grove, Illinois: InterVarsity Press, 1980.

[Strong 1997]   Douglas M. Strong, *They Walked in the Spirit: Personal Faith and Social Action in America*. Louisville: Westminster John Knox Press, 1997.

[Thurston 1993]   Branson L. Thurston, *The United Methodist Way: A Brief Overview of the History, Beliefs, Mission, and Organization of the United Methodist Church*. Nashville: Discipleship Resources, 1993.

[Tyson 1986]   John R. Tyson, *Charles Wesley on Sanctification: A Biographical and Theological Study*. Grand Rapids, Michigan, Asbury Press, 1986.

[UMBoD 2004]   *Book of Discipline of The United Methodist Church (U.S.)*, United Methodist Publishing House. Nashville: Abingdon Press, 1992.

[UMBoW 1992]   *The United Methodist Book of Worship*, The United Methodist Church (U.S.), United Methodist Publishing House. Nashville: Abingdon Press, 1992.

[UMCPrimer 2002]   *The United Methodist Primer*, Revised Edition. Nashville: Discipleship Resources, 2005.

[UMCTeacher 2002]   The United Methodist Church, *What Every Teacher Needs to Know*. Nashville: Discipleship Resources, 2002.

[UMH 1989]   *The United Methodist Hymnal: Book of United Methodist Worship*, United Methodist Publishing House. Nashville: Abingdon Press, 1989.

[UMSBoH 1966]   *Supplement to the Book of Hymns*. Nashville: United Methodist Publishing House, 1982.

[UMTFWS 2000]   Hoyt L. Hickman, General Editor, *The Faith We Sing*. The United Methodist Church. Nashville: Abingdon Press, 2000.

[Vickers 2000]   John A. Vickers, *A Dictionary of Methodism in Britain and Ireland*. Peterborough, England: Epworth Press, 2000.

[WCC 1982]	*Baptism, Eucharist, and Ministry,* Faith and Order Paper 111, WCC Publications, Geneva, Switzerland, July 1982.
[WCC 1998]	*The Nature and Purpose of the Church: A Stage on the Way to a Common Statement,* Faith and Order Paper 181, WCC Publications, Geneva, Switzerland, 1998.
[Wesley 1746]	John and Charles Wesley, *Hymns of Petition and Thanksgiving for the Promise of The Father,* Whitsunday, Bristol, 1746.
[Wesley 1754]	John Wesley, *Explanatory Notes Upon the New Testament.* London and Peterborough, England: Epworth Press, 1754 (1976 Edition).
[Wesley 1765]	John Wesley, *Expanatory Notes Upon the Old Testament.* Bristol: William Pine, 1765.
[Wesley 1784]	John Wesley "Directions for Renewing Our Covenant With God," Third Edition, 1784. http://wesley.nnu.edu/john_wesley/covenant/index.htm (copy of Edition 1, 1780, provided in Frank Whaling, Editor, *John and Charles Wesley: Selected Prayers, Hymns, Journal Notes, Sermons, Letters, and Treatises.* New York: Paulist Press, 1981).
[Wesley 1812]	John Wesley, *Minutes of the Methodist Conferences,* Vol. 1 (1744-1798), London: Cordeux, 1812.
[Wesley 1894]	John Wesley, *A Plain Account of Christian Perfection* (Edited by Thomas O. Summers). Nashville: Publishing House of the M.E. Church, South, 1894.
[WesleyC 1889]	Charles Wesley, *A Collection of Hymns, for the Use of the People Called Methodists,* with a New Supplement [*Methodist 1889 Hymnal*]. London: Wesleyan-Methodist Book-Room, 1889.
[WesleyC 1997]	Charles Wesley, *The Journal of Charles A. Wesley: The Early Journal 1736-1739,* New Edition. Taylors, South Carolina: Methodist Reprint Society, 1977.
[WesleyS 1711]	Susanna Wesley, *Journal Notebook (1709-1718),* May 17, 1711, "Headingley Manuscript A," Wesley College, Bristol, England. See Charles Wallace, Jr., Editor, *Susanna Wesley: The Complete Writings,* New York: Oxford University Press, 1997 [Entry 47], p. 235.
[Whaling 1981]	Frank Whaling, Editor, *John and Charles Wesley: Selected Prayers, Hymns, Journal Notes, Sermons, Letters, and Treatises.* New York: Paulist Press, 1981.
[Wheeler 1995]	Sondra Ely Wheeler, *Wealth as Peril and Obligation: The New Testament on Possessions.* Grand Rapids, Michigan: W.B. Eerdmans Publishing Company, 1995.
[Willard 2006]	Dallas Willard, *The Great Omission: Reclaiming Jesus' Essential Teachings on Discipleship.* San Francisco: Harper, 2006.
[Willimon 1990]	William H. Willimon, *Why I Am a United Methodist.* Nashville: Abingdon Press, 1990.
[WorksBH 1984ff]	Frank Baker and Richard P. Heitzenrater, General Editors, *The Bicentennial Edition of the Works of John Wesley,* Nashville: Abingdon Press; and Oxford: Clarendon Press, 1984ff. Volumes 1-4, *Sermons,* Albert C. Outler, Editor (1984-1987) Volume 7, *A Collection of Hymns for the Use of the People Called Methodists,* Franz Hildebrandt and Oliver A. Hildebrandt, Editors. Volume 9, *The Methodist Societies: History, Nature, and Design,* edited by Rupert E. Davies Volume 11, *The Appeals to Men of Reason and Religion and Certain Related Open Letters,* Geral R. Cragg, Editor, 1975. Volumes 18-24, *Journal and Diaries,* edited by W. Reginald Ward (journal) and Richard P. Heitzenrater (manuscript journals and diaries), 1988-1993. Volumes 25-31, *Letters,* Frank Baker, Editor
[WorksJ 1984ff]	Jackson, Editor, *The Works of John Wesley,* Third Edition, Complete and Unabridged, Fourteen Volumes. Grand Rapids, Michigan: Baker Book House, Reprinted 1979 from the 1872 Edition issued by Wesleyan-Methodist Book Room. Volume I, *Journals from October 14, 1735 to November 29, 1745* Volume VII, *Sermons on Several Occasions,* Second Series Concluded; Third, Fourth, and Fifth Series [Sermon CXVI, *Causes of the Inefficacy of Christianity (1789), pp. 261-290*].
[Yrigoyen 1996]	Charles Yrigoyen, Jr., *John Wesley: Holiness of Heart and Life.* Nashville: Abingdon Press, 1996 (with a study guide by Ruth A. Daugherty).
[Yrigoyen 2001]	Charles Yrigoyen, Jr., *Belief Matters: United Methodism's Doctrinal Standards.* Nashville: Abingdon Press, 2001.
[Yrigoyen 2005]	Charles Yrigoyen, Jr., *Praising the Grace of God: The Theology of Charles Wesley's Hymns.* Nashville: Abingdon Press, 2005.

B.3 WEBSITES

African Methodist Episcopal Church	http://www.ame-church.com/
Bibliographies in Methodism	http://www.gcah.org/umbib.htm
Christian Methodist Episcopal Church	http://www.c-m-e.org/
Cokesbury (Disciple)	http://www.cokesbury.com/disciple_controller.aspx?pageid=202&id=17
Cokesbury Bookstore	http://www.cokesbury.com/
Discipleship Resources Bookstore	http://www.upperroom.org/bookstore/category_search.asp
Explanatory Notes on the New Testament	http://new.gbgm-umc.org/umhistory/wesley/
Free Methodist Church	http://www.freemethodistchurch.org
Hymns of Charles Wesley	http://gbgm-umc.org/umhistory/wesley/hymns/#hymns
Journal of John Wesley	http://www.ccel.org/index/author-W.html
Library, Wesley Theological Seminary	http://library.wesleysem.edu/
Methodist Articles of Faith	http://www.godonthe.net/cme/methdist/articles.htm
Preacher's Magazine (Church of the Nazarene)	http://www.nph.com/nphweb/html/pmol/index.htm
Sermons of John Wesley	http://gbgm-umc.org/UMhistory/Wesley/sermons/http://wesley.nnu.edu/john_wesley/sermons/intro.htm http://www.cyberhymnal.org/bio/w/e/s/wesley_c.htm
Star of Zion (African Methodist Episcopal Zion Church)	http://www.starofzion.org/
Upper Room Bookstore	http://www.upperroom.org/bookstore/default.asp
Wesley Ministry Network	http://www.wesleyministrynetwork.com/
The United Methodist Church	http://umc.org/
The Wesleyan Church	http://www.wesleyan.org/

Appendix C: Glossary

C.1 ACRONYMS AND OTHER ABBREVIATIONS

AME	African Methodist Episcopal (Church)
Ch	Church
KJV	*King James Version of the Holy Bible*
NIV	*New International Version® of the Holy Bible*
NKJV	*New King James Version of the Holy Bible*
NRSV	*New Revised Standard Version® of the Holy Bible*
TNIV	*Today's New International Version® of the Holy Bible*
UM	United Methodist
WTS	Wesley Theological Seminary

C.2 DEFINITIONS (FIRST USE IS MARKED WITH THE SYMBOL "*")

Aldersgate (Street) Experience. The first perception by John Wesley of a personal assurance of God's forgiveness of *his* sins, which occurred on May 24th, 1738, and often referred to as his evangelical conversion.

Analogy of Faith. That connected chain of Scripture truths that constitute the very core of Christian teaching, those doctrines essential to the story of salvation [Runyon 1998, p. 19]. Understanding the Word of God "as a whole rather than through individual or obscure passages" [Manskar 2004, p. 73]. "The connection and harmony there is between those grand, fundamental doctrines, Original Sin, Justification by Faith, the New Birth, inward and outward holiness [Preface to *Explanatory Notes on the Old Testament*; Wesley, 1765, p. ix].

Assurance Confirmation. by God through the Holy Spirit that one's *own* sins have truly been forgiven. "The complete and absolute knowledge of one's state of salvation. . . . Wesley . . . held that the internal witness of the Spirit, and a holy life, assure the believer of his or her own salvation." [González 2005, p. 20]. "A sure confidence in God, that through the merits of Christ, his sins are forgiven" [*A Plain Account of Christian Perfection*, 1894, §13, p. 34].

Atonement. "The saving work of Jesus Christ on the cross" [González 2005, p. 20]. The "reconciling act ['at-one-ment'] of God in Jesus Christ, especially but not exclusively through his passion and death, that mends the broken relationship between God and humanity caused by sin" [Migliore 2004, p. 405].

Awakening. The awareness of one's sinful condition and the need for forgiveness, made possible due to God's prevenient grace.

Christian Perfection. Loving both God and neighbor fully, to the exclusion of all else—the logical result of Wesley's belief that sanctification is a process of growth in holiness. "Pure love reigning alone in the heart and life—this is the whole of scriptural perfection" [*A Plain Account of Christian Perfection*, §19 pp. 77-78]. Two other expressions are frequently used for Christian perfection: "entire sanctification" and "perfection in love." "The goal of the Christian life—not as something that one attains, but as a gift from God" [González 2005, pp. 130-131].

Conversion. Often a synonym for repentance, justification, and the experience of the new birth. "If justification refers primarily to what God does *for* us in Christ, conversion, strictly speaking, may be seen primarily as the transforming work of God *in* us by the Spirit, literally 'turning [us] around.'" [Runyon 1998, p. 57] "Turning away from sin" [González 2005, p. 152].

Convicting or Convincing Grace. That form of God's grace that makes personal conviction of sin and repentance possible. "Salvation is carried on by *convincing* grace, usually in Scripture termed *repentance*; which brings a larger measure of self-knowledge, and a farther deliverance from the heart of stone. Afterwards we experience the proper Christian salvation; whereby, 'through grace,' we 'are saved by faith'; consisting of those two grand branches, justification and sanctification" [*On Working Out Our Own Salvation*, §II.1(emphasis in the original)].

Conviction. Confirmation by God through the Holy Spirit that personal forgiveness of sins is necessary and possible, through cooperation by the Holy Spirit. Conviction of sin is a necessary part of repentance [*The Witness of the Spirit, I,* §II.1]. "A conviction of our utter sinfulness, and guiltiness, and helplessness" [*The Repentance of Believers,* §Intro.2].

Doctrine. Literally, "teaching"; often referring to "those considered views and tenets that characterize a particular group within the church" [González 2005, p. 47]. The "exposition of an important article of Christian faith" [Migliore 2004, p. 408].

Ecumenical. Literally, "universal." In recent times, the term has been used concerning "the effort to bring the various churches all over the world into closer connection," [González 2005, p. 51], for the sake of unified Christian witness and mission.

Enthusiasts. A derogatory term used by contemporaries of John and Charles Wesley. The term often came in the context of Christian perfection, especially its "inward emphasis" [found, for example in John Wesley's 1732 sermon, *Christian Perfection;* see Lesson 12].

Entire Sanctification. The ultimate goal of the process of growing in holiness, which John Wesley believed was possible for believers before their death . Also known as the "Second Blessing" (after the first blessing of conversion) in some Wesleyan traditions. See also Christian Perfection. "Entirely changed…wholly transformed into the image of him that created us" [*The Repentance of Believers,* §III.2]

Eschatology. "The doctrine of the 'last things' or the completion of God's works of creation and redemption" [Migliore 2004, p. 409]. As the "basis of Christian hope and joy, eschatology is the expectation and assurance that in the end God and God's love will prevail" [González 2005, p. 54].

Faith. The act of belief and the content of that belief. "A divine evidence and conviction of God, and of the things of God" [*Original Sin,* §III.3]. "A sure trust and confidence that God both hath and will forgive our sins, that he hath accepted us again into his favor, for the merits of Christ's death and passion" [*Justification by Faith,* §IV.3]. "Personal response of trust and confidence in the gracious God made known in Jesus Christ" [Migliore 2004, p. 410].

Fear of God. To be in awe and wonder of God. The fear of the Lord or fear of God is to stand in awe of what God has created

Forgiveness. "God's free and gracious acceptance of sinners decisively declared in Jesus' teaching, ministry to sinners and outcasts, and death for the salvation of the world" [Migliore 2004, p. 410].

Glorification. "Our deliverance from the very presence of sin" [Maddox 1994, p. 190], usually occurring at the moment of death.

Gospel. Literally, "good news"; more particularly, the message of Jesus Christ. "The 'good news' of salvation through the free and unmerited grace of God in Jesus Christ" [Migliore 2004, p. 411].

Grace. "The unmerited love of God, which both forgives and transforms the sinner" [González 2005, p. 69]. The free and unmerited act through which God restores his estranged creatures to himself" [Harvey 1964, p. 108].

Grand Depositum. A treasury of traditions, practices, and ideas passed on by a group of people from one generation to another. Used by John Wesley to refer to Christian perfection as the particular contribution of Methodism to Christianity.

Heathen. Non-Christian.

Holiness. The state of being set apart, especially for relationship with God in Jesus Christ. Wesley called holiness "Christ's righteousness infused in the heart of the believer" [Heitzenrater 1995, p. 221]

Holy temper. A habitual pattern of living that results in a virtuous and holy life, through grace. See "temper" below. Holy tempers may be thought of as "synonymous with the fruit of the Spirit in Gal. 5:22-33" [Manskar 2004, p. 7].

Hope. "A gift of God [that] anticipates the fulfillment of God's promises to and purposes for the world" [Migliore 2004, p. 412].

Infirmities. "All inward or outward imperfections which are not of a moral nature" [*Christian Perfection,* §I.7].

Justification. Pardon, the forgiveness of sins, when Christ's righteousness becomes our righteousness. To be declared blameless (as in a court of law). "The act by which God brings [humans] back into proper relationship to him" [Harvey 1964, p. 135]. "God's gracious pardon and acceptance of sinners, not on account of their own virtues or good works, but solely because of God's sheer grace embodied in Jesus Christ and received by faith" [Migliore 2004, p. 414].

Justifying Grace. The active grace of God manifested toward us in Jesus Christ, resulting in the forgiveness of sins due to Christ's atoning death for us, which is the foundation for new life. "The righteousness of Christ is the whole and sole foundation of all our hope. It is by faith that the Holy Ghost enables us to build upon this foundation. God gives us this faith. In that moment we are accepted of God, and yet not for the sake of that faith, but of what Christ has done and suffered for us" [*The Lord Our Righteousness,* §II.13].

Kingdom of God. The reign of God as a "new and different order" rather than a place, which has an eschatological dimension (at hand, about to break in, already come) and a radical upheaval of the present order (e.g., the first shall be last) [González 2005, p. 92]. Life in the presence of the Holy One of Israel, characterized by new kinds of relationships between God and humans, humans and humans, and humans and creation (that is, by God's righteousness becoming reality). As we cooperate with God's grace in Jesus Christ, we begin to recognize the imminence and signs of actualization of the Kingdom of God that are central to the good news of Jesus Christ.

Latitudinarianism. Literally, to permit wide variation. (a) The doctrine that "every man's view of revealed religion is acceptable to God, if he acts up to it; that no one view is in itself better than another, or at least that we cannot tell which is the better" [Newman 2004]. (b) "A movement within the Church of England [that] advocated religious toleration [Fieser 2006]. "After 1688, the latitudinarians sought to end religious controversy, to make the established church [of England] as inclusive as possible, to provide toleration for dissent, and to minimize the importance of doctrine and forms of worship in the interests of 'reasonableness'" [Armentrout n.d.].
Speculative Latitudinarianism—Indifference regarding essential doctrines
Practical Latitudinarianism—Indifference regarding the importance of practicing public worship.

Liberty. Our human "capacity to enact or refuse to enact our desires and inclinations" [Maddox 1994, p. 69].

Love. The "act of seeking and maintaining the good of another. In Scripture, the steadfast love of God for Israel (*hesed*) and the self-giving love of God for the world in Jesus Christ (*agape*) define the essential nature of God" [Migliore 2004, p. 416].

Means of Grace. "Outward signs, words, or actions, ordained of God, and appointed for this end, to be the ordinary channels whereby he might convey to men, preventing, justifying, or sanctifying grace" [*The Means of Grace,* §II.1].

Ministry. The discipleship of every baptized Christian acting in love for others.

Moravians. Pietist Christians from the German Lutheran tradition who followed the teachings of Wesley's contemporaries, Nicholas Ludwig von Zinzendorf and August Spangenberg.

New Birth. The transformation that God works in the soul when God brings it into life; specifically, restoring a right relationship with God and others, which God does in us by the Holy Spirit, beginning the reconstruction of the image of God in our lives [*The New Birth,* §II.5]. The new birth often occurs simultaneously with justification, but is theologically distinct from it, since the new birth is the beginning of (gateway into) sanctification.

New Creation. The coming of the new heaven and the new earth as described in Rev. 21. The process of making the Kingdom of God real throughout all creation, the full restoration of the image of God in this world.

One Thing Needful. To recover the image of God wherein [a person] was created, especially renewal in the love of God [*The One Thing Needful,* §§II.2,3]. The "one thing needful" is a life-long journey, which we call the Way of Salvation, beginning with prevenient grace, justification, and the new birth; and culminating in Christian perfection.

Oracles of God. Holy Scripture.

Ordinances of God. The "instituted means of grace; the basics of Christian discipleship that draw us to Christ and keep us with him" [Manskar 2004, p. 23].

Original Sin. The state of humankind that reflects its separation from God, where the intended relationship with God is replaced by a corrupted relationship marked by human insecurity, anxiety, false pride, and irresponsibility. "The classical way of referring to the fact that sin pervades all human life from birth, and is therefore more than mere acts we commit, a state in which we live" [González 2005, p. 124].

Perfection in Love. Faith in Christ's full atoning sacrifice and trust in the gospel of forgiveness of sins. A never-ending aspiration for all of love's fullness. [Runyon 1998, pp. 90-91] See Christian Perfection.

"Perfection [means] perfect love . . . love excluding sin; love filling the heart, taking up the whole capacity of the soul. It is love "rejoicing evermore, praying without ceasing, in everything giving thanks." [*The Scripture Way of Salvation*, §I.9]

Pluralist. The belief that all religious teachings are a true revelation of God and that no religion has final and definitive truth.

Predestination. The teaching that "God has foreordained all things, especially that God has elected certain souls to eternal salvation and others to eternal punishment" [Manskar 2004, p. 53]. "The view that God has determined beforehand who is destined for eternal life" [González 2005, p. 138].

Prevenient or Preventing Grace. The grace that comes before our justification; grace that, through the power of the Holy Spirit, awakens us to our sinful condition and brings us to repentance.

Providence. God provides for our wellbeing and, moreover, God has "foreknowledge" [González 2005, p. 142]. God as the Provider; the teaching that "God unceasingly cares for the world, that all things are in God's hands, and that God is leading the world to its appointed goal" [Migliore 2004, p. 421]. Note: "Awful providence" means bad personal circumstances. that may nonetheless be used by God for our good.

Quietism. The belief that one should not practice the means of grace "until one receives the assurance of faith" [Manskar 2004, p. 73]. In general, "any doctrine or practice that suggests that the role of humans in their relationship with God is one of absolute passivity—a passivity that is reflected in a similar attitude via-á-vis the life of society" [González 2005, p. 144].

Real Christians. Those who have both "the form and the power of Christian religion" as contrasted with "almost Christians," who have the form without the power. Real Christians "earnestly love God with all their heart, soul, mind, and strength," expressed in "an inner transformation of assurance and the new birth; and a love for their neighbors as themselves. Real Christians do all in their power to grow in that love." [Manskar 2004, p. 50].

Redemption. God's "forgiveness of sins" [*The Way to the Kingdom*, §II.11]. "The action whereby God in Christ overcomes sin" [González 2005, p. 161].

Repentance. Turning back toward God, seeking renewed relationship with God. "An inward change, a change of mind from sin to holiness" [*The Repentance of Believers*, §I.1]. "The recognition, rejection, and abhorrence of one's sin. . . . The Greek word in the New Testament that is usually translated as "repentance" in fact means also turning away from sin, and thus may also be translated 'conversion'." [González 2005, p. 152] (1) sorrow on account of sin; (2) humiliation under the hand of God; (3) hatred to sin; (4) confession of sin; (5) ardent supplication of the divine mercy; (6) the love of God; (7) ceasing from sin; (8) firm purpose of new obedience; (9) restitution of ill-gotten goods; (10) forgiving our neighbor his transgressions against us; (11) works of beneficence, or alms-giving. [*True Christianity Defended*, §I.7].

Righteousness. (a) "The life of God in the soul" [*Upon Our Lord's Sermon on the Mount I*, §I.11] (b) "Righteousness . . . is the image of God, the mind which was in Christ Jesus. It is every holy and heavenly temper in one; springing from, as well as terminating in, the love of God, as our Father and Redeemer, and the love of all men for his sake." [*Upon Our Lord's Sermon on the Mount II*, §II.2] (c) The state of being justified—"the justification that flows from [God's] mere grace and mercy, freely forgiving our sins through the Son of his love, through the redemption which is in Jesus" [*The Righteousness of Faith*, Intro.2]. (d) Righteousness also refers to the character of one who is justified. For example, Christian Righteousness is said to have two forms: outward righteousness (characterized by ones acts: zealous of good works; full of mercy and good fruits) and inward righteousness ("gentleness, meekness, long-suffering"); moreover, Christian righteousness has two "great branches"—love of God and love of neighbor. [*The Way to the Kingdom*, §§I.7,9] (e) The Righteousness of God (in the Kingdom of God) expected at the Second Coming of Christ includes the return to right relationships between God and humans, humans and humans, and humans and other parts of creation.

Sacrament. "An outward sign of inward grace, and a means whereby we receive the same" [*The Means of Grace*, §II.1]. A "sacred practice of the church based on a scriptural mandate and made effective by the Spirit of God as "means of grace" to confirm the presence and promise of Christ to believers" [Migliore 2004, p. 423].

Salvation. Reconciliation with God through Jesus Christ. "deliverance from guilt and punishment... and a deliverance from the power of sin" [*Salvation by Faith*, §III.2]. "Rescue from mortal peril, deliverance from sin and death, and the gift of fulfilled life in communion with God [Migliore 2004, p. 423]. Restoration to God. Implies both justification and sanctification.

Sanctification. The process of growing in "inward and outward holiness" [*The New Birth*, §IV.3]. "Recovery from that vile bondage, the love of his creatures, to the free love of our Creator" [*The One Thing Needful*, II.9]. The process by which a believer is brought closer to the will of God" [González 2005, p. 155]. "Total renovation of spirit, soul, and body" [Charles Wesley, *Awake Thou that Sleepest*, §I.2]

Sanctifying Grace. The grace that comes after our justification; grace that, through the power of the Holy Spirit, leads and empowers us to growth in holiness.

Sin (Inward). "A voluntary trangression of a known law" [*On Perfection*, §§II.9, III.9]. "Willful, voluntary transgression of the known will of God" [Heitzenrater 1995, p. 229]. "Any sinful temper, passion, or affection; such as pride, self-will, love of the world, in any kind or degree; such as lust, anger, peevishness; any disposition contrary to the mind which was in Christ" [*On Sin in Believers*, §II.2]. "Willful disobedience of God; violation of God's commands" [Manskar 2004, p. 14].

Soteriology. The doctrine of salvation. "The doctrine of the saving (reconciling, liberating, renewing) work of Jesus Christ and participation of believers in the new life in Christ by the power of the Holy Spirit" [Migliore 2004, p. 425]. See Salvation.

Theology. The study of God and things that pertain to God. More generally, theology is faith seeking understanding. "The entire corpus of Christian doctrine [and] reflection about it" [González 2005, p. 170].

Way of Salvation. A description of the reception of grace in a person's life: God's plan for humanity to be restored in God's image.

Witness of the Spirit. "The assurance of salvation given to Christians when they accept the grace of God in Jesus Christ and trust in him and only him as Savior and Lord" [Manskar 2004, p. 60]. A reference to Rom. 8:16 "It is that very Spirit bearing witness with our spirit that we are children of God" (NRSV). Wesley writes [*The Witness of the Spirit, II*, §II.1,V.2]:

> the testimony, the sum of what God testifies in all the inspired writings, "that God hath given unto us eternal life, and this life is in his Son. . . . is given by the Spirit of God to and with our spirit. He is the Person testifying. What he testifies to us is, "that we are the children of God." The immediate result of this testimony is, "the fruit of the Spirit;" namely, "love, joy, peace, long-suffering, gentleness, goodness"; and, without these, the testimony itself cannot continue. . . . The true witness of the Spirit is known by its fruit. . . .

Works righteousness. The belief that it is by our own efforts that we can be accepted by God; that is, not solely relying on God's grace.

C.3 MEANING OF TERMS USED BY JOHN AND CHARLES WESLEY IN MODERN ENGLISH (FIRST USE IN THE SERMON TEXTS IS MARKED WITH THE SYMBOL "*")

Term Used	Meaning in Modern English
barely	merely; only
bowels	center of emotion; often what we mean by "heart"
charity	love (especially, self-giving love)
conversation	(often means) manner of life
disinterested	impartial (e.g., "disinterested love for all")
divers	many
end	(often means) purpose, goal (e.g., "to what end?")
event	result
evidently	made clear
experimental	(often means) experiential (what one could or has experienced)
filial	pertaining to sonship (e.g., "filial love")

gay (world)	sophisticated; also, that part of the world given to social pleasures [from *Webster's Third New International Dictionary*]
in order to	(when preceding a noun, often means) "in order to do/have"; "in order to receive/obtain" (e.g., "in order to faith")
intercourse	interaction, relationship
meet	fit, proper
open (a text)	explicate; explain the meaning of (the text)
peculiar	("peculiar people") particular, distinct
prevent	(often means) precede; the Wesleys used the term "preventing grace"
prevenient	preceding (literally, "coming before")
primitive	early, original (e.g., "the primitive church")
prove	(often means) come to know by experience
several	different, various (e.g., "at two several places")
singular	distinct; not conforming to the crowd
styled	called, known as
temper	attitude, temperament, disposition; "an enduring or *habitual* disposition of a person" [Maddox 1994, p. 69].
to own	(often means) to acknowledge
vulgar	popular, common, colloquial
want	(often means) need or lack rather than desire (e.g., "go to those who want you most" means "those who need you most.") to own
Source:	Expanded from a list originally compiled by Dr. Howard A. Snyder of Asbury Theological Seminary for The Wesley Center for Applied Theology, Northwest Nazarene University (http://wesley.nnu.edu/john_wesley/wesley-vocabulary.htm).